The constitution of poverty

Toward a genealogy of liberal governance

Mitchell Dean

London and New York

First published 1991
by Routledge
11 New Fetter Lane, London EC4P 4EE

Simultaneously published in the USA and Canada
by Routledge
a division of Routledge, Chapman and Hall, Inc.
29 West 35th Street, New York, NY 10001

© 1991 Mitchell Dean

Phototypeset in 10pt Times by
Mews Photosetting, Beckenham, Kent
Printed and bound in Great Britain by
Mackays of Chatham PLC, Chatham, Kent

British Library Cataloguing in Publication Data

Dean, Mitchell *1955–*
    The constitution of poverty : toward a genealogy of
    liberal governance.
    1. Great Britain. Poverty, history
    I. Title
    305.5690941

Library of Congress Cataloging in Publication Data

Dean, Mitchell, 1955–
    The constitution of poverty : toward a genealogy of liberal
    governance – Mitchell Dean.
        p. cm.
    Includes bibliographical references.
    1. Public welfare – Great Britain – History. 2. Poor – Great
    Britain – History. 3. Poor laws – Great Britain – History. 4. Great
    Britain – Social policy. I. Title.
    HV245.D348 1991
    362.5'0941 – dc20

                                                          90-35004
                                                          CIP

    ISBN 0-415-04355-7
        0-415-04356-5 (pbk)

Contents

Acknowledgements

This book began life as a doctoral dissertation which was submitted to the School of Sociology at the University of New South Wales in 1988. I want to express my heartfelt appreciation to that school as a whole for the help and support it gave me during more years than I care to recall. In particular, I would like to give recognition to the patience, assiduity, intellectual guidance, and encouragement, of my supervisor, Stephen D'Alton. I must also mention the significant contribution of an earlier supervisor, Lois Bryson, who read my earliest attempts to make sense of this project, and who made vital and valuable comments on the final draft of my thesis. I must also warmly thank Michael Bittman for his friendship, support, and encouragement for this project over the years, Boris Frankel for his comments on a version of the thesis manuscript, and Colin Bell for starting me on the road to this by proposing that I study in Britain for a year. I accepted that proposal in 1979 thanks to the financial support afforded by an Australian Government Commonwealth Postgraduate Scholarship.

The crucial work of doctoral examiners remains largely unheralded. In my case the swift and helpful responses of David Walsh, Paul Hirst, and Jeffrey Minson, were greatly appreciated. Whatever merits the present book contains is in no small part due to their comments and criticisms. Together with the significant redirection afforded by my first anonymous referee at Routledge, their contribution gave me the opportunity to reshape this book into a substantially bolder, broader, and more challenging work. I hope I have accepted that opportunity. I would also like to acknowledge my colleagues in the Department of Sociology and Politics at Phillip Institute for the kindness they have displayed while I have been rewriting this during 1989, and to the staff at Routledge, particularly Chris Rojek and Lynda Goldman, for their tireless efforts on behalf of a book written on the other side of the earth by someone they had not met.

There would be no finished volume before you without those sacrifices, both large and small but always demanding, which my family has had to make both in the preparation of my doctorate and in its rewriting as a book. It has called upon reserves of tolerance, patience, moral suport and simple endurance, particularly from my wife, Deborah Southon, but also from my two sons, Terence and Alistair, which I doubt I would have possessed in similar circumstances. I hope that this book serves as some small compensation for them. Indeed, I hope the book warrants at least some of the efforts of all those who have contributed to it.

I am grateful to Oxford University Press for their permission to reproduce extracts from their edition of Adam Smith's *Wealth of Nations*, © Oxford University Press 1976. Reprinted fom *An Inquiry into the Nature and Causes of the Wealth of Nations* by Adam Smith, edited by R.H. Campbell, A.S. Skinner, and W.B. Todd (1976) by permission of Oxford University Press.

Introduction

Early in the course of researching this study, while reading Karl Polanyi's *The Great Transformation* (1957), I found a sentence which simply and clearly stated a proposition which I had been struggling to formulate. At that moment, I understood its thesis had been implicit in my own investigations. It revealed that the terrain I had stumbled on to had already been assiduously charted and gave me renewed confidence and provided inspiration to persist with what became the present study. It read: 'The figure of the pauper, almost forgotten since, dominated a discussion the imprint of which was as powerful as that of the most spectacular events in history' (Polanyi 1957: 83–84).

In hindsight the value of this statement for the present study was more of the order of rhetoric than an explicit historical proposition. The force which it possesses depends on the juxtaposition of the solitary, almost elemental creature whose existence stands only as a figure (of speech or of frame?) against the weight of history, popularly conceived as that singular totality which encompasses the glory and might, heroism and tragedy, of the endeavours of humankind. Moreover, the statement juxtaposes in order to identify. On the space of this history, it discloses a filiation between the lowly pauper and the 'most spectacular events'. The statement suggested, from that moment of first reading, that pauperism could be treated as an *event*, even if it lacks the spectacle of war, revolution, and the rise and fall of princes and dictators.

'Pauperism and political economy', Polanyi commented with equal flourish, 'together form part of an indivisible whole: the discovery of society' (1957: 103). The merits of Polanyi's approach can be grasped as genealogical, in Foucault's sense (Foucault 1980b: 83), in so far as it leads us to entertain the claims of 'minor' discourses and events and to place these in relation to those knowledges which claim the legitimacy and authority of science. The event of pauperism is about the relations between specific forms of theoretical and strategic knowledge. It is about the practical inscription of 'scientific' discourse within specific policies and means of administration of poverty. It will lead us not to uncover

1

the social determinants of knowledge, after the fashion of the sociology of knowledge (Mannheim: 1936), nor to analyse discourse simply as an autonomous, self-referential structure, but to show the effects of knowledge in so far as it embodies a programme towards social reality. The discussions of pauperism, in the eighteenth and nineteenth centuries, for all their ignoble concerns with 'morality' and 'behaviour', are a part of the genealogy of the science of society in its practical relations, and remind us of that continuing dimension of the *social* sciences which maintains the mark of what in the eighteenth century were called the *moral* sciences.

Another statement, to be found in Marx's *Grundrisse* (1973), a text which uncovers something of the moral premises of political economy, discloses a key to the reasons for this 'imprint' of pauperism upon history.

It is already contained in the concept of the *free labourer*, that he is a *pauper*: virtual pauper . . . . If the capitalist has no use for his surplus labour, then the worker may not perform his necessary labour; not produce his necessaries. Then he cannot obtain them through exchange; rather, if he does obtain them, it is only because alms are thrown to him from revenue . . . . This exchange is tied to conditions which are accidental for him, and indifferent to his organic presence. He is thus a virtual pauper. Since it is further the condition of production based on capital that he produces ever more surplus labour, it follows that ever more necessary labour is set free. Thus his chances of pauperism increase.

(Marx 1973: 604)

This makes plain that the event of pauperism is not of mere antiquarian interest. It is among the *conditions of existence* of wage-labour, of that labour which Marx says it is 'absolute poverty' in so far as it is stripped of all objective wealth at the same moment as it is the general possibility of wealth (1973: 295–296).[1] Similarly, for Weber, the 'free labour' of capitalist society is borne by those 'who are not only legally in the position, but are also *economically compelled*, to sell their labour on the market without restriction' (Weber 1927: 277, emphasis added). The event of pauperism is, of course, about class and property relations, but never quite in the ways in which theory suggests.

This study develops these fundamental sociological insights but not in order to substantiate what the classical theorists already knew. Rather, it seeks to show that what they grasped in terms of theoretical models of capitalism was part of the explicit, often calculated, strategic, and above all practical presuppositions of its genesis and functioning. It demonstrates that pauperism belongs to the conditions of emergence of our present, its 'historic preconditions' or 'history of formation', as

Marx said (1973: 459). But it also shows that pauperism is among the political and discursive forms which secured the conditions of existence of the first national capitalist labour market (cf Cutler *et al* 1977, 1: 222–229). These conditions are what we hope to condense in the phrase which this study seeks to explicate, 'the constitution of poverty'.

While the veritable war on pauperism in the nineteenth century may be the reverse side of the historic movement of the generalisation of wage-labour, it is much else besides. The event of pauperism is as much about 'morals', forms of everyday life, families, breadwinners, households, and self-responsibility, as economics, the state, poor laws, and poor policies. It is about the formation of particular categories of social agent, and of specific class and familial relations, in so far as they are promoted by governmental practices. Indeed, the discussion of pauperism, in which the constitution of poverty can be discerned, stands at the centre of a political and epistemic complex from which contemporary modes of governance emerged.

Method

The narrow temporal boundaries of this event, as defined by intellectual histories such as J.R. Poynter's *Society and Pauperism* (1969), are marked by the dates 1795 and 1834. The former stands for both the repeated agrarian scarcities which beset England in the final years of the eighteenth century and the major statements concerning poor policy made by Thomas Malthus, Jeremy Bentham, F.M. Eden, and others. The latter date is that of the passing of the Poor Law Amendment Act, which occasioned the most fundamental change in the administration and practice of poor relief since the inception of the poor laws during the Tudor monarchy.

It might be thought that the changing nature of relief and administration of poverty in this period is a rather unpropitious terrain for any species of social theory. It is the contention of the present study, however, that this field of study can yield a greater degree of insight into present-day social and political arrangements than has been acknowledged by conventional intellectual and institutional historiography. The discourses, policies, and relief practices under examination here are dated from a period which presents certain difficulties for historical analysis, particularly that which seek naïvely to employ common-sense categories of economics and politics and to read discursive and governmental events and formations in terms of economic interests and forces. As Karel Williams (1981: 21–51) has shown, the recent economic history of the pre-1834 poor law has been hampered by its preoccupation with the application of a marginalist economic theory which presupposes a universal calculus of economic rationality by *homo oeconomicus*. This study follows those which remain wary of the employment of categories and concepts which it regards as products of the transformations it is seeking to analyse (cf George 1985: 199–203). For example, L.J. Hume (1981: 33) has recently argued that economics, in the form of political economy, had not yet separated itself, even towards the end of the eighteenth century, from the two related fields of 'police' and 'oeconomy', and employed the latter concepts to provide a non-anachronistic reading of eighteenth-century conceptions of government. To view eighteenth-century poor policies as the implementation of particular *economic* theories would be disastrous.

It will become clear in what follows that the approach to history manifested in historical specialisms, and the division of labour they presuppose, must be challenged to appreciate the full significance of this event. By cutting across this division of labour, the full, ruptural nature of pauperism will be made evident, as it was to near contemporaries. According to Chevalier (1973: 134–136) the French social investigators of the 1840s knew that the discussion of pauperism marked a fundamental rupture in matters of social assistance and the application of knowledge to the framing of policy, law, and administration. It is time that late twentieth-century historians and sociologists shared this knowledge.

But what does the treatment of pauperism as an event entail and how might it differ from alternative treatements? 'An event is a portentous outcome; it is a transformation device between past and future', stated Philip Abrams (1982: 191). As Abrams points out (190–226), there are no theoretical or methodological grounds for sociology to abandon events to the province of history since events are always theoretically constructed as objects of knowledge. Events are crucial to analyses of social, discursive, and governmental transformation because they are markers of transition. This insight opens on to one of the key dimensions of Michel Foucault's celebrated reworking of the genealogical perspective. He described his work as a process of '*eventialisation*' (Foucault 1981: 6–7), registering singularity instead of invoking underlying historical necessities or logics in order to bring about a 'breach of self-evidence' and a suspension of commonplace assumptions. For Foucault, events can only be made intelligible through a progressive, and always necessarily incomplete, consideration of multiple domains of reference. In order to grasp the meaning of such a method some examples are called for.

Determinative logics abounded in what might be retrospectively called the post-war historical sociology of the welfare state. Its least sophisticated arguments were for a broad continuity between the welfare ideals of state responsibility embodied in the Tudor poor-law legislation and those of contemporary social services. Bruce discerned (1968: 7) the basis and essence of the welfare state in the Elizabethan 'common weal'. More complex were the arguments derived from T.H. Marshall's seminal essay of 1948 (1983) that the modern welfare state was a part of the broad evolution of citizenship in which the Elizabethan poor law and its later permutations (especially 'Speenhamland') figure as the premature embodiment of modern social rights. Another argument posited a broad *societal* logic in which social policy is an 'organic process' of industrialism (e.g. Beales 1946). In these approaches, the economic, social, and demographic changes of the 'Industrial Revolution' were said to issue a need for the poor-law reform (Henriques 1979: 1–3). By contrast, this study will suspend all arguments that the 'coming of the welfare state' is the end product of an ideal, political, economic, or societal logic or of the adjustment of society to needs generated by industrialism.

Pursuing this position in relation to a theoretically developed historical sociology, one could derive from Marxian and Weberian social theory an analysis of pauperism as a feature of the rationalisation of the administration of poverty in terms of the logic of capitalist development. Such an analysis would provide a degree of intelligibility: Benthamite critiques, and the reforms of the 1830s, would be understood as expressing rationalising concerns, in so far as they sought to move poor-law administration from its local, complex, and particular forms rooted in the parish and executed by elected officials, to a national, uniform, universalistic central-state form run by a corps of professional officers. Similarly, the revolution of the poor laws after 1834 has major implications for the formation of a national labour market and can be understood in terms of class relations, possibilities which are explored in this study. Whatever its merits, in its quest for global explanation this approach would fail to come to terms with the complex linkages of discourse, policy, and practice around the event of pauperism and its manifold consequences for legal, administrative, familial, and economic practices and relations.

More generally, it is necessary to eschew a teleology in which the characterisation of discursive and governmental practices is established by their anticipation of, or inadequacies in relation to, a putative end-form (such as 'social policy', 'the welfare state', 'sociology', etc.) from which judgement is passed (cf Bruland and Smith 1981: 469). The following analysis seeks to make intelligible the practices under examination in their own terms, an approach which is also implied by the critique of 'recurrence' made by Foucault (1972: 187–188), and, more generally, the French history of science (Tribe 1978: 18–23).[2]

If this study seeks to 'eventalise' pauperism, it is because pauperism-as-event reveals something more than is found in inexorable logics which serve only to reassure us of the necessity and virtue of current forms of state and its policies. For many accounts it is precisely the turn manifested by the debate on pauperism and the 1834 law which presents major difficulties to the search for such necessity. Such analyses seek to smooth over the ruptural aspects of pauperism by denying it as event. Thus Briggs (unwittingly?) approves the Fabian view of the *'laissez-faire'* state as an 'aberration' which was in any case never completely realised, with the 1834 poor law as a 'substitute for social policy' and a threat to the link between traditional 'historic rights of the poor' and modern working-class politics (Briggs 1961: 233–236). For others there is a 'profound disjunction' in both 'aims and policies' between the 1834 Act and the welfare state, so that the latter 'represents, at least in theory, the total reversal of nineteenth-century attitudes' (Henriques 1979: 268). Something of this reversal of attitude is contained in T.H. Marshall's claims that 'we' – in this case the members of 'democratic-welfare-capitalism' – have rejected the old ideas that poverty is necessary, has evolutionary benefits, is a work incentive, and is 'the inevitable and perpetual deposit of personal failures' (Marshall 1972: 28).

These positions serve to distance present social arrangements, policies, and values from those which are thought to be manifested by the event of pauperism. On the one hand, the post-war accounts of the welfare state seek a profound continuity and necessity in the passage from ancient poor law to modern welfare state. On the other, the effect of claiming an exception for the 1834 reform is to underplay the significance of pauperism. Indeed, it is to underplay the significance of the liberal break in poor policy. The present study renews this search for continuity and rupture in the history of poor policies. Its aim is to reform the presuppositions of historical interpretation so it is understood that:

1 the event of pauperism is more than a simple negation of the 'enlightened' knowledges, policies, and practices of the late twentieth century;
2 the governmental and discursive practices around pauperism can and do increase the intelligibility of debate in our own period of reaction to welfare-state measures without denying the evident reality of state transformation of the last two centuries; and
3 the growth of state 'interventions' since the early nineteenth century is insufficient to differentiate modes of governance.

The final point is absolutely crucial to this study. While we shall take the view that the poor law and pauperism are in no way equivalent to the welfare state and contemporary social policy, we shall emphasise that the classical liberal mode of government always contained the active possibility of the expansion and centralisation of state activity within its form of economy in a way which traverses empty oppositions between individualism and collectivism, *laissez-faire* and interventionism, etc.

Durkheim's sociological method and Nietzsche's genealogy have warned, in remarkably similar terms, against the teleological confusion of 'efficient cause' with later 'function', of 'origin' with 'utility', present 'employment', and 'purpose'.[3] The assumption of such an identity in the present case would serve as a debunking exercise to highlight the unsavoury origins of social policy and social science and to reject a view of governance as an Enlightenment project of a rational mastery of the human world for benevolent purposes. This assumption is certainly evident, as Minson demonstrates (1980: 13–18), in Nietzsche's (and Foucault's) 'revaluation of all values' theme in which lofty values are shown to have base origins. However, while taking note of such problems, this study is placed within a revamped genealogical project which constructs intelligible trajectories of events, discourses, and practices without determinative origin or end (Minson 1985: 108).

In order to do so it is necessary to undertake meticulous and detailed studies which refuse the quest for either pristine origins containing a truth undiminished by time or the promise of a truth to which history haltingly proceeds. The present work is not intended as an exposé of base origins or an uncovering of ancient wisdom. Nor is it the detection of an immutable movement towards a (un)happy ending. Rather, it is simply a case-history of the government of poverty.[4] Although conducted within definite geographic and temporal limits, this case-history can illuminate issues of governance and knowledge, the moral regulation of categories targeted by policies, and the relation between theoretical discourse and administrative programme. If the sociology of knowledge can be said to have the aim of the 'reconstruction of the systematic theoretical basis underlying the single judgements of the individual' (Mannheim 1936: 52), the aim here is the reconstruction of the systematic theoretical basis of the statements and treatment of poverty at a particular time and place.

The crux of this case-history is to register a major break between the classical governance of poverty and that which preceded it. In a further study, I shall defend the argument that this break is more fundamental than any which has succeeded it, as evidenced by the uneven development of welfare provision, and by current debates around the 'crisis of the welfare state' and various policies of privatisation, monetarism, economic rationalism, neo-liberalism, and so on. For the time being this second argument must be left to the reader's own reflection. However, if it pits the present work against the post-war welfare-state historians, the thesis here will require some reformulation of the frameworks from which it arose, particularly Foucault's arguments around biopolitics.

The debate on pauperism, which commenced at the end of the eighteenth century, went on fully for forty years before the 1834 reform, and continued in some quarters into the next century, must be understood as the key component in a fundamental transformation in modes of governance, which has effects down to the present day. The full theoretical significance of this transformation is dramatised as the *constitution* of poverty.

The exposition of this concept requires some care in order to appreciate the implications of its two dimensions, the epistemic and the normative. What is undertaken here is an analysis of the *discursive* constitution of poverty within particular policies and ways of knowing. To do this it is necessary both to avoid the effects of empiricist epistemologies and to be wary of the reductive possibilities of representational sociologies of knowledge. Against the former, to grant pauperism its proper weight as an event implies a 'bracketing-out', at least in the first instance, of the empiricist assumption that discursive entities such as 'poverty', 'pauperism', 'the poor', and 'the labouring poor' can only be analysed by their degree of adequacy to the extra-discursive reality of poverty, to the 'flesh-and-blood' existence of the poor awaiting only accurate observation and investigation. Certain historians of the welfare state (e.g. Briggs 1961: 252) have argued that the debate over pauperism was characterised by a dogmatism derived from political economy which would only later be overcome by the empirical studies (of Charles Booth and Seebohm Rowntree) which revealed the true nature of poverty. Poverty does not exist in relation to pauperism as empirical truth to stigmatising dogma. Both are equally (and sometimes interconnected) products of the formation and transformations of definite discursive and governmental practices.

From the perspective of the sociology of knowledge, these concepts would be understood as elements of a *Weltanschauung* which is 'relational' to the social (class) position of those who utter them (Mannheim 1936: 67–74). As in so many other areas, Polanyi (1957: 77–101) is exemplary. He can be understood as fulfilling such a project by placing arguments about poverty and poor relief in relation to characteristics which are conceived as elements of the world-view of various social classes and the social forces which they represent. In such a schema, the defenders of the old systems of poor relief are identified with the 'paternalism' (a concept which reminds us of the patriarchal nature of the relations involved) and the labour-regulation beliefs of the landed gentry and their representatives, the magistracy. These beliefs are held to reflect the rural, local, and hierarchical social order. Similarly, the advocates of abolition of relief are viewed as expressing the '*laissez-faire*', naturalistic, and individualistic attitudes of the bourgeoisie rising on the wave of the Industrial Revolution and the progressive extension of the market.

The approach of this study is somewhat different. This is not to say that issues either of the validity or social determinants of knowledge should not be posed, but simply that we avoid giving them a primary explanatory power in our analysis. Moreover, while it can be acknowledged that the second of these approaches has provided some fundamental insights, it is improbable that its sociologism could yield any further intelligibility to our event. The epistemic aim is thus a non-reductive one: to make intelligible the conditions under which poverty appears in various forms of discourse, whether theory, policy, or empirical social investigation. Such a move is certainly not without precedent in contemporary critical theory. Keith Tribe's (1978: 5–23) ground-breaking analysis of the formation of economic discourse rejects both these approaches in its attempt to specify the discursive conditions which constitute economic science.

Yet it is also necessary to go beyond 'discourse analysis', if by that we mean an analysis which regards discourse purely as a structure within which concepts and explanations are formed. The constitution of poverty is integral to the formation of the theoretical discourse of the economy. Notions of poverty, however, are produced not only in economic and other forms of theoretical discourse but also in a variety of ethical and theological debates, political polemics, obscure tracts, and official reports. Poverty is thus constituted in other equally, if not more, important ways in relation to matters of policy, legislation, and administration, and in moral and political arguments. If the constitution of poverty concerns an epistemic shift, it is also implicated in a shift in modes of moral regulation and governance. Hence it is not possible to rest content with a purely 'discursivist' account, such as that of Tribe, or Williams' (1981: 235–368) Barthesian analyses of social investigations. While the great merit of such accounts has been to produce exemplary analyses of the specificity of, and differences between, discursive forms, it is simply not sufficient to grasp the full character of our event.

The fact that poverty is the site of the intersection of scientific and theoretical knowledges with the constitution of practical problems implies a movement beyond a self-contained discourse analysis. It becomes necessary to attend to that face of theoretical discourse which turns towards the provision of a practical rationality and that aspect of governmental practice and state intervention which is strategic and calculating. A minimum thesis is that the discursive constitution and moral-political governance are so interlinked that they may be regarded as determinative of, yet irreducible to, one another. The campaign against pauperism is the hinge of a transformation which has two sides, one concerning ways of theorising, knowing, and classifying; the other, forms of treatment, relief, discipline, deterrence, and administration. The result is the production of poverty in a definite historical form. The object of this case-history might therefore be called the constitutive-regulation of poverty, except for the inelegance of that construction (cf Corrigan and Sayer 1985: 2).

As a case-history, this study does not seek an exhaustive reconstruction of the past. Instead it aims to provide a necessarily incomplete understanding of certain theoretical discourses and more practical knowledges, social policy (providing we are aware that the adjective is problematic in this context), modes of state administration, and other social and institutional practices. The initial focus on the discussion of pauperism thus requires examination of various cognate fields.

Some brief examples can be given. The Malthusian dimension of the poor-law debate not only calls for an understanding of the trajectory of notions of population and prior discussions of poor policy but also demands that the question of the effects of political economy be put, which, in turn, raises the problem of what distinguishes the new economic discourse. Further, once such a theoretical problem is posed, others, involving the transformation of frameworks for policy, require resolution, and issues of the supposed shift from ethical to economic grounds of policy (and back again) become germane. So too do the themes of the relation between *moral* economy, *political* economy, and *social* economy (a series drawn by Corrigan 1977: iii), of the old notions of paternalism (or, indeed, patriarchalism) and deference, and of the 'demoralisation' of both policies and knowledges as much as that of individuals and targeted social categories.

Yet even then the intelligibility of our event has not been exhausted. If we take up problems of state administration of poor relief, we are drawn into debates over Benthamism and utilitarianism, of the revolution in government, of the relations between political economy and state administrative strategies, and the characterisation of the distinctiveness of the liberal style of state administration from the 1830s. It is to Polanyi's enduring credit that he sought to displace the opposition between '*laissez-faire*' and 'interventionism' by arguing that economic liberalism was systematically *enforced* by the state, including under the reforms of 1834 (1957: 147–152).[5]

These theoretical-historical problems require a consideration of a range of topics which are adjacent to that of pauperism and the constitution and moral regulation of poverty. The ones explored here include 'mercantilist' discussions of 'the Poor', poor relief and provision, the archaic concept of police in European political discourses, Adam Smith's analyses and the formation of economic discourse, the institutions, agents, and practices of poor relief and their transformations before and after 1834, and the discussion of the conditions of the labouring population in the 1830s and 1840s, among others. Needless to say, these adjacent issues form only a small part of what could have been investigated. For instance, the histories of philanthropy, migration, colonisation, forcible transportation, and the 'Irish question', which enter into the history of poor policy at many critical points, are bypassed or only occasionally touched upon.

Finally, it must be acknowledged that the present study, in seeking to provide a framework for the analysis of the transformation in poor policy, has not sought to link its findings in a systematic way to the history of popular struggles. While conceding that the full intelligibility of governmental transformation cannot be given unless such a task is undertaken, this is not an oversight. It is rather a deliberate theoretical strategy to attempt to displace conventional historical and social–theoretical accounts and hence establish the nature of the liberal transformation of governance on a sounder footing. It is the conviction of this study that the genealogy of the governance of poverty needs yet to be secured, and only when this has been done can it be confidently linked with the history of the social struggles and resistance of the propertyless.

The liberal mode of government[6]

The terms 'liberal' and 'government' are both rather troublesome. Although they are recognisable from everyday usage as well as from political and intellectual discourse, they are both plagued by a lack of specificity and a surplus of significations which makes them elusive vehicles of communication. Given this, to couple them to make a further term, the liberal mode of government, may seem highly problematic. Why indulge in such a neologism, it may be asked, when there are adequate expressions which, if not wholly unambiguous, at least possess a degree of consensual usage in the social sciences? If the topic is a definite political formation, why not use the term 'liberal state'? If it is a political doctrine under examination, isn't 'liberalism' sufficient?

First, this term distinguishes the general terrain of the present study from an exclusive concern with the liberal state. 'Government' is used in a manner which suspends its nineteenth-century restriction to the problem of the state, i.e. to the question of the basis of political sovereignty and the institutions which secure it, exemplified by James Mill's celebrated article (1978; Halévy 1928: 419–424). Our reworked use of the term is also intended to avoid the impasse into which the debate over the 'nineteenth-century revolution in government' was led by its focus on the relation between 'Benthamite ideas' and the state administration of the 1830s. The sense of the term here is closer to the concept of government found in the final phase of Foucault's writings and lectures (1979a: 5–21; 1982: 221–224).

Foucault suggested (1982: 221) a return to the broader sense of the term current in the sixteenth century. He argued (1979a: 5–9) that this encompassed the government of oneself in the revival of Stoicism, of souls in pastoral thought, of children in pedagogy, of families by 'oeconomy', and, only later, of the state by the Prince. The point of rescuing this polyvalent meaning here is not to devalue the role of the state (which Foucault often appeared to do) but to note that *political* government is only one possible means or dimension of regulating or directing what is done, and that its intelligibility is given in relation to other such means or dimensions. Government is here used as a general term which includes any relatively calculated practice to direct categories of social agent in a particular manner and to specified ends.

There is an extremely important consequence of this use of the term government. It directs analysis not solely to the features of that body which claims the right to the sole legitimate use of force in a given territory (after Weber), but to the relations between such a body, its legal, administrative, and security apparatuses and practices, and other institutions and domains of practice. One key feature of this liberal mode of government of poverty will be shown to consist in a particular set of relations between the sphere of the state and its practices of poor relief and the domain of personal responsibility which is constituted around familial and domestic arrangements.

Second, the term distinguishes our present concerns from those which focus on liberalism as a political and economic doctrine. It does this both in the way its historical domain is constructed and in terms of the perspective adopted.

An investigation into liberalism, and its influence upon the stage of world history, would be compelled to address the philosophies of the social contract, the doctrines of the revolutionaries, utilitarianism, the 'New Liberalism', and so forth. By contrast, the use of the word 'liberal' is applied in this study to particular configurations of discursive and governmental practices rather than to the theoretical or ideological foundations of a specific type of polity. One such configuration may be discerned to be constructed around the 1834 poor-law reform. Here the title 'liberal mode of government of poverty' is applied to those practices which are broadly consistent with the means, strategy, and objectives of this reform. In recognition that this mode may take other forms, it will occasionally be referred to as the 'classical liberal governance of poverty'.

This use of the term 'liberal' also coincides with its application in the early nineteenth century to denote 'Whig-liberal' political positions, explored by Halévy's classic study (1928) and in Corrigan's exemplary thesis (1977). Raymond Williams (1976: 148–150) suggests that it was first applied by conservatives in the second and third decades of the nineteenth century to those of advanced Whiggish or Radical views. Such a desgination roughly covers the political affiliation of the discourses described here as liberal. It should be noted, however, that this formation consisted of intellectual positions which had been stated at least a generation earlier (from the 1790s) and that it did not have significant legislative impact until the reforms of the 1830s.

More importantly, the focus on the liberal mode of government implies a disjunction between mode of government and political doctrine which often goes unnoticed. Liberalism is usually presented as a doctrine concerned with the optimisation of the sphere of individual freedom and rights, and the preservation of this sphere against any arbitrary encroachment by the state. It thus posits a sphere of private autonomy which is opposed to a domain of public intervention. The term 'liberal mode of government' does not so much deny as contextualise this opposition. In this regard, the term implies two postulates. The first is that the private sphere, far from being inviolate, is already the effect of a multitude of state and other governmental interventions which loosely cohere around the objective of the promotion of a specific *form of life*. Second, it is argued that, at least in regard to matters of poverty, the private sphere is not so much one of personal freedoms and rights but of the economic responsibilities of a certain category of social agent, the male breadwinner. To achieve this 'responsibilisation' of the poor, the liberal mode of government, far from guaranteeing certain rights, must oppose arguments for, and remove practices which secure rights to, subsistence for various social categories. Since Marx, the critique of liberalism has never tired of showing the contradictions between the tenets of liberal philosophy and the actual operation of capitalist relations of exploitation. For us, the problem must be repositioned not so much as a contradiction between theory and practice but as the complex and subtle confrontations between a universalistic, ethical discourse of rights and the particularistic, practical logics of government.

Forms of life

An examination of the debate on pauperism leads to a consideration of the liberal mode of government. However, in order to understand the role of pauperism in marking out the domain in which poverty can be made *administrable*, it is necessary to employ a further concept, that of 'forms of life'.[7] This concept allows us to address the issue of the *moral* effects of poor relief, a theme which has attracted the attention of major social and political theorists from Alexis de Tocqueville in 1835 (1986: 27–40) to T.H. Marshall (1972: 25). Whereas the former objected to public poor relief on the grounds that it destroyed work motivation by ensuring survival and gave legal status to inferiority, the latter gave consideration to the relations between 'the authoritarian, or paternal character of welfare' and the consumer's 'exercise of choice' and 'initiative and self-reliance'. One of the recurring themes of this book is to take a critical distance from the opposition between the free individual exercising choice and the regulation of choice by the state. What does paternalism mean in this context? Is this critique of paternalism a critique also of patriarchal social relations? Or, is it, as Carole

Pateman suggests (1988), a subtle defence of the *fraternal* patriarchy of liberal governance and capitalism?

'Forms of life' is here used in order to address the way in which the (in)action of the state and other agencies is a calculated attempt to structure behaviour and options within a given field of social practices for specified categories of social agent. A prime example of this is the official strategy enunciated in *The Poor Law Report of 1834* (Checkland and Checkland (eds) 1974: 341–374) in which the objective was to convert paupers into 'independent labourers', a form of life with characteristics such as industry, frugality in matters of domestic economy, and foresight with regard to marriage and procreation. Such a policy presupposed certain economic and affective relations within families and attempted to calculate its effects in terms of 'private' practices of savings, domestic economy, philanthropy, and so forth. In principle, and without assuming that policies and strategies are necessarily consistent among themselves or completely effective, it would be possible to map the forms of life which are promoted by each mode of government in the intersection of state-administrative and other governmental practices.

A form of life is the grid of everyday existence which is constructed through a multiplicity of governmental practices, one aspect of which defines the division between a sphere of private responsibility and autonomy and a sphere of public responsibility and intervention. This concern with everyday life as a target of administration may be read as an alternative to the focus on the body which was typical of Foucauldian genealogy in the 1970s. There the genealogy of 'modern' forms of power considered 'the body' as both the privileged point of application of bio-power and the site of resistance to power (e.g. Foucault 1979b; 1977a). From the present perspective, this approach has the effect of reducing complex issues of the government of the minutiae of everyday life of subject populations to matters of the body. The term 'form of life' seeks to preserve this positive attention Foucault has given to the construction of the body along different dimensions of government (such as health, sexuality, and punishment) but also includes practices whose objects are not directly corporeal or which are irreducible to the regulation of bodily capacities, needs, and desires. For example, the role of charities, savings banks, and friendly societies become of vital interest as practices implicated in governmental aims of defining the responsibilities of agents in matters of the financial support of dependants, increasing the propensity to save, improving domestic economy and hygiene, and so on.

The theme of forms of life is perhaps closer to an aspect of Weber's thought than to 'middle-period' Foucault. If one follows the reading of his analysis of Protestantism offered by Hennis (1983: 141), Weber was concerned with the 'genealogy of the rational *Lebensführung*', i.e. with the historical genesis, located in Christian asceticism, of a *conduct of life* based on the methodical pursuit of a calling. In contrast to Weber, this study is not concerned with the genesis of rational asceticism in religious ethics but with the promotion of a certain ascetic life style among the propertyless by particular policies through definite administrative means.

It may or may not prove to be the case that Weber's rational *Lebensführung* and the form of life promoted by this liberal government are closely related. This is a matter for further investigation.[8] However, the present study is also concerned with how this form of life, promoted by definite state-adminstrative practices, was linked to the securing of the conditions of existence of wage-labour in the first capitalist national economy. Since it cannot be assumed that there is a necessary correspondence between strategy and consequence, this linkage becomes a matter for positive demonstration. This problem brings us to the crux of Polanyi's powerful thesis concerning the poor law and the 'commodification' of labour. If Polanyi's thesis is correct, then the liberal mode of government of poverty, far from being an epiphenomenon determined by underlying social and economic transformation, would have to be considered as a necessary component of early capitalist social relations.

Organisation

This study proposes that the constitution of poverty can be dated to a fundamental transformation of governance which is still less than two centuries old. This constitution, manifested in the debates over pauperism, must be understood in the context of the advent of a *liberal* government of poverty. It is thus first necessary to comprehend what the liberal mode displaced. This is the purpose of the first three chapters. They construct a general framework for understanding statements about poor policies in the seventeenth and eighteenth centuries through an examination of tracts on poor relief, make-work schemes, and workhouses. The arguments and concepts which are characteristic of these texts display a remarkably consistent way of addressing issues which will be called 'the Discourse of the Poor'. The first two chapters are concerned with the examination and exploration of the central themes of this discourse. Moreover, the coherence of this discourse can best be understood in terms of the requisites of what was known during this period, particularly in continental Europe, as 'police'. This is the subject of chapter three.

The defining ambition of the police of 'the Poor' was its concern with the utilisation and fostering of the 'numbers of the Poor'. Hence it relied upon a specific conception of population. The disruption to this conception effected by Malthus' principle of population will be dealt with in the following two chapters. Chapter four examines the nature of the Malthusian intervention by comparing its conception of population with others of the eighteenth century, principally that of Joseph Townsend, and by drawing out its implications for poor policy. Chapter five considers the question of the effectivity of this intervention in relation to Christian philanthropy and wider intellectual and political opinion. These considerations provide the basis for an evaluation of the relation between Malthus' view of the ethical responsibilities of the poor and the reform of the poor law in 1834.

A key aspect of the Malthusian intervention was its introduction of arguments about poor policy of a specifically *economic* order. The meaning of the application of such a theoretical rationality to matters of poverty must therefore be explored. To this end, chapter six examines a widely shared but rarely explicated historical schema of a shift from an ethical to an economic conception of public policy. The general claims which are made as a result of adherence to this schema are problematised. Moreover, the particular claims made for one text in the accounts of this shift, Adam Smith's *An Inquiry into the Nature and Causes of the Wealth of Nations* (1889), are interrogated in chapter seven. This chapter will also develop the implication of Smith's 'moral economy of exchange' for poor policy. Chapter eight situates these implications in relation to the great outpouring of solutions, plans, and theories concerning the poor in the 1790s, and the innovations of classical political economy in the early nineteenth century, instanced by Ricardo. This chapter thus explores the links between the rise of an economic approach to poor policy and the constitution of poverty.

The final three chapters are founded on the contention that the administrable domain of the liberal mode of government of poverty was defined through the notion of pauperism. To support this, the challenge presented by Polanyi's claims concerning the significance of pauperism is taken up. Chapter nine consists of an examination of Polanyi's thesis that the reform of the poor laws in the 1830s was necessary to overcome the obstacles to the formation of the first national capitalist labour market. Chapter ten moves on to an examination of the notion of pauperism in various tracts, with special attention given to Bentham's tracts on pauper management. Finally, chapter eleven contains an analysis of the notion of pauperism in both the new literature of police, exemplified by the work of Patrick Colquhoun, and a range of social-investigatory literature, in order to illustrate how it could be used to define a form of life for the labouring population.

The conclusion highlights the implications of the liberal break in the governance of poverty in two ways. First, it sketches some of the elementary consequences of the study by contrasting it with features of Marx's and Weber's accounts of the conditions of capitalism. It then foregrounds some issues of rupture and continuity, taking up themes of the pre-liberal, and illiberal, basis of the theory and practice of liberal governance, the formation of the 'social question', notions of self-responsibility, and the transformation of patriarchal relations. In the course of this study we shall be compelled to consider whether this liberal mode of governance was a break with the patriarchalism of earlier systems of the police of relations between the rich and 'the Poor'.

Chapter one

The discourse of the poor

The liberal transformation of the government of poverty was first signalled by a radical inversion of the way in which arguments concerning population figured in discussions of poor policy. This can be evidenced by a note David Ricardo was to enter in the second edition of his *Principles of Political Economy and Taxation* (Ricardo 1951, 1). After arguing that the operation of the poor laws increased the frequency of improvident and early marriages, Ricardo asserted that

> The progress of knowledge manifested upon this subject in the House of Commons since 1796 has happily not been very small, as may seen by . . . the following sentiments of Mr Pitt, in that year. 'Let us,' said he, 'make relief in cases where there are a number of children a matter of right and honour, instead of a ground of opprobrium and contempt. This will make a large family a blessing, and not a curse; and this will draw a proper line of distinction between those who are able to provide for themselves by their labour, and those who after having enriched their country with a number of children, have a claim upon its assistance for support.'

(Ricardo 1951, 1: 109)

Pitt's statement had been made in argument for allowances for large poor families. His ill-fated Poor Bill (1796–7), vigorously attacked by Bentham and others, had among its various provisions allowances for every child after the second for poor men, and after the first for widows (Bahmueller 1981: 42–52; Hammond and Hammond 1978: 99). For Ricardo, a policy based on the assertion that poor relief should reward the poor for their fecundity appears not only as backward and naïve but as dangerous. The political economist of 1818 is separated from the statesman of 1796 by a gulf which renders the latter's 'sentiments' almost incomprehensible. The aim of the first three chapters of this book is to bridge that gulf by providing a way of understanding the form of discourse which could sustain pronouncements such as that made here by the younger William Pitt.

18

How did it come about that, in only a few years, the objective of poor policy shifted from the encouragement to the discouragement of the poor's fecundity? It is well known that Malthus' *Essay on the Principle of Population*, first published in 1798, espoused the view that the poor laws encouraged the poor to procreate without regard to the availability of the means of subsistence. The nature of Malthus' theoretical transformation of conceptions of population and his subversion of earlier poor policy, together with the relation of this shift to the formation of economic discourse, will be discussed in chapters four and eight. For the present, however, Ricardo's satisfaction at the progress on this subject in parliament raises many other, no less important, questions. His footnote forces us to ask what conception of the poor, what notion of population, and what theory of state policy, could have allowed such a view to be expressed by so prominent a political figure only two years before the publication of Malthus' doctrine. Is it possible to construct the form of discourse by which statements such as this can be made intelligible? If so, can we discover the mode of government to which such statements were connected?

It will be argued in this and the next chapter that in the century and a half before the publication of Malthus' first *Essay on the Principle of Population* (1798), poor policy was discussed, formulated, and undertaken in a remarkably consistent fashion. In numerous pamphlets petitioning parliament, discourses on trade, and in the works of statesmen, political oeconomists, and jurists, can be found a single but accommodating conceptual architecture in which a notion of 'the Poor' was constructed in relation to the concerns of national policy, chief among which stood the augmentation of national wealth.

This form of discourse will be called the Discourse of the Poor, the capitalisation of which will distinguish it from the mass of historical discourses concerning poverty and denote the specific character of the object of this discourse.[1] Many of the texts which exemplify its features are commonly designated by the term 'mercantilist'. There is no reason to object to the application of this term to seventeenth- and eighteenth-century texts and policies which define national wealth in terms of a favourable balance of trade and an industrious population. However, in this study it has been necessary to join those who have taken a distance from those conventional, retrospective histories of economic thought which treat mercantilism as merely a flawed prevision of classical economics and as a body of doctrine solely concerned with trade and international exchange, or as a pre-modern policy of state tutelage of the economy (George 1985; Meuret 1981/2). As will be shown here, the key terms of these texts cannot be read as simple precursors of economic theories of value, profit, and production. Moreover, the content of this mercantilist discourse covers themes of internal political 'oeconomy', among which stands the central issue of 'the Poor'. The term Discourse of the Poor thus may be thought of as distinguishing from among mercantilist writings those statements which directly construct the Poor as an object of knowledge, and as a field of national policy and practice.

In order to maintain vigilance against anachronistic use of the discourses of the period, it is necessary to address certain fundamental premises of particular historical and sociological approaches to their historical context. This is the first task of the present chapter. We shall then summarise this foreign terrain and detail its conceptions of the 'numbers of the Poor' and the 'wealth of nations'. The next chapter will examine the policy implications of this discourse as encapsulated in the aim of 'setting the Poor to work' and the problem of idleness. Chapter three will show how the archaic signification of the term 'police' provides a viable alternative framework for understanding the mode of government to which this discourse is wedded.

History and genealogy

The texts under analysis here date from the middle of the seventeenth to the end of the eighteenth century. This is the period following the English Civil War of the early 1640s, especially after the 'settlement' of 1688, until the late eighteenth century.

For the Marxist historian, Christopher Hill, the 1640s and 1650s 'marked the end of medieval and Tudor England', a veritable 'revolution in government' (1969: 135; Corrigan and Sayer 1985: 72–3). He argues that this was true in many different dimensions, including agrarian relations (146), trade, colonial, and foreign policy (155), finance and taxation (180), and, importantly for our present purposes, industry and internal trade, when the central government lost its power to grant monopolies and to administer poor relief in 1641 (169). For Hill all this, coupled with 'the religious and intellectual revolution of the sixteen-forties and fifties' (190), makes this a time of bourgeois revolution, the beginnings, it might be said, of a 'capitalist modernity'.

Some caution needs to be expressed over applying such a schema to the course of the governance of the Poor. This period certainly marked the end of one phase of the English poor law. However, as we shall show, the style of administration of relief it inaugurated was hardly conducive to capitalist relations and could not be said to have embodied a capitalist economic rationality. Indeed, it was this very aspect of government which would form the central focus of the political economists' attacks in the early nineteenth century. Let us briefly summarise its main features before returning to the problem of the relation between the eighteenth-century governance of the Poor and capitalism.

While the celebrated Act of 1601 (43 Elizabeth c.2) is often taken to mark the beginning of the old poor law, it is in fact a re-enactment of a 1597 Act (39 Elizabeth c.3) which, as Webb and Webb note (1963a: 64), did little more than systematise and simplify the legislation of 1572–1576. The one important difference in the later legislation is that it brings to the fore civil authority by requiring the appointment, for the first time, of overseers of the Poor in every parish. The duty of these officers was to see to it that all classes of the Poor were provided for, that those who were able be set to work, that the sick be relieved, and that children receive an education. This comprehensive measure for the relief of the indigent was one of a 'package' of legislative measures of 1597–1601, including measures concerned with the punishment of rogues, vagabonds, and sturdy beggars, the regulation of charitable endowments, the erection of hospitals or 'abiding and working houses' for the Poor, the maintenance of tillage, and the prevention of the decay of townships.

The period 1590–1640 was also marked by what Webb and Webb call the 'administrative hierarchy' which sought a centralised control and supervision of the governance of the Poor by a national authority under the Privy Council (1963a: 65–70). While there is some dispute over whether the effect of the Puritan Revolution was a collapse in the institutional framework of the poor law (Pearl 1978: 206–209), it is true that central control broke down during the Civil War. A continuing feature of the old poor law was the high degree of discretion exercised by the local agents of the governance of the Poor, the justices of the peace, and the parish overseers. Moreover, after the Restoration, a second pillar of this localised administration was put in place, the law of settlement.

This law, which dated from 1662 legislation (14 Charles II c. 12) ironically entitled 'An Act for the Better Relief of the Poor of this Kingdom', sought to specify who were the legitimate members of the Poor of each parish, and thereby to identify potential or actual applicants for the relief the parish was bound to provide (Oxley 1974: 18–21, 39–43; Hammond and Hammond 1978: 70–77; Webb and Webb 1963a: 314–349; Bahmueller 1981: 20–28). It thus sought to prevent potential relief applicants from wandering from their place of birth or usual place of abode and empowered the justices to order forcible removal. To obtain a settlement was a complex procedure, caught in a web of apparently contradictory regulations concerning birth, legitimacy, the marital status of women, the payment of taxes, the serving of apprenticeships, and the holding of public office. The usual way of obtaining a settlement on the part of the labourers, however, was the notification of their new place of abode to the churchwardens or overseers of the Poor, who would then deliver a certificate forty days after the date on which a settlement would be granted. During that time, these officials could apply to the justices for the removal of the new inhabitants unless the newcomers rented a tenement over ten pounds a year or gave security to the parish, attested to by two justices, for indemnity against relief.

Can such changes in state administrative practices be regarded as the consequence of a 'bourgeois revolution'? Does the poor law after 1640 abruptly turn towards creating the conditions of a capitalist modernity? These are very large questions, which will be placed in abeyance for the time being. As Corrigan and Sayer concede when reviewing Hill's position, it is hard to sustain the claim that the Civil War was such a revolution, if that implies a 'set-piece struggle between clearly defined class groupings, with the victorious bourgeoisie emerging in secure possession of political power' (1985: 84-85). Their well-drawn history of English state formation, working largely within the umbrella of a Marxist historical sociology, finds that it is simply not possible to match political actors with economic interests in the events spanning from 1640 though the Restoration of 1660 to the settlement of 1688-9. Further, such an approach notices that capitalism was still fundamentally mercantile and commercial and had not yet revolutionised production. This is presented as a paradox of an at least partially bourgeois state, or at least a state which 'fostered both capitalist enterprise and the con-solidation of the bourgeois ruling class', but which could not be understood as a rationalised instrument of the capitalist classes who were its principal beneficiaries (88).

For Corrigan and Sayer (1985: 87-113), nowhere is this paradox more evident than in the particular political formation of the period which later came to be known as 'Old Corruption'. This formation, found during the century following 1688, has been characterised by E.P. Thompson (1978: 322) in terms of a 'social stasis' which witnessed the degeneration of ruling institutions, the spread of corruptions, and the entrenchment of, and increasing dissatisfaction with, a narrow elite comprising the Whig oligarchy which monopolised key positions in the state. Corrigan and Sayer point out, however, that 'it is not enough . . . to see capitalist development as something that occurred entirely independently of this "parasitism". Old Corruption was conducive to capitalism, if in complex and contradictory ways' (1985: 89). While accepting that such an approach may grant a high degree of intelligibility to the broader history of English state formation, the present study opts for a different line of attack on the genealogy of poor policy. It suggests that it may be possible to understand the government of the Poor during this period in terms of the measures and the goals of the specific programmes and policies in which it is embodied, rather than in its relation – no matter how complex and contradictory we might wish to make it – to capitalism. Despite the evident revolution in government in the mid-seventeenth century, the government of the Poor should not, at least in the first instance, be prematurely judged from the *telos* of modern political and economic formations.

A similar point could be made about paternalism, the eighteenth-century version of which is so vividly described by Thompson (1974). One of the ways in which this political formation encouraged capitalism, according to these authors, was the constitution of a 'capitalist ethos' through 'theatrical representations of social propriety and deference' and 'paternalist paradigms of master and servant' (Corrigan and Sayer 1985: 94). Now while there is certainly an important issue involved in conceptions of proper relations between rich and poor, is it necessary, and indeed helpful, to assume capitalism as their ultimate referent? To answer the question, it is useful to examine a body of written material which is evidence of patriarchalist relations of submission and dominance, of obedience and rule, and of rights and duties. But, as we shall see, there is much to this form of discourse which certainly does not resemble a nascent capitalist ethos, including its notions of labour, wealth, and profit. Such a discourse must be challenged, and its characteristic concepts displaced, before the liberal transformation of governance, which *will* be conducive to capitalist relations, is complete. Our first aim should be to approach these discourses in such a way that their irreducible *otherness* to more familiar concepts and categories is maintained.

In order to do so, it is necessary to examine the claim that the discussion of the Poor did not undertake the 'explicit application of social theories' and did not offer 'general economic analysis' (Poynter 1969: 21). Following our earlier warnings of the dangers of recurrential readings of texts, it would appear that these observations are, at the very least, well-founded starting points. However, we should not draw the conclusion from such lacunae that there were 'few coherent views on poverty' at this period, that writings and comment were 'for specific purposes' and less systematic than moral literature (21–22).

While it gives explicit recognition to issues of anachronism, this type of intellectual history presupposes the pertinence of categories and concepts drawn from social theory and economics as much as one which reads every text as a precursor of modern knowledges. Thus the reading of the 'debate before 1795' is as much filtered through the norms of the social theories and economic discourses of the twentieth century as one which seeks everywhere precursors of scientific knowledge. Here, however, the discourses under analysis are read negatively as those which lack such norms and are hence without any internal order. The consequence of such an approach is profoundly anti-genealogical. It does not allow us to entertain the claims of the history of discourses on poverty and the Poor and to interrogate the formation of economic science from

23

such a standpoint. A far more useful assumption would be that, even in the absence of such things as a theoretical conception of the economy or a notion of social totality, the discourse and mode of government of this period possesses an intrinsic logic or rationality, that is to say, its own form of coherence. A history of ideas which writes from the perspective of the contemporary social sciences, and knows only their rationality, needs to be replaced by a genealogy of government which is able to constitute the immanent rationality which inheres in the diversity of statements and policy formulations available in forms of discourse.

Related to this argument is the issue of the supposed isomorphism between the discourse and institutional treatment of the Poor in the eighteenth century. While our genealogy of government seeks to erase the effects of sterile division of intellectual labours, it is also necessary to avoid a premature elision of aspects of the history of 'ideas' with those of 'institutions'. To do this, we can examine the presumption that the fact that 'the old Poor Law was constructed by practical men reacting to local problems with varying degrees of intelligence, integrity and zeal' is enough to demonstrate the lack of explicit theories or general arguments concerning the Poor and their treatment (Poynter 1969: 21).

We have already mentioned the post-Restoration local nature of relief administration. One of the legacies of the revolutionary period was to loosen the governance of the Poor from the 'administrative hierarchy' and to place it within the framework of the local social and political order, particularly under the laws of settlement. Poor relief was administered on a mostly local basis for the next century and a half in the tiny administrative unit of the parish by officials elected by ratepayers assembled in 'vestries'. The next central administration, that of the 1830s, would have to deal with an estimated fifteen thousand parishes and it was something of an achievement that 13,691 parishes had been incorporated into 583 Poor Law Unions before the end of that decade (Henriques 1979: 42).

Moreover, it is true that the agents of administrative superintendence were – given the patriarchal nature of this mode of governance – *men* who were, one assumes, of practical bent. The poor-law administration revolved around that pivotal figure of English governance dating from the Middle Ages, the justice of the peace, Maitland's 'county gentleman commissioned by the King'. The JP's judicial-cum-police powers to arrest, to commit to gaol, and to demand sureties dated from the fourteenth century. His explicit statutory responsibility for matters pertaining to the Poor dated from the 1349 Statute of Labourers, under which he was given authority over the enforcement of maximum wage rates (Corrigan and Sayer 1985: 38–40). In 1601 the Poor Law and its immediate agents, the overseers, were placed under his charge and from 1662 he was to issue warrants for the removal of paupers. Through the justices, whose selection entailed a severe property qualification, 'the central state capacity in England . . . was based upon a high degree of involvement of local ruling elites in the exercise of governance' (16).

Thus the government of the Poor was fundamentally a local matter in terms of both the unit and agents of administration, run by the parochial community which supplied the poor rates and administered by the local gentry in their role as justices of the peace. While it is worth keeping all this in mind, there are no *a priori* grounds on which to assume that knowledges and discussions of the Poor will take on the same localised and practical nature. It is necessary to make the relation between the intellectual and institutional forms a matter for positive demonstration. Indeed, this and the following chapters will demonstrate that the knowledges and policies concerning the Poor in the eighteenth century possessed a systematicity and generality which did not respect local, regional, or perhaps even national boundaries. If this genealogy is premised on the search for the complex interlacing of knowledge, policy, and practice, it cannot afford to make, and then reductively traverse, a dogmatic distinction between ideas and institutions.

The numbers of the Poor and the wealth of nations

A summary view

The Discourse of the Poor may be said to be concerned, either implicitly or explicitly, with the question 'Who are the numbers of the nation's Poor?' There are other questions which are prominent in this literature, such as those seeking the causes of the distresses of the Poor and the burden of the poor rates, but, as will become clear, these can only be answered in the terms established by this first basic question and its solutions, which may be read as governing statements. I shall begin this exposition with an overall summary of the basic architecture of this discourse.

There are three possible responses to the attempt to define who constitute the Poor in this discourse, and each may be approached in terms of its relation to the notion of 'work'. The numbers of the Poor are constituted by: first, those that *cannot* work; second, those that *will* work; and third, those that *will not* work. Thus a late seventeenth-century author defines the duties of the parishes under the poor laws as 'work for those that will labour, punishment for those that will not, and bread for those that cannot' (Dunning in 1685, quoted by Eden 1928: 36). Similarly, three-quarters of a century later, an historical account of the poor laws divides the Poor into three classes, each with a corresponding category of statutes. The classes of the Poor and the objective of the respective types of legislation are: servants, labourers, and artificers, for whom employment should be provided; rogues and vagabonds, who are to be encouraged to labour; and the impotent, who are the objects of maintenance (Burn in 1764, quoted by Eden 1928: 64).

The numbers of the Poor are thus subject to a threefold classification from which arises a threefold policy imperative. The first category, those that cannot work, comprises the sick and impotent Poor, who, it is universally agreed, are the legitimate objects of relief and maintenance. The second category, those that will work, comprises all those of the Poor who are employed in occupations which are profitable to the nation. The remedy for any distresses of this category of the Poor is for them to be set to work. As we shall see, however, it would be premature to argue that this discourse, and the Elizabethan poor law, recognised a formal *right* to employment on behalf of the Poor and a *duty* of the state to provide such employment. Hence, neither the legislation nor the discourse can provide a concept of want of employment as unemployment, i.e. as an effect of economic factors over which political government has little or no direct control. Since it is within the province of the state to provide employment for those who are able, the existence of those idle through want of employment must be the result of a failure of the policies of the sovereign. By the beginning of the seventeenth century the means of providing such employment comes to be thought of in terms of the workhouse, the discursive function of which is to link the greatest numbers of the Poor to the wealth and strength of the nation. However, this means of provision does not exhaust the possibilities of effecting such a link within the Discourse of the Poor which also propounds a low-wage theory of the incentive to labour. The third category, those that will not work, comprises the idle Poor, afflicted by the 'taint of slothfulness', seduced by the luxury of the alehouse, and liable to punishment as rogues and vagabonds, terms which in themselves are subject to elaborate attempts at classification. The 'encouragement' of this category consists of such measures as the suppression of beggary, corporal punishment, and forced labour schemes of many sorts.

The category of the impotent Poor, or those that cannot work, remains relatively stable within this discourse. It occasions little controversy with a widespread acceptance of the legitimacy of the maintenance of those in this category under the poor laws. The other two categories are not so stable and, under specific conditions, cease to be mutually exclusive. Thus it is possible to argue that there are numbers of the Poor who are idle through 'want of work' and that these may be rendered industrious by the provision of work by means of workhouses or other forms of public works. However, it is also possible to argue that not only are the idle Poor unwilling to work and that there is already ample employment for all the Poor, but also that the industrious Poor have become gradually corrupted into the ways of idleness by bad work, domestic

and leisure habits, and so succumb to the taint of sloth. There i
flexibility for lively controversies to emerge within the shifting
between the two categories.

The great practical problem which is evinced by this threefold
of the numbers of the Poor is the question 'How will the Pooi be set
to work?' The answers include the provision of a 'parish stock' after
the fashion of the Elizabethan legislation, the establishment of institutional manufactures or workhouses, and the effective 'regulation' of the
Poor so that they will take up already existing employments. This
regulation includes not only the punishments and forcible transportation
meted out under the Vagrancy Acts but also techniques of lowering wages
and raising the price of provisions, both of which were said to stimulate
the labourer to a regular and industrious mode of existence. The objective of this classificatory system and its ruminations on the various means
by which the Poor are to be compelled to labour is not to relieve the
sufferings of those in a condition of poverty but to formulate the numbers
of the Poor in such a way as to promote most effectively the policy
objectives of increasing the wealth and strength of the nation.

The numbers of the Poor

The Discourse of the Poor, then, does not ask 'What is poverty and what
are its social and economic conditions and determinants?' In asking 'Who
are the numbers of our Poor?' it asks something quite distinctive and
very different from late twentieth-century texts of social science and social
policy. This question depends above all on a particular conception of
the relation between populousness and the wealth of nations. To illustrate
this linkage let us cite a passage by a well-known political arithmetician
of the seventeenth century and then the views of an early twentieth-
century historian of mercantilism.

In his *Treatise of Taxes and Contributions* of 1662, William Petty
argues that

> Fewness of people is real poverty; a Nation wherein are Eight Millions
> of people is more than twice as rich as the same scope of Land where
> are but Four; For the same Governours which are the great charge,
> may serve near as well, for the greater, as the lesser number.
> Secondly, if the people be so few, as that they can live, *Ex Sponte
> Creates*, or with little labour, such as is Grazing, etc., they become
> wholly without Art. No man that will not exercise his hands, being
> able to endure the tortures of the Mind, which much thoughtfulness
> doth occasion.
>
> (Petty 1963:34)

Petty's 'Political Arithmetick' may be taken as typical of the thought concerned with the 'oeconomy' and 'police' of the nation from the second half of the seventeenth century. It is common to find writers of this period arguing that the population of their nation was too small for its territory and advancing remedies for this condition. Both the reasons for taking this position and the means of remedying it vary widely. Hence Petty argued for a large population on the grounds that it meant a proportionate decrease in the charge of politicians and was conducive to the stimulation of more thoughtful or artful types of activity. However, a more universally recognised benefit of population increase was the lowering of wages which in turn was held to ensure greater industry on the part of the labouring Poor. The means of ensuring this increase were also diverse, ranging from religious toleration, which would both encourage immigration and diminish the emigration of native non-conformists (Furniss 1957: 34), to D'avenant's calls (1771, 2: 191) for rewards for the married to be apportioned to the number of their children and penalties for the unmarried.

Turning now to Furniss' classic study of mercantilism one finds a repeated insistence in mercantilist literature that people, by virtue of their 'industry', are the real foundation of national wealth (Furniss 1957: 16–17, 22–23). Thus Barbon wrote in 1690: 'The people are the riches and strength of the country', and, a decade earlier, Petty had argued that 'People are the chiefest, most fundamental and precious commodity, out of which may be derived all sorts of manufactures, navigation, riches, conquests, and solid dominion'. As early as 1664, Thomas Mun had suggested that 'Where people are many and the arts good, there the traffic will be great and the country rich'. Such assertions continue throughout the eighteenth century and were put perhaps most succinctly by the Quaker, John Bellers: 'Regularly labouring people are the kingdom's greatest treasure and strength'. By the middle of the century, Henry Fielding sought to define the status of such an assertion: 'That the strength and riches of a society consists in the numbers of the people is an assertion which hath attained the force of a maxim in politics'.[2]

One target of administration commonly identified and much discussed in such writings is 'the Poor'. By contrast, the notion of poverty – with its far more familiar ring today – usually refers only to the conditions pertaining in large geopolitical unities, above all the nation but also the city. 'Poverty' fulfils only a very narrow discursive function and does not comprehend an attribute or condition of either individuals or classes. Moreoever, the Poor are not treated as those afflicted by poverty but as a category which bears upon the well-being of the nation. The rationale for the political concern with the Poor is not the alleviation or even amelioration of poverty but the regulation, management, and proper ordering of, and provision of employment for, the nation's Poor. Consider, for example, how the theme of the relation between numbers and wealth is brought to bear on the riches or poverty of the city and nation in Josiah Child's *A New Discourse of Trade*, written in 1669:

> The riches of a City, as of a Nation, consist in the multitude of Inhabitants; . . . and if a right course be taken for the Sustenation of the Poor, and setting them on Work, you need invent no stratagem to keep them out, but rather to bring them in. For the resort of the Poor to a City or Nation well managed, is in effect, the conflux of Riches to that City or Nation; and therefore the subtil Dutch receive, and relieve, or employ all that come to them, not enquiring what Nation, much less what Parish they are of.
>
> (Child 1669: 64)

Child thus moves from the characteristic identification of numbers and wealth to a consideration of how to attract the Poor to the nation or city by means of provision for their relief and employment. 'Setting the Poor to work' is the predominant practical solution to the question of how to link the numbers of the Poor to the augmentation of national wealth and strength in this literature, although it would meet some notable and occasionally effective opposition.

There are, nevertheless, definite limits to the identification of numbers of inhabitants with the real wealth, strength, and greatness of the nation. In *A Discourse Touching Provision for the Poor* (1683) Matthew Hale argues that the absence of the provision of employment and the bringing up of children in poor families in the ways of begging and stealing leads to 'a successive multiplication of hurtful or at least unprofitable people, neither capable of Discipline nor beneficial Employment'. He continues:

> But with us in England, for want of a due regulation of things, the more populous we are, the Poorer we are; so that, that wherein the Strength and Wealth of a Kingdom consists, renders us the weaker and the poorer.
>
> (Hale 1683: The Preface)

Here populousness coincides with wealth on the condition that it is made up of those able to provide their own sustenance by means of 'profitable' employments and not by the 'burdensome trades' of begging and stealing. The link between the two terms depends on increasing the numbers of the industrious Poor and decreasing the numbers of the idle Poor. Others, such as Daniel Defoe, rework this condition of the coincidence of populousness and wealth in the form of a paradox so that England becomes a 'lazy, diligent Nation' which is at once populous, rich, and flourishing as well as poor and clogged with burdensome people (1704: 26, 9).

The wealth of nations

A way of increasing the intelligibility of these statements is to render intelligible their notions of the 'stock of labour' and 'the wealth of nations'. This can be done by examining the use of such terms in light of recent investigations into governmental discourses (including Political Oeconomy) which emerged in the context of the rise of the administrative nation states from the sixteenth century. We shall return to specific aspects of these discourses in later chapters but, for the moment, it is worth summarising certain salient features. These features are:

1 An *oeconomic* or 'householding' rather than economic conception of the art of government (Tribe 1978: 80–84; Bruland and Smith 1981: 474–476; Foucault 1979a: 5–21);
2 A presupposition of a prior constituted polity and the agency of the *sovereign* or *statesman* (e.g. Tribe 1978: 85, 104) in the absence of a theoretical conception of the economy as an autonomous entity;
3 An assumption of *patriarchal* relations of service and obligation between monarch and subjects, and between the heads of individual households and their wives, children, servants, and labourers (Foucault 1979a: 16–17; Bruland and Smith 1981: 474–475; George 1985: 205–209; Corrigan and Sayer 1985: ch. 4; Hill 1964: ch. 12); and
4 A *distributional* problematic, in which the task of the wise administration of the nation referred to the maintenance of all its objects (persons, things) in their rightful place (George 1985: 210; Tribe 1978: 81–85).

Foucault noted that 'the word "oeconomy" can only refer to the wise government of the family for the common welfare of all' and that 'prior to the emergence of population, the art of government was impossible to conceive except . . . as the management of a family' (1979a: 10, 17). The art of government so conceived entailed certain qualities of stewardship on the part of governors, as is evident in Calamy's instruction to MPs in 1641 that they first must reform their own families, i.e. servants, wives, and children, before reforming the family of God (Corrigan and Sayer 1985: 81). The household was both model for the patriarchal state and an element in its constitution, a model of governance and the means by which the sovereign governed. There was a complete continuity within the patriarchal state in the relations which existed between monarch and subjects, governors and governed, master and servant, husband and wife, and father and child. The sovereign, in fact, sought to enforce this patriarchal authority and to define the prerogatives of householders. Thus only merchants, noblemen, and gentlemen (and not artificers, journeymen, husbandmen, and labourers) were permitted to read the Bible in their households under Henry VIII (34 and 35 c.1), and Elizabethans (35 c.1) were fined if their children or apprentices failed to attend church (Corrigan and Sayer 1985: 81). The Tudor monarchy deliberately fostered the power of the husband and father in the conjugal relation (Hill 1978: 456). The enforcement of familial responsibility for the maintenance of 'poor, lame, blind, and impotent' family members, and 'those without labour', was a clause in the Elizabethan poor law (Corrigan and Corrigan 1979: 6).

It is thus no surprise that Tribe (1978: ch. 5) finds that Political Oeconomy is not an economic discourse in any recognisable sense of the term. It is not built upon a theoretical conception of the economy, that is, of processes of the production and distribution of wealth and their agents, which are conceptually autonomous from the political order and its actors. In this discourse, national wealth is not conceived as equivalent to the aggregate of value produced and/or realised within a definite political–geographic unit, but rather as a process of circulation within the polity composed of trading households. 'Economic' operation is thus conceived in terms of domestic finance in which 'households of the oeconomy trade with each other, realising circulatory gains in so far as they can buy cheap and sell dear' (Bruland and Smith 1981: 475).

This circulation has various possible origins, including labour (Tribe 1978: 90–91). Labour is connected with wealth not through production but by virtue of its position at the origin of the circulation of commodities and money, although, as in the case of physiocratic doctrines, it may in turn give way to land as the origin of wealth. To argue that labour is the source of wealth in such a discourse is simply to nominate an origin of the process of circulation. For mercantilists such as Child and Hale the establishment of manufactures, including in workhouses, can be understood as attempts to augment the number of patriarchal trading households of the nation in order to bring in numbers of the industrious Poor, and to discipline the idle Poor, and thereby increase circulation and wealth.

Labour does not signify a kind of constitutive activity but merely the numbers of the industrious Poor. The 'stock of labour' which makes up the nation's wealth is not the value-generating activity of nineteenth-century classical or Marxist political economy but the members of a specific category of the populace, the industrious or labouring Poor (Tribe 1978: 103–104). The Discourse of the Poor, as a discourse on the actual or potential members of this category, hence intersects with Political Oeconomy's objective to increase the numbers of the labouring or industrious Poor.

Wealth here is also a quite particular entity – primarily, money wealth. The earliest mercantilist writers conceived the wealth of nations in terms of the quantity of bullion within the country (Furniss, 1957: 9). Any foreign trade which brought an inflow of specie into the country was considered to increase national wealth and any which occasioned an outflow decreased that wealth. Therefore, trade was deemed favourable or unfavourable depending on whether it brought money metal into the country or sent it out. A more sophisticated variant was later introduced to defend merchants who exported precious metals in the course of foreign trade (Furniss 1957: 9–11). Thus the annual balance of foreign trade became the deciding factor. If this balance indicated a flow of specie into the country, then foreign trade had been favourable to an increase in national wealth.

These doctrines on national wealth became considerably more complex by the beginning of the eighteenth century while still retaining the balance-of-trade approach. At that time it was argued that it is not the quantity of money which is crucial but its function of facilitating circulation (Furniss 1957: 63–66). Money is no longer an end of national policy in itself. It has become a means of the augmentation of the circulation of commodities and the increase in employment it allows.

Prosperity is commonly conceived by a physiological metaphor, as in this passage by an anonymous writer in 1700:

> The money in a kingdom or commonwealth is . . . the blood that circulates through the veins and arteries of the body and communicates life and vigour to every part, without which the members would become dead and uncapable to assist or comfort one another.
>
> (quoted by Furniss 1957: 65)

What is significant is that this image of the body is an attempt to conceptualise relations between population, money, exchange, production, and wealth without the benefit of the theories of production and distribution which are constitutive of economic discourse. In the tracts and pamphlets which make up the Discourse of the Poor there is a conception of wealth which relies on the circulatory processes of the body politic rather than a theoretical mechanism of its production by and distribution to specific agents in a national economy. Thus Defoe argues that 'the wise Queen' (Elizabeth) directed public employment projects under the poor law because she realised that 'it was the Manufactures brought the People thither, and Multitudes of People make Trade, Trade makes Wealth, Wealth builds cities, which Enrich the Land round them, Land Enrich'd rises in Value, and Value of the Lands Enriches the Government' (1704: 5). It will be noted that the end of this process of circulation between the patriarchal trading households, here encouraged by the establishment of manufactures, is the royal treasury. Political Oeconomy thus deals with the proper practices for the management of the national estate (George 1985: 212) and the Discourse of the Poor deals with the administration of that category of subjects, within patriarchal relations of domination and subordination, which is of critical importance to the augmentation of that estate. Wealth is national wealth. The Discourse of the Poor shares with eighteenth-century Political Oeconomy the use of population as a way of assembling its object and the theme of population representing wealth (Tribe 1978: 90–92). In both, the population can be said to represent wealth because it is possible to divide it into productive and unproductive employments for the purpose of arguing about the policies to be followed by the sovereign or statesman. Within Political Oeconomy, these arguments concern the relative merits of agriculture and manufactures; in the Discourse of the Poor, of industry and idleness.

However, any attempt to read the concept of population as an index of the *modernity* of political discourses is deeply problematic. This is the position on the concept of population afforded by Foucault's account of the emergence of biopolitics (1979b: 139–143). Biopolitics involves the constitution of the population as a field of (state and non-state) regulation in particular forms of knowledge, such as vital statistics and census taking, in tandem with calculated strategies of the management of its health, welfare, hygiene, and living conditions. For Foucault, this double entry of the population as a field of knowledge and target of government marks the crossing of the 'threshold of modernity' in the 'West', and the beginning of an 'era of governmentality' (1979b: 142–143; 1979a: 20). In a later lecture (Foucault 1979a: 21), the entry of the population as a target of Absolutist nation states is said to be best understood as the 'governmentalisation of the State'. The principal form of knowledge which is the correlate of the government of populations is political economy.

This last innovation brings Foucault's conceptual elaboration closer to the concerns of this book. Nevertheless, *pace* Foucault, the concept of population in eighteenth-century thought on government is strikingly different from its classical liberal (and more recent) uses. It entails neither the formulation of policies and political action by reference to an explicit economic rationality which is characteristic of liberal governance nor the welfarist focus on the enhancement of the life of 'individuals'. It would seem necessary, in this instance at least, to follow earlier formulations of Foucault which decisively reject this kind of totalising cultural analysis of the teleology of the West (e.g. 1972: 204; 1977b: 139–164; cf Dean 1986: 44–61).

While the Discourse of the Poor constitutes the population as a terrain of political government, it does so in way which excludes the possibility of the dominance of policy by a theoretical conception of the economy. Indeed, a simple demarcation cannot be made between government of the population and householding government, as Foucault seems to imply (1979b: 17). Gregory King's estimate of the size of the English population for 1695 was based on the household unit, and indeed was later criticised for understating the population by using too small a multiplier (Glass 1973: 14). Similarly Sir James Steuart's 1767 *Political Oeconomy* (1966) both clearly sustains the householding conception of governance and enunciates and operates within the framework of a definite conception of population. Although these discourses are the site of the entry of concern for the conservation and utilisation of human beings as valued resources of the state, their end is not the positive enhancement of the life of individuals but the augmentation of the national estate. This conception of population in matters of the Poor may be viewed as a means of constructing arguments and policies on pertinent aspects of employment, trade, migration, poor relief, and so on, in a form typical of Political Oeconomy and in a way which is entirely distinct from an economic science or a set of welfare imperatives. It should not be surprising, therefore, to find that the mode of formulating poor policy in eighteenth-century England had more in common with a discourse which arose in German-speaking regions at about the same time, *Polizeiwissenschaft*, or the science of police, than with economics as we know it. This theme will be taken up in chapter three. The aim of the next chapter is to examine the various means by which it was possible, in the Discourse of the Poor, to link the population of the Poor with national goals.

Chapter two

The problem of idleness

The problem of harnessing the numbers of the Poor to national goals is resolved into the practical imperative of 'setting the Poor to work'. To understand the various solutions to this problem, we must understand both how the idle Poor could be transformed into the industrious Poor, and, conversely, how the industrious could be corrupted into idleness, within the terms of the Discourse of the Poor. On the one hand, we must examine the advocacy of make-work schemes, including the most renowned one, the workhouse. On the other, we should attempt to understand the moral diagnosis of the Poor embodied in the criticism of make-work schemes.

Such a task will lead us to consider themes of the 'taint of slothfulness', and the ensuing 'corruption of morals' of the *labouring* Poor, which were said to be induced by the alehouse and other 'luxury'. It will also bring to the fore the widespread use of measures such as low wages, high prices, and anti-recreational campaigns as remedies to idleness.

This is the ground covered in the present chapter. It concludes with a brief discussion of the phases of the debate on the existing system of poor relief before the 1790s.

Setting the Poor to work

To understand the Discourse of the Poor, it is necessary to elaborate upon the linkage of 'numbers' and 'wealth' and the crucial discursive condition of this linkage, that the Poor must be made 'industrious' and be engaged in 'useful employment'. To do so, it is helpful to return to the question which governs the Discourse of the Poor, 'Who are the numbers of our Poor?' This question encapsulates the general pre-occupation with populousness which arises from the association of the size of the population with the considerations which fall under the headings of the 'wealth, strength, and greatness' of the nation. Moreover, the specific condition of this association of numbers and wealth requires a means of discrimination between certain habits, customs, and behaviours of the Poor. This means is provided by the distinction between the industrious Poor and the idle Poor which distributes the positively- and negatively-valued features of the Poor into two separate categories.

Nevertheless, these categories are not mutually exclusive under all conditions. This can be illustrated by the strategy of setting the Poor to work. In such a strategy work is used as a technique of transform- ation of the idle into the numbers of the profitably and usefully employed. This transformation should be viewed *not* as a moral reform of the individual but as a way of properly utilising the nation's most valuable resource, its population. As the ubiquity of the 'Great Confinement' (or the continent-wide movement to sequestrate the poor in enclosed institu- tions) shows, the possibility of realising such a transformation predicates the entire edifice of poor policy in Europe in this epoch (Foucault 1965: 38–64).

In a complementary shift, moreover, the problem of idleness comprehends rather more than the 'sturdy beggar' and 'the rogue and vagabond'. The sin of sloth is able to taint more than those who can give no account of themselves or their occupation. It reaches into the labouring populace itself to corrupt its industry and therefore waste the wealth of the nation. We must examine both the transformation of the idle Poor into the industrious Poor and the discovery and excoriation of idleness from its lodgings within industry. The former is the topic of this section. The latter will be dealt with in following sections.

The proper employment of the Poor is pertinent to the linkage which is supposed to exist between numbers and wealth in a nation. There are two ways within the Discourse of the Poor in which this can be achieved by the action of the state. The first of these may be instanced both by William Petty's discussion (1963: 29–31) of the 'Publick Charge' for the care and employment of the Poor and also by the raising of funds for the establish- ment of a parish stock (of flax, hemp, etc.) under provisions of the Tudor poor law (Webb and Webb 1963a: 91–92). In the latter case, the Webbs cite evidence from parochial reports of parishes setting the Poor to work with or without the provision of such a stock. Tiny rural parishes report possessing small amounts of 'town stock' to 'set the Poor on work as need', or to be 'bestowed in hemp and employed to set such Poor on work as want'. Another reports the stock was 'disbursed to poor people . . . to set them to work', presumably in their own homes. Still other parishes claim that 'the Poor are otherwise set on works' in the absence of the existence of such a stock. The nature of such works may be gleaned from sugges- tions by Petty who, it may be noted, advocated lower taxes in all cases *except* the relief and employment of the Poor.

Petty recommends 'receptacles' for invalids, hospitals for the sick, and institutions for 'orphans, found and exposed' (1963: 29). He even adds the patriarchal justification of the latter that such children would 'afford the King the fittest Instruments for all kinds of his Affairs, and be as firmly obliged to be his faithful servants as his own children' (29). Given that arrangements are made for these categories, and provided that the 'lazy and thievish' be restrained and punished, he proposes public employment for all other indigent people. This would include the cutting and scouring of rivers, the planting of trees, the making of bridges and causeways, working in mines, quarries, and colleries, and the manufacturing of iron (29–30). Petty claims that all such works are wanting in the nation and that they would introduce new trades requiring 'much labour and little art'. These suggestions, like those of the small-scale experiments with the parish stock in the first half of the seventeenth century, remind us that the imperative to set the Poor to work need not be fulfilled by a specific institutional form.

Another point worthy of note here is that the objective of such public employment is not, for Petty, limited to putting the Poor to work on useful labour. Such works 'would keep their minds to discipline and obedience, and their bodies to a patience of more profitable labour when the need shall require it' (Petty 1963: 31). Petty even suggests that it would not matter if this labour was as useless as building a pyramid upon the Salisbury Plain or carting the stones from Stonehenge to Tower-Hill! Such tasks could be justified because employment for the Poor removes the evil habits attendant upon begging and stealing and the possibility of an indisposition to labour (30).

The linkage between the numbers of the Poor and the wealth of the nation by the provision of labour cannot be reduced to the economic mobilisation of a reserve army of labour or the like. Rather, it should be understood in terms of the complete requisites of the proper administration of the Poor as vital to the welfare of the nation, and as a means of security by establishing and maintaining patriarchal relations of command and obedience. In this regard Matthew Hale argues that poverty 'leaves men tumultuous and unquiet' and the relief of the poor is 'an Act of Civil Prudence and Political Wisdom': 'Where there are many very poor, the Rich cannot long or safely continue such; Necessity renders men of phlegmatick and dull natures stupid and indisciplinable; And men of more firey or active constitutions rapacious and desperate' (Hale 1683: Preface). It would be problematic to translate the projects for employing the Poor into one of making their labour a source of profit on capital outlays on the means of production. The terms 'profitable employment' and 'useful labour' would be better understood as referring to a wide range of national considerations including those of internal security, military strength, and political allegiance, among which the augmentation of national, rather than individual or private, wealth can be counted. It is true, however, that the theme that the Poor must be profitably and usefully employed attains some prominence in certain of the writings which argue for the establishment of workhouses.

The workhouse, along with the house of correction, the house of industry, and the later labour colony, falls in the second and dominant category by which this discourse seeks to govern the numbers of the Poor to achieve national goals. The year 1557, in which the former Royal palace of Bridewell was converted into a house of correction which was both an embodiment of patriarchal governance and a hive in which some twenty-six arts and trades were practised, might serve as the date for the inauguration of such projects (Evans 1982: 49–50). Indeed, it became a model for the institutions established under the enabling legislation of 1576, 1597, and 1609, in which the house of correction was the punishment for failure to work on the parish stock (George 1985: 242–250). Such houses were indeed punitive, and discipline was achieved by means of ritual inscription of sovereign power upon the body of the idle or dissolute, but they were also refuges and almshouses.

The public workhouse, however, does not make its appearance until after the Civil War. Among the earliest of the workhouse projectors in England were the Chief Justice, Sir Matthew Hale, and the Chairman of the East India Company, Sir Josiah Child. Hale is very sanguine about his scheme:

> The prevention of poverty, idleness, and a loose and disorderly Education, even of poor children, would do more good to this Kingdom than all the Gibbets, and Cauterizations, and Whipping Posts, and Jayls in this Kingdom, and would render these kinds of Disciplines less necessary and less frequent.

(Hale 1683, The Preface)

Hale (1683: 7–9) argues that, despite the Elizabethan poor law, it is rare to see any provision of a stock in most parishes for the relief and employment of the Poor. He offers the following reasons for this failure. The churchwardens and overseers are unwilling to raise the rates lest they displease their neighbours. In any case, there are those poor parishes with a preponderance of tradesmen and labourers in which it is impossible to raise the rates. Furthermore, there is the lack of consideration of the benefits accruing from a more far-sighted approach. Thus the law is deficient as there is no compulsion, nor is there a provision for contiguous parishes to unite to raise a common stock. The law does not even enable parishes or unions of parishes to hire or erect a 'common Work-House'.

Hale then propounds a remedy which consists of empowering the justices of the peace to unite the parishes for workhouse financing and construction, to employ a master, and to provide 'a stock to set the Poor within those precincts on work' (1683: 9–10). Upon doing this, the law should be backed up by force so that 'if any person that is able to work, and not able to maintain himself, shall refuse to do so he may be forced thereunto by Warrant of two Justices of the Peace by Imprisonment, and moderate correction in such Work-House' (10).

Child's arguments, written a decade later, bear a remarkable similarity to Hale's, locating the failure of the poor law in the laws themselves, their 'radical error' being the leaving of the care of the Poor to every parish singly (1693: 58–61). He proposes an experiment 'in those parts of the Kingdom which are the Vitals in the body politick' (65). London, Westminster, and surrounding districts would be united into one province or 'line of communication' for the relief and employment of the Poor. These duties would be then entrusted to an assembly incorporated by an Act of Parliament, titled the 'Fathers of the Poor', and elected after the manner of the East India Company by the 'livery-men' of London (64–72). This assembly would have the power to purchase lands, erect and endow workhouses, hospitals, and houses of correction, erect 'petty Bancks and Lumbards', send numbers of the Poor to overseas plantations, tax playhouses, and hold the patent for farthings (67–68).

Child reiterates the theme of making the Poor useful to the Kingdom and suggests that the scheme would save the public purse some hundreds of thousands of pounds per annum (1693: 56). However, his list of the 'benefits to this Kingdom' appears to leave out considerations of profitability altogether. He argues that the Poor could find work without wandering in search of it, the rich would know where to disperse their charity, and, following from this, beggary would be eliminated, the foreign plantations would be well supplied with servants, and the proposed assembly in its wisdom would doubtless provide for visiting the sick and instructing children in learning and the arts (73–74). Expectations of a regular return on the outlays of capital are striking only by their omission.

Hale's text brings out the complexity of this conception of profitability even further. For instance, he argues (Hale 1683: 11) that his scheme would bring the Poor and their children into a regular, orderly, industrious course of life which would become as natural to them as the begging and stealing they are currently engaged in. Thus a certain 'course of Life' may be a profitable one. If the term is broken down further, it becomes evident that such a profitable life has a minimum requirement that 'every Body (be put) into a capacity of eating his own Bread' (12). The profitable employment of the Poor does not necessitate a surplus in excess of the production of the labourer's means of subsistence but refers to the capacity of a certain course of life to be (if only potentially) self-sustaining:

> And were there no other Benefit to the Kingdom, in general, nor to the particular Places where such Work-Houses shall be settled but

this, although the Stock were wholly lost in four years, it would be an abundant recompense, by the accustoming the poor sort to a civil and industrious course of Life, whereby they would soon become not only not burdensome, but profitable to the Kingdom and Places where they live.

(Hale 1683: 1)

It is possible, therefore, to be profitable to the Nation or the locality even if the 'Stock' on which the Poor are to be set to work is completely lost over a period of time. Such is hardly the language of the Weberian rational capitalist entrepreneur! Where pecuniary considerations do enter into these arguments they are not concerned with the means of expansion of private wealth but with the problem of taxation. To become profitable is to practise a specific way of life which includes the capacity to provide or to contribute to one's own subsistence so that it will become in 'every way more easy for them that are to pay' for the care and maintenance of the Poor (Hale 1683: 15). The workhouse thus allows the Poor to be educated in civility and industry, to gain a trade which will provide greater means of support than the contributions of the poor rate, and to be weaned off relief.

The numbers of the Poor are linked to the wealth of the nation by the mechanism of the workhouse. This is not because these are institutions for the generation of surplus value. Rather, the workhouse would halt the flow of money out of the kingdom to pay for imports by means of the establishment of manufactures which provide for domestic consumption and thus make 'our Trade Outward . . . exceed our Trade Inward' (Hale 1683: 12–13). This argument is typical of the make-work schemes of the mercantilist period (Furniss 1972: 46–52). Useful employment for the idle Poor is conceived in terms of either the replacement of previously imported manufactures or the working up of raw produce into manufactured exports. Thus Hale proposes the establishment of woollen manufactures throughout the kingdom for the knitting of 'Stockings, Caps, Waist-coats, and the like' and manufactures for 'Linnen Cloth, Laces of all sorts, Nets, Sails, etc.' (1683: 13–14). These textile manufactures would prevent the importation of such items from Holland, France, and Flanders. The course of encouraging new manufactured, as opposed to raw, exports was widely advocated provided that care was taken not to deprive other industrious Poor of employment (Furniss 1972: 48). Even Daniel Defoe in his protracted diatribe against make-work schemes admits that the establishment of a new export trade or a new item of domestic consumption is 'so much clear Gain to the General Stock' as to be 'something extraordinary' (1704: 16).

The first workhouse experiments were made in the decades after the proposals of Child and Hale were put forward. Thomas Firmin, who had set men and women to clothing manufacture after the plague in 1665, purchased a spacious building in 1676 to employ the Poor in linen manufacture. This 'private' workhouse employed able-bodied tradespeople (carders, flax dressers, combers, spinners, and weavers) at low wages as well as children from the age of three, the aged, and the nearly blind, and lasted until his death some twenty-one years later (Webb and Webb 1963a: 106–107). The workhouse was one of the major origins of the textile concentrated enterprise. The houses of correction in the West Riding became centres of woollen manufacture, and the provision of spinning was the most common make-work vehicle of both mercantilism and poor-law projects (George 1985: 245). The first legislation for the incorporation of parishes was the Act of 1696 allowing the City of Bristol to establish a Corporation of the Poor for the whole city for the purpose of constructing a workhouse. The Act was passed in response to local notaries, including the Mayor and Alderman, and local merchants, including John Cary who had written an influential pamphlet on the project published in the previous year (Webb and Webb 1963a: 119–120). During the next fifteen years thirteen further towns applied and received Acts for such an incorporation for workhouse construction. An enabling act of 1723 – Knatchbull's Act (9 George I c.7) – for workhouse construction, which also gave the first legislative recognition of the deterrent function of the workhouse, brought in response over a hundred more of these institutions and a fresh round of applications for incorporation, not only in the towns but also in the rural parishes (Webb and Webb 1963a: 120–121).

From the pamphlets of its proposers, the workhouse emerges as the ideal institutional solution to the problem of linking the numbers of the idle Poor to the wealth and strength of the nation. The form of the workhouse was a condensed solution to a multi-faceted problem of transforming the idle into the industrious. The workhouse was to provide the Poor with livelihoods, to suppress beggary, to instruct poor children, and to give an education in civility, discipline, and obedience. It would, it was hoped, equalise the poor rates among the parishes and harness charitable endeavour to positive national goals. Its greatest aspiration was to put the idle in the way of earning their own subsistence rather than marshalling their labour for the production of profit. Even when it failed to do this, as it would throughout the following century, the breadth of the functions which it was held to fulfil, and the over-riding concern that the Poor be set to work evinced in mercantilist labour policy, ensured that this massive experiment would not be easily abandoned.

Nevertheless, the sanguine attitude towards the prospects and advantages of setting the Poor to work was not shared by all mercantilist commentators. The problem of linking the Poor to national goals

41

showed the less benevolent face of paternalism in its approach to the problem of idleness.

The taint of slothfulness

'Giving alms no charity'

In the Discourse of the Poor there is another position which ultimately leads to a rejection of make-work schemes as futile and injurious to the nation. It asserts that the numbers of the industrious Poor are rendered less profitable by their proclivity to idleness and their affliction with the taint of slothfulness, and that there is sufficient work for those that want it. This position is often associated with low-wage/high-price theories of the industry of the Poor and with anti-recreational campaigns and movements for moral reform in the eighteenth century.

Among the earliest and best examples of this position is the sharp rebuke to half a century of workhouse programmes delivered in Daniel Defoe's pamphlet *Giving Alms No Charity and Employing the Poor a Grievance to the Nation* (1704). It would appear that this publication met with some success as a response to a bill which had actually passed through the House of Commons. This bill would have established in each parish something of the public workhouse, with its employment, educative, and relieving functions, which had been advocated by numerous writers in the previous decades (Webb and Webb 1963a: 113–114). Since the avowed aim of the text was to plead the case against the public employment of the Poor, whether in the form of the workhouses or parish stocks, it took the form of a petition to the 'Knights, Citizens and Burgesses in Parliament assembled' (Defoe 1704: 3).

The Webbs interpret Defoe's pamphlet as a 'blow to the compassionate efforts' of the make-work projectors, throwing into the debate 'the hardest possible stone of economic disillusionment and worldly cynicism' (1963a: 114). Polanyi (1957: 108–109) reads it as an early economic argument against public employment as displacing private manufactures. Whatever the cynicism involved, there is no textual support for the implication that this pamphlet foreshadows the later subjugation of the question of poverty to an emergent economic rationality. Defoe's statements are continuous with the aims of mercantilist domestic policy and the form of the Discourse of the Poor, repeating its tenets regarding population and national policy and its conception of circulation as dependent upon manufacturers and trade. The text does not disturb the previously existing calm of charitable impulse but is an instance of how all the characteristic arguments of the Discourse of the Poor could be marshalled towards a conclusion opposed to that drawn by the advocates of workhouses. The way in which this discourse conceived the numbers of the Poor always contained within itself the possibility of the declamation of the most cherished ambitions of enforced labour.

Defoe begins with an 'Account of how we came to be a rich, flourishing and populous Nation' (1704: 9) by affirming the benefits brought about by the Elizabethan poor-law provision to set the poor to work. He argues that this provision was designed to establish cloth manufacturers using the assistance of refugees from the Low Countries fleeing Spanish religious persecution. Defoe suggests that 'the wise Queen knew the number of inhabitants are the Wealth and Strength of a Nation' and that the poor-law establishment of textile manufacturers was the means of securing 'multitudes of people' whose trade would build cities and enrich the land, and lead to an increase in the national treasury (7). In all key respects, Defoe's text is typical of the Discourse of the Poor with its emphasis on sovereign power, populationism, and mercantilist trade theory. Like the workhouse projectors, Defoe argues that manufactures are a means of attracting numbers of people and encouraging trade which ultimately augments national wealth.

Also like them, Defoe poses the question of poverty at the level of large geographical and political unities, mostly the nation state. For Defoe, the wealth and poverty of the nation exist in dichotomy. While the former is defined in terms of an industrious population, the latter refers to the absence of manufactures, the fleeing of trade, the depopulation of the cities, and the existence of a 'crowd of clamouring, unimploy'd, unprovided for poor people, who make the Nation uneasie, burthen the Rich, clog our parishes' (Defoe 1704: 9). Moreover, Defoe partakes of the householding conception of policy of the Discourse of the Poor enunciated by the workhouse projectors. The sovereign figures as the foundation of a wise policy of providing employment so that 'every Family might live upon their own Labour' (13). Employment remains a core policy objective. For Defoe, however, it is the means by which this objective is secured which leads him to differ from many of his contemporaries.

What of the question of the relation between the forced establishment of new manufactures and the existing employments of the Poor, from which so much has been inferred? Here the problematic of circulation within the *oeconomic* organisation of the nation enables this pamphlet to establish the terms of the argument against public works for the Poor. Having established the wisdom of setting the Poor to work in the Elizabethan period, Defoe then turns to a survey of the contemporary scene in which

> The Manufactures of England are happily settled in different Corners of the Kindgom, from when they are mutually convey'd by a Circulation of Trade to London by Wholesale, like Blood to the

Heart, and from thence disperse in lesser quantities to the other parts
of the Kingdom by Retail.

(Defoe 1704: 17-18)

The body politic here would seem less a metaphor than a means of conceiving the different functions of specific locations in the nation. For
Defoe, the establishment of public manufactures to set the Poor to work
is therefore a 'Breach of the Circulation of Trade [which] must necessarily
distemper the Body' (18). The effect of such meddling with the happily
settled manufactures of different parts of the kingdom is to put a vagabond
into an honest labourer's employment (17).

These criticisms should not be interpreted as an argument for the free
market in labour or a defence of wage-labour as the best means of provision for the Poor. Nor should they be taken as an early example of
the plea for private investment over expenditure on public employment.
Defoe's position is a defence of existing manufactures which are
themselves the result of a previous initiative by the sovereign. His
pamphlet serves only to warn against tampering with the existing distribution of manufactures throughout the nation, those 'Arcanas of Trade'
which, although established by 'casual circumstances' and the 'consequences of time', 'to alter or disorder . . . would be an irreparable
damage to the Publick' (1704: 17). These are not the arguments of proto-liberalism but those of a national mercantilism.

Defoe's case against make-work schemes rests on an objection not
to the degree of state intervention into a self-regulating market, but to
the transposition caused to the established system of circulation and the
current dispersion of manufactures within the nation. He argues, rather,
that the proposed erection of workhouses for manufactures would
occasion all sorts of disorder. They 'will turn thousands of Families out
of their Employments and take the Bread out of the Mouths of diligent
and industrious families to feed Vagrants, Thieves and Beggars' (Defoe
1704: 23). But they would also upset the present settlement of families,
make towns and cities independent of one another, damage the dignity
and reputation of English goods abroad, cause ruin to all carriers, and
end in a 'strange Confusion and particular Detriment to the general
circulation of Trade' (21-22).

These schemes signify a confusion as to who makes up the numbers
of the Poor. Defoe's statements should not be read as an instance of
incipient liberal anti-statist themes but as an elaboration of one particular
way of answering the question which governs the Discourse of the Poor.
Having established the harmful effects of make-work schemes, Defoe
(1704: 23-24) argues that the level of wages is such as to show that there
is more 'Work' than 'Hands', and that, as in the case of his own well-paid labourer, high wages coexist with the parochial support of the

wives and children of labourers. Moreover, the difficulties officers have in pressing men into the army indicates that labourers live in plenty and ease and that steady employment is readily available (24).

According to Defoe there is more than sufficient employment for those 'that will work'. Therefore, not only does the provision of workhouses and parish stocks injure the existing system of circulation but it is also completely unnecessary. The solution to the distresses of the Poor is to be found in a better mode of 'regulation' rather than any employment scheme (Defoe 1704: 28). Unfortunately, he refrains from informing the reader what this regulation might be, preferring to leave that to the wisdom of the legislature.

Who, then, make up the numbers of the Poor, given the circumstance of plentiful employment? For Defoe the 'Poverty and Exigence of the Poor' is derived from either 'Casualty' or 'Crime' (1704: 25). He thus discounts the possibility that there exists a class of indigence which is derived from the inability to procure employment of those willing and able-bodied. Defoe quickly passes over the first of his causes, concurring with his contemporaries that those unable to work through infirmity and age are legitimate objects of parochial relief. However, his discussion of the latter cause, crime, illustrates one way of using two of the categories of the Poor: "Tis the Men that *won't work*, not the Men that *can get no work*, which makes up the numbers of the Poor' (Defoe 1704: 27, original emphasis).

Defoe speaks of the crimes of luxury and pride which lead to the distress of the Poor. He exemplifies them by a contrast which will become familiar in the literature on the Poor in the eighteenth century. There are men who, 'with good husbandry', honestly entrust their earnings to their wives' management. There are others, however, who drink their earnings away at the alehouse, leaving their wives and children starving and in rags to become unwitting charges upon the parish (Defoe 1704: 26). But beneath these crimes is the 'general Taint of Slothfulness' which has marked the Poor (27) . This view echoes those expressed in John Locke's report to the Board of Trade of 1697 which attributed the burdensome nature of the Poor to the 'relaxation of discipline and corruption of morals' (Eden 1928: 38–39; Webb and Webb 1963a: 109–112).

From this perspective, the problem of the Poor is not how to set the sturdy beggar and vagabond, or even the idle labourer, to the discipline of work and to useful employment for the benefit of the nation. It is, rather, a problem of the labouring Poor, those already in work and their families, and the luxury and sloth which inheres in their character, or what Defoe terms their 'temper and genius'. This is a problem of the coincidence of high wages with the distress which leads to applications for poor relief. It is a problem of the irresponsible use of patriarchal authority by the Poor man. For example, Defoe swears

I am ready to produce to this Honourable House the Man who for
several years has gain'd of me by his handy Labour at the mean
scoundrel employment of Tile-making from 16s. to 20s. per Week
Wages, and all that time would hardly have a pair of shoes to his
Feet, or Cloaths to cover Nakedness, and had his wife and children
kept by the Parish.

(Defoe 1704: 24)

Defoe locates an anomaly between wages and living conditions in the
'luxury' of one set of labourers. This luxury is illustrated by only one
example, the drinking habits of the English labourers who consume
alcohol 'three times as much in value as any sort of Foreigners' (Defoe
1704: 26). This results in the vivid contrast between the happy living conditions of the Dutch workmen and the wretchedness of the English (26).
The villain of the piece hence becomes the alehouse. But this institution
is not simply the site of overspending. It is where Poor men come after
working and then proceed to drink themselves into debt and their wives
and children into penury. It is the place where the 'general Taint of
Slothfulness' upon the Poor can be most acutely observed. Defoe testifies
that 'from hence comes Poverty, Parish Charges, and Beggary' (27).

Just as the workhouse fulfils the educative function of teaching the
idle an industrious mode of life, so the alehouse functions to transform
the Poor, but in the exact opposite direction. If the vagabond and beggar
and those idle but wanting work represent problems to be solved by the
administrative utopia of the workhouse, the high-waged labourer whose
wife and children are supported by parochial relief is highlighted against
the background of the alehouse. In many respects the figure of the
labourer at the alehouse, where he risks the moral dangers of drinking,
gambling, and other entertainments, and is even open to political
discussion and organisation, is far more threatening in the eighteenth
century than the vagabond or beggar. For this labourer is the head of
a household, no matter how humble, over which he has patriarchal
governance, and which can follow him into distress. Here it is not a matter
of turning present waste to the future advantage of the nation, but of
identifying the process and institution at the source of the moral corruption and political mobilisation of the nation's most valuable resource,
its industrious Poor, the consequent dependence of their wives on parish
relief, and the education of their offspring in the ways of idleness and
worse.

Alternative and complementary solutions

Thus the problem of idleness does not simply concern those who are
unwilling or unable to work. It has the labouring Poor as a central target

of concern. It encompasses the rhythms of their work and leisure, their use of time during the day and the week, and their calendar of festivals and holidays. Several writers have noted and explored the sustained anti-recreational campaign during the eighteenth century (George 1985: 273–288). We can refer to, for example, E.P. Thompson's vivid account of the work patterns of the eighteenth-century town and village labourers, particularly the punctuation of the working week with 'alternate bouts of intense labour and of idleness', the association of the weekend with drinking, the widespread custom of holding 'St. Monday' sacred, and the popular culture of wakes and feasts celebrated throughout the year (1967: 70–86).[1]

It would seem that a concern with the work–leisure nexus in the lives of the Poor can be traced back some way. Appleby cites the late seventeenth-century view that 'the Poor, if Two Dayes will maintain them, will not work Three', and the complaints of Thomas Manley that the labourers had grown so independent as to be 'too proud to beg, too lazy to work, when 'tis either too hot or too cold, and will choose their own time and wages, or you may do your work yourself' (1978: 145–146). E.P. Thompson (1967: 72) himself cites John Houghton to the effect that framework-knitters and stocking-makers spent their Mondays and Tuesdays at the alehouse or at ninepins when they received high wages, and that weavers were commonly drunk on Monday, hung over on Tuesday, and had out-of-order tools on Wednesday. 'As for the shoemakers', Houghton continued, 'they'll rather be hanged than not remember St. Crispin on Monday . . . and it commonly holds as long as they have a penny of money or pennyworth of credit.'

The problem of idleness thus confronted these writers as a double problem of not only setting the idle Poor to work, which was encapsulated in the Elizabethan poor law and the mercantilist hopes for the workhouse, but also of removing that sloth which had become ingrained in the habits and customs of the Poor. Calculations of the waste to the nation of holidays can be found from the end of the seventeenth century, while Henry Fielding distinguished between the Rich, whose problem is to kill time, and the Poor, who are born to labour for six days under the command of God (George 1985: 274–275). During the eighteenth century there were sustained attempts to use the law to curb the recreation of the Poor, by withholding fairground licences, treating travelling entertainers as vagrants, withdrawing access to commons and wastes on grounds of public security, and, more generally, to undermine the Poor's collective and leisure activities (276). There was also the campaign against licentiousness and profanation on the Sabbath from 1690–1710, and the concerted campaign in manufacturing districts from 1786–7 of the Committee for the Reform of Manners Among the Lower Orders to regulate virtually every aspect of the lives of the Poor (277–288). In all this the key agents are the Justices of the Peace, both in assuming judicial functions over these 'minor' matters of local governance and as leading lights of such committees and campaigns.

Concomitant with the prolonged anti-recreational campaign are those measures designed to promote work-discipline, including the division and supervision of labour in workshops and factories, the reduction of activity to quantifiable labour time by the introduction of clocks, fines, bells, and timetables, and the general moral preaching directed at the Poor (E.P. Thompson 1967: 79–90). However, there was another, more pervasive, and simpler solution to the problem of idleness among the working population, that which Furniss (1957: ch. 6) has chillingly called the 'utility of poverty' or, more precisely, the utility of low wages.

The doctrine of low wages as a spur to industry did not receive universal assent in this period. Appleby, for example, cites various writers at the end of the seventeenth century who argued that the Poor must have 'a reasonable fruit for their Labours' (1978: 147–148). However, these writers, among them the initiators of the workhouse movement, Child and Hale, advanced such arguments to show the benefits of make-work schemes or to attack levels of wages inadequate to procure subsistence provisions. Indeed, Furniss (1957: 177–178) notes the development of something like a subsistence theory of wages over the course of the eighteenth century and a debate on what constitutes a fair and reasonable subsistence. Nevertheless, despite Hume's view that the labourer should 'enjoy the fruits of his labour, in full enjoyment of all the necessaries and many of the conveniences of life' (quoted by Furniss 1957: 178), and Adam Smith's predisposition in favour of a 'liberal reward for labour' (1976, 1: 99), (see chapter seven), the position most often taken is that high wages and low costs were the interchangeable causes of idleness and that, conversely, low wages and high costs were the motivation of industry.

This literature has been dealt with thoroughly elsewhere (Furniss 1957: 118–125; George 1985: 270–273). We may, however, note the colourful language of Arthur Young: 'Everyone but an idiot knows that the lower classes must be kept poor or they will never be industrious' (quoted by Furniss 1957: 119). Young illustrated this in his accounts of his tours through the southern and northern counties of England (1768; 1771), the east of England in 1771, and France in 1793. He claimed to find that the manufacturing labourers of Norwich earning sixpence a day were much happier than those on two or three shillings a day, that Yorkshire colliers reduced their work hours with high wages, that high-waged Manchester manufacturing labourers spent half a day in the alehouse from which 'no bribe' could tempt them, and that the affluent northern agricultural labourers scarcely worked more than three days a week and spent the rest of the week drinking (Furniss 1957: 119–120). For

Young high wages were the correlate not only of idleness spent at the alehouse but also of political disorder. The southern riots of the 1740s, he claimed, involved the best paid workers of whom he said: 'The more these fellows earn, the more succeeding time and money they have for the alehouse and disorderly meetings' (quoted by Furniss 1957: 120).

But what is the rationale for such a linkage of low wages/high costs with the industry of the Poor? From Petty to Child to Young, one finds what amounted to a doctrine that hard times, by encouraging the labouring Poor to unremitting industry, were good for them since by being industrious they 'lived better. At times the solution to the riddle seems rooted in human nature, as in the argument of Temple in the mid-seventeenth century that 'mankind . . . are naturally so fond of ease and indolence, that they will not labour while they have the means of idleness in their power' (quoted by Furniss 1957: 124). Roger North claimed that this propensity to idleness was 'so perverse' that when the prices of corn and other foodstuffs were low, 'so that Labourers might live by half Charge, yet they would not abate, but rather enhanced their Labour, and made the Ballance good by their Idleness the better half of their Time' (1753: 58–59).

Idleness, then, can be so deceptive that it may assume the guise of a short-term increase in industry.[2] It is only where an urgent necessity forces itself upon the Poor that one can be sure of the performance of continuous and unremitting labour. The problem then was to establish such necessity by raising the price of subsistence items of the labouring Poor and lowering their wages. Thus there was widespread support for the establishment of public granaries, the placing of excises on foodstuffs, and schemes for encouraging population and the supply of labour, such as immigration, the relaxation of naturalisation laws, and the granting of allowances to large families (Furniss 1957: 134–136, 140–144).

These various policies return us to the identification of numbers and wealth which is characteristic of the policy framework of the Discourse of the Poor and completes a search stimulated by Pitt's statement in favour of his ill-fated Poor Bill. It was this identification which we found in Petty's advocacy of public works and in the writings of the workhouse projectors. Yet we have seen it was not merely a dogma uncritically absorbed and propounded by a myriad writers but a means of assembling arguments for a multitude of particular policies to be pursued by the state in its quest to make the Poor industrious. The position of Pitt, which Ricardo was to find so incomprehensible, is not, therefore, a naïve and backward adherence to a pre-scientific doctrine, or simply an example of paternalism towards the Poor. It is one instance of a systematic and coherent conception of poor policy throughout the century-and-a-half before 'Malthus' intervention into the debates concerning population and the poor laws.[3]

Three clear phases within the Discourse of the Poor can be distinguished in the writings surveyed by F.M. Eden at the end of the eighteenth century which broadly correspond to the periodisation of 'attitudes to the poor' provided by Coats (1976: 103–110).

The first phase extends almost until the end of the seventeenth century and its primary concern is the projection of ways to set the Poor to work. There are several pamphlets to this end prior to the writings of Child, Hale, and Firmin, which criticise the poor law for its tendency to relieve rather than provide employment for the Poor, thereby encouraging the Poor to remain idle and do nothing but beg and steal and habituate their children in these ways (Eden 1928: 26–33). The favoured projects of this era call for the extension of the linen trade as a means of employing the Poor. Towards the end of the century, the problem of make-work begins to emerge in full relief with the strong demand for the incorporation of parishes for the construction of workhouses. This is the period of local, and often private, workhouse initiatives, as well as the Bristol workhouse and its multitude of successors. It is the high tide of classical confinement of the Poor.

As Coats has suggested, 'From the beginning of the new century . . . a strident note of hostility became more widespread' in the attitudes toward the Poor (1976: 107). Defoe's pamphlet is evidently representative, as is Locke's report. In this second period, the increase in the poor rates is frequently noted and put down to the luxury and idleness of the Poor. Dunning in 1698 lists 'dietary profuseness' and separate housing as two of the reasons for rate increases as well as the more conventional complaints of idleness and the excessiveness of relief grants (Eden 1928: 40). The workhouse is still praised as an alternative to poor relief in Dunning's time but now the emphasis has shifted on to its deterrent value, its noted propensity to drive away 'foreign beggars' and to reduce the number of locals applying for relief. The legislation of 1723, Knatchbull's general Workhouse Act, empowered parishes to build a workhouse singly or in union with other parishes and provided that a person refusing workhouse relief was to be 'put out of the book' (Henriques 1979: 17).

The shrillness of tone of this period is opposed to the sanguine views of the earlier one and is evidenced in the calling for greater and more brutal methods to set the Poor to work and greater surveillance of those that were likely to become chargeable on the rates. In the former category is the suggestion by Alcock in 1752 that three-time offending rogues and vagrants be transported and enslaved (Eden 1928: 57–58). Into the latter fall the earliest plans for the taking of the census and a project for the inspection of the Poor in their homes so that parish officials would be in a position to know who were suitable objects for relief and employment or for more punitive measures (57). During this period no alternatives have been put forward which might constitute a threat to the principle of setting the Poor to work although the structure of the administration of the poor laws comes under virulent attack. These attacks, however, are still made within the conceptual armoury of the Discourse of the Poor. Fielding, for example, in 1753 refuses to criticise the principle of setting the Poor to work but argues that the problem has arisen in the way in which the parish overseers are selected (the vestry system) and the way in which they put the principle into operation (59–60). Other writers charge that the poor law, particularly those aspects of its administration relating to the law of settlements, was depopulating.

The jurist Burn argued that these laws encouraged parish officers to pull down cottages, to drive out as many inhabitants and admit as few as possible (Eden 1928: 66). The laborious and litigious execution of the settlement law was now so identified with the poor law that others, including Kames, made the charge of depopulation against the totality of the existing system of relief (70). The poor law was attacked on these grounds in the writings of Roger North (1753), Massie in 1758 and Young in 1767 (Furniss 1957: 37), to which we may add the famous denunciation of Adam Smith (see chapter seven). The charge of depopulation was repeatedly made against the existing poor law, particularly the local policies which saw parish officers pulling down cottages, seeking to restrain marriage among the virtuous segment of the Poor, and removing pregnant women.

For most of the eighteenth century, the question of the poor laws was considered within the terms of reference established by the Discourse of the Poor. The problem remained what it had been for the Elizabethan legislation: the proper administration of the Poor so that those able to work might be usefully employed, those unable to work properly relieved, and those unwilling to work restrained and punished. The inability of the poor laws to achieve such goals as the suppression of beggary, a reduction of the distresses of the Poor, or even of setting the Poor to work, was not put down to some underlying flaw in the objectives or principles of the laws but to their maladministration.

It was not until the final decades of the century that this tacit acceptance of make-work schemes and belief in the ability to institute a proper administration of public relief and employment seem to have run out of steam. The next period represents a break with the characteristic interpretations of the poor law in the Discourse of the Poor in at least three ways: the emergence of a strong abolitionist strain towards the poor law; the insistence that voluntary charity is morally superior to the compulsion inherent in the poor rates; and the substitution for make-work schemes of various contributory methods, including life annuities, insurance plans, and mutual assistance or friendly societies.

The final period marks the end of this form of discourse and the rise of the discursive, if not administrative, conditions for a liberal mode of government of poverty. Since this phase, acutely manifested in the 1790s, will be explored in detail in later chapters, it is possible to put it to one side for the moment, and to move to a characterisation of the mode of government to which the Discourse of the Poor was wedded.

Chapter three

The police of the poor

How can the 'problem of idleness' in the seventeenth and eighteenth centuries be characterised and understood? How can the ubiquitous desire to set the Poor to work, which is common to those who projected the institutional solution of the workhouse and those who remained opposed to it, be interpreted?

In the first instance, one might be led to construct a thesis based on a gloss of several of Max Weber's comments and notes. This discourse, which persistently affirms the remedy of labour for the ills of the Poor, would be viewed as an instance of the application of the social and ethical consciousness formed by Protestant asceticism to mercantilist policy. In fact, Weber (1985: 177–8, 268) specifically refers to the English poor law as an illustration of the effect of Puritanism and claims that it was the new religious sects which initiated the 'deterrent system of workhouses'. Moreover, in his *General Economic History*, Weber contrasts the 'Christian socialism' of the Stuarts, characterised by a 'friendly' attitude to the Poor, with Puritanism 'which saw every poor person as work-shy or as a criminal' (1927: 349). One could, with Weber, thus construct a contrast between inherited medieval religious ethics and those of the Reformation. The former not only tolerated begging and understood it as an occasion for doing good works but made it sacred by the encouragement of the mendicant orders. The new ethic, on the other hand, not only condemned begging and indiscriminate almsgiving by the Church but also demanded compulsory public employment for the idle Poor. The workhouse would then appear as the embodiment of a dual Puritan-inspired objective of the suppression of beggary and the enforcement of work.

There are, however, major problems with such an account. First, Weber's conception of mercantilism as 'carrying the point of view of capitalistic industry into politics' in which 'the state is handled as if it consisted exclusively of capitalistic entrepreneurs' is, at best, partial and, at worst, highly anachronistic (1927: 347). Far more apt is his characterisation of national mercantilism after the Civil War as 'the last time irrational and rational capitalism faced each other in conflict' (350). Perhaps Weber would have included under the former type of capitalism all those policies applied to the provision and relief of the Poor in the following century-and-a-half which we have examined in earlier chapters.

Second, in respect of claims concerning Puritanism, the confinement of the idle and the desire to set them to work in the seventeenth century is a phenomenon of European-wide dimensions, practised both in Protestant and Catholic countries, as Foucault makes clear in his account of the *hôpitaux généraux, Zuchthäusern*, workhouses etc. (1965: 38–64). Moreover, the history of poor policy shows that the earliest plans for the assumption of public responsibility for poor relief and the provision of employment were made and executed in the early sixteenth century in both those 'countries in which the Reformation had already prevailed and those in which the Roman Catholic Church was still dominant; and to have emanated from both Catholic and Protestant theologians and administrators' (Webb and Webb 1963a: 30).

A distinctive formula for the government of the Poor was promulgated across the continent during the first half of the sixteenth century by figures ranging from Luther himself to the Spanish Catholic humanist, Juan Luis Vives (Webb and Webb 1963a: 29–41). The principles on which this formula rested were that all those who could work should be made to do so, that begging would not be tolerated, and that refuge be given in reformed hospitals and almshouses to those unable to work. For Vives, for example, these institutions would treat the sick, sequestrate the insane, and educate poor children. He proposed the appointment of officers to investigate the circumstances of the Poor in their homes, to ensure the return of beggars to their homes with journey-money, and to provide employment for those who remained. He also suggested small pecuniary assistance for those who were willing but unable to work due to want of employment.[1] This is certainly not very far from the central tenets of the Tudor poor law which would be codified in the Elizabethan legislation of 1597–1601.

The final problem with the 'Weberian' schema is that it assumes that calls for the suppression of mendicancy were made under an ethical regime which inaugurated a new valuation of labour. The history of statutory law in feudal England reveals something quite different. While the Catholic Church may have had to wait until 1516 when John Major at the Sorbonne delivered a theological argument against begging and in favour of public poor relief, there existed a solid body of feudal legislation dating from the ninth and tenth centuries of 'ever-increasing severity against vagrants, whether as sturdy beggars or rogues addicted to crime and disorder, or as labourers who abstracted themselves from their obligations to the manor or parish to which they belonged' (Webb and Webb 1963a: 23–24). These statutes, which span a period of some seven hundred years, were aimed at such categories as 'landless men', 'beggars able to labour', 'idle persons living suspiciously', and everyone 'having no land-master, nor using any lawful merchandise, craft or mystery, able to give no reckoning of how he doth lawfully get his living'. The existence of this body of legislation vitiates any attempt to identify such poor-law concerns as setting the Poor to work and suppressing beggary with imperatives derived from reformed religious ethics. Both these policy objectives have a far longer historical trajectory which, despite its distinctly Puritan bent in the seventeenth century, corresponded to a set of more fundamental political requisites.[2]

Without entering further into these arguments, I would now like to propose the concept of *police* as a way of understanding the policies, state administration, and various projects and practices, directed towards the Poor in those centuries which preceded the liberal transformation of government.[3]

As Minson (1985: 102) has pointed out, the concept of police is one which has been used only infrequently to describe and interpret the social, political, and economic developments in Europe during the epoch which commences at the waning of the Middle Ages. Indeed, the term 'police' is quite uncommon in learned discourse in English prior to the nineteenth century. The outstanding exceptions are the lectures delivered by Adam Smith at Glasgow University in 1762–4 but not collected and published until 1896 (Smith 1956), and the commentaries of the jurist, William Blackstone (1830). For the former, police, justice, revenue, and arms were the four 'great objects' of law (Smith 1956: 154); for the latter, 'public police and oeconomy' meant the 'due regulation and domestic order of the kingdom' (Blackstone 1830, 4: 162). Even given these references, one can cite the French visitor to London in about 1720 who exclaimed: 'Good Lord! How can one expect Order among these People, who have not such a Word as *Police* in their Language' (quoted by Radzinowicz 1956: 1). Despite such ignorance, the term was a pervasive point of political reference in continental Europe from the thirteenth century, particularly in German regions and in France, and gave rise, after the seventeenth century, to a distinct *science* of police, *Polizeiwissenschaft*.[4]

The archaic sense of the term may be contrasted with that which is designated by its more familiar namesake. Today, the term police is identified with a body of officials or officers, some of whom are uniformed, a police *force*, whose rationale is the prevention and detection of crime, or 'keeping the peace'. However, the sense of a body which would administer legal regulations and codes was first clearly implied only in the course of the eighteenth century in the writings of de Lamare, Bielfeld, William Midmay, John Fielding, and Jonas Hanway, and then only as one of the many branches of the subject (Hume 1981: 43–44).

For example, the 'prevention of robberies' formed one of the eight branches of police in the Empress Catherine's *Instructions* of 1768 (Hume 1981: 34–35) and Blackstone's concept of the patriarchal state grounded in the rule of law precluded the possibility of police as an institution (Radzinowicz 1956: 418–429).

So what, then, can one make of 'that strange word' if it does not refer in the first place to a particular social agency? According to Knemeyer (1980: 172–181), police was both the condition of order in the community and the regulations (ordinances) which sought the institution and maintenance of that order in fifteenth- to seventeenth-century German statute law. At other points police appears to go beyond matters of order. Thus from the sixteenth century the term began to denote a wider set of meanings, embracing the concept of commonality itself in humanistic and theological literature. Nevertheless order remained the paramount focus so that when, in the seventeenth and eighteenth centuries, a science of police (*Polizeiwissenschaft*) was formed, it was concerned with the content of that order, and so theorised the specific conditions of its institution and maintenance. This science thus led to an evaluation of the objectives of the *state* and the proper form of *state* activity.

Two points about the development of police can be made. The first concerns its range of regulation. *Polizei* was said to exist when freemen or subjects behaved in an 'orderly, modest, courteous and respectful fashion' in every aspect of life (Knemeyer 1980: 174). Police was thus equated with a society of good manners, polite society. At first police ordinances dealt primarily with 'sumptuary' problems of the blurring of distinctions between the estates, such as the wearing of extravagant clothing, the appropriate behaviour of each subject at church or during festivals, the performance of trades and occupations, and the behaviour of servants and journeymen towards their masters (Knemeyer 1980: 177). Later were added concerns over monopolies, unseemly vendors, weights and measures, usury, extravagance in all areas, fires, public buildings, and streets (Knemeyer 1980: 177; Hume 1981: 33–34).

The difficulty of defining the primary purposes of police is that its attempts at regulation respected few bounds, particularly of a 'private' realm, and extended to manners, morals, and the minutiae of everyday life. One way of arriving at a definition, however, would be to emphasise the municipal concerns of police, defined by de Lamare as the 'public order of each town' (Hume 1981: 33). It is certainly the case that police was widely regarded as a matter of local authorities, or 'the inferior parts of government' as Adam Smith put it, concerned with public cleanliness and security, and cheapness and plenty (1956: 154). Such a police could be characterised – at least in its 'oeconomic' dimension – as the outlook of a relatively isolated community, with a narrow and largely closed market, which dealt with perishable goods of limited supply, and was liable to famines, traders' rings, forestallers, and dishonest practices (Hume 1981: 33). Despite its partial adequacy, such a definition is largely a static one, missing the crucial dynamic of police in relation to state formation, as well as its 'moral' dimension, the latter nicely expressed as the police of 'general morality and respectability', or in Catherine's *Instructions* as the police of 'public decency' (Hume 1981: 34–35).

Second, the development of police, and its movement beyond 'sumptuary' laws to a police of general morality, can be understood, at least in continental Europe, in the context of the specific devolution of authority from the estates to the newly-forming local, municipal, and central-state structures. In fact, it has been argued (Knemeyer 1980: 178–81) that police encompassed matters of the regulation of manners as the estates declined and legislative responsibility came to be located in more centralised governmental apparatuses. However, it would seem that this is not quite so simple a matter. In the late medieval period the multiple sources of police regulation included 'municipalities, guilds, charities, principalities, ecclesiastical and seigneurial authorities as much as from royal command' (Minson 1985: 104). The emergence of the sovereign state saw not simply a take-over of police prerogatives exercised by the estates, but the concentration of some police functions and a sublimation of others into an emergent private sphere around issues of social morality. The result of this is that police had slowly become identified with the distinctive political sphere, the sovereign state, and the estates were depoliticised (Minson 1985: 104–105). This can be exemplified by the eighteenth-century theme of a lack of fit between the treatment of national and local issues, a theme in which police is linked to the pervasive Enlightenment calls for an effective, clear, and simple body of sovereign-made law (Hume 1981: 34–40). This too is how it is possible to understand the definition of police given by Von Justi at the end of this long evolution as 'the enlargement of the internal power and strength of the state' (quoted by Knemeyer 1980: 181).

Considering the ubiquity and difficulties of administration and enforcement, it has been suggested that police was both a precondition of and an obstacle to the formation of the sovereign state (Minson 1985: 104). It could well be argued that these are limitations of police only from the point of view of the theory and practice of sovereignty as it developed in the eighteenth century, particularly in its drive for legal codification and effective implementation. It was these political developments which were at the root of the transformation of police from a *condition* to be attained by the proper government of the kingdom into a *technique* for attaining certain goals, a police force, a force charged with the effective administration of police measures.

The Poor, whether in relation to the questions of begging and vagrancy or as a general category, were a central object of this police. The early sixteenth-century ferment of experimentation in the municipal and secular provision for the Poor which emerged across the continent was often contained in regulations of police or conceived as a matter of police. Thus in 1530 the German Emperor, Charles the Fifth, issued a *Reichspolizeiordnung* in which each city and commune was directed to maintain its poor along the lines of a number of towns and cities which, following Luther's scheme of an 'Ordinance for a Common Chest', had prohibited begging and appointed guardians of the Poor (Webb and Webb 1963a: 30–32). Similarly, in 1521 the parliament of Normandy issued an ordinance for a *police des pauvres* to be established at Rouen. By 1534, the city had established a *bureau des pauvres* which, under a board of jurists, councillors, and churchmen, appointed officers, collected funds, set the idle to work, distributed relief, and established an almshouse for infants, the sick, and the aged. In France during this period tracts describing the systematic provision and organisation of the Poor by city and municipal authorities referred to this development as police. Webb and Webb cite (1963a: 33–35) two old pamphlets dealing with the police of the Poor at Lyon in 1530, one of which is entitled *La Police de l'almonse de Lyon*, and a third dealing with a similar organisation in the capital, *La Police des pauvres de Paris*, published in 1544.

The Poor were a department of police throughout the entire epoch. This is instanced by Pasquino's (1978: 46–47) comparison of a late-medieval set of 'Regulations of police of the city of Nuremberg' with Duchesne's 1757 analysis of police, *Code de la Police*. While the former included the regulation of beggars, *Bettelordung*, the latter, some four centuries later, devoted a separate chapter to the 'police of the poor'. Similarly, Catherine's *Instructions* of 1768 directed that police should be understood to cover the relief of the sick and the impotent and provision for the able-bodied Poor (Hume 1981: 34–35).

One could distinguish, after Minson (1985: 102–106), between two general phases or aspects of police: the first concerns the re-forming of feudal relations and codes; the second, the mercantilist, biopolitical problem of the utilisation and fostering of the population.

In the first phase, police consists in a conservative ambition. Unlike the 'preventive' police we have inherited from the nineteenth century, police does not refer to the negation of future acts injurious to persons, property, and the state, but to the *re*-formation, in the sense of 'putting back into shape', of the existing order of things. Pasquino (1978: 47) proposes that at the end of the Middle Ages police regulations are a 'labour of formation' of the social body, an attempt to regulate all that goes unregulated in a society of orders or estates, *Standegesellschaft*. In this way, police already presupposes a breakdown of the estate-based feudal order, however minor, and the development of spaces in which 'the feudal world's traditional customs, established competences and clear relations of authority, subordination, protection and alliance cease to hold sway' (47). Within the ken of such a notion would fall the Statute of Labourers in England of 1350 and the regulations of sumptuary police.

The statute can only be properly understood in the context of the crisis in feudal relations in the fourteenth century which was, if not caused, at least accelerated by the wave of pestilences which culminated in the Black Death of 1349 (Zeigler 1970: 236–247; Webb and Webb 1963a: 23–29). The gross depopulation associated with the Black Death led to an increased commutation of labour services into cash rents. This caused a doubling of wages and an increased mobility of labour, while leading to a sharp fall in the price of agricultural products and a rise in the cost of manufactured products. Landlords, particularly on manors in which the land was poor or which had been severely affected by the plague, were unable to afford wage increases or enforce manorial obligations. Consequently they were forced to let off parts of the demesne for money. Villeins were thus in a position to slip away from their manors and labourers to demand wage increases. In the years immediately following the Black Death there arose measures specifically aimed at checking the commutation of services into cash rents and halting the rises in wages and the movement of labour (Zeigler 1970: 237–240).

Such a crisis could be read as a crisis of police and such measures as instances of the conservative aspect of police in so far as they are concerned with a re-formation of feudal social relations and codes of obligation and service by means of the regulation of the plebeian masses. Such a police would hence be concerned with securing the conditions of feudal servitude and bonded labour by juridical rather than customary measures.

The Statute of Labourers (Webb and Webb 1963a: 23–28) was the outstanding example of such measures. It dealt with the regulation of the relations between masters and labourers, the fixing of wages and hours, and the giving of alms to idle persons. It demanded that all those without means of support and able to labour be made to serve any master at rates customary prior to the pestilences and appended a long table of rates to guide such a purpose. Moreover, it forbade the combination of labourers for the purpose of the raising of wages and prohibited almsgiving so that labourers would be compelled to labour. Another statute at the time demanded that the runaway man be 'burnt on the forehead with an iron formed to the letter F in token of his falsity' (Webb and Webb 1963a: 26). While it is true that such measures were designed to prevent disorder, violence, and crime, their primary function would seem to be the re-formation, by juridical means, of relations of authority and service which had been previously ensured by the customary bonds of the serf to his manor and the labourer to his master. These relations and bonds were the 'truth' which underwrote the cruel inscriptions betokening falsity.

Minson (1985: 104) notes that authorities often issued police regulations without any effective means of their enforcement. This is certainly not the case with the Statute of Labourers. As with so many other aspects of the government of the Poor, and local governance generally, the key agent of the enforcement of the Statute of Labourers and vagrancy regulations was the justice of the peace. This institution, which dates from the early fourteenth century, exemplifies the peculiarity of English political formation, i.e. that England possessed an early, comparatively well-developed central state which rested on the high degree of involvement of local ruling elites and agents (Corrigan and Sayer 1985: 16). Indeed, it could be argued that the justices from the start fulfilled a police as much as a strictly judicial function. Thus they had powers to 'keep the peace' – to arrest, commit to gaol, demand good behaviour sureties, exercise powers of summary conviction (after 1388), and try most crimes in quarter sessions. Germane here was the power to compel labourers to work at statutory rates under the Statute of Labourers of 1350, and to intervene in master–servant relations in textile manufactures under laws of 1467. The justices would also play key roles in the administration of both the poor law of 1601 and the law of settlement after 1662.

The justices symbolise the peculiarities of the history of the police of England. It involved less a devolution of authority from local to central organs of government than a continuous realignment of local–central state relationships and competences. At least until the 1830s, when the poor-law reformers would seek to undermine their authority over the granting of relief, the strengthening of central capacity meant the further empowerment of the propertied classes as local agents. The absence of a notion of police in eighteenth-century England may be due to the early development of its central state and the effective securing of police functions by these local agents.

It would not be stretching the point to cite the multitude of regulations concerning the suppression of vagrancy as attempts to maintain good police in the face of the dislocation which resulted from the breakdown of serfdom. These laws repeatedly attempt to specify all those classes who, for whatever reasons, have escaped or been expelled from the strictures of bonded labour, those who are landless or 'masterless', without proper station in the social hierarchy, a potential source of crime and disorder, and representatives of a breakdown in relations of authority and subservience. This is well exemplified by the (now seemingly) bizarre collection of cases deemed 'rogues and vagabonds' in the Vagrancy Act of 1597, the 'wandering scholars seeking alms', 'shipwrecked seamen', 'idle persons using subtle craft in games or in fortune telling', 'pretended proctors, procurers or gatherers of alms for institutions', 'fencers, bearwords, common players or minstrels', 'jugglers, tinkers, peddlers and petty chapmen', 'able-bodied wandering persons and labourers refusing to work for current rates of wages', 'discharged pensioners', 'wanderers pretending losses by fire', and, of course, 'Egyptians or gypsies' (Webb and Webb 1963a: 351).

Additions and deletions were made through the centuries to the list of those deemed vagrants. The masterless man and the labourer refusing to work at customary rates held sway until, in the sixteenth century and later, administrative attention was given to 'idle and disorderly persons'. It was not until the second half of the eighteenth century that such statutes became concerned with classes of vagrants suspected of being a danger to property such as poachers, those frequenting public places with the intent to commit felonies, and those being in the possession of 'burgularious implements' (Webb and Webb 1963a: 352). In short, until very late in its history, the law for the suppression of vagrancy was more concerned with establishing the status of those within its purview, unmasking their fraudulent acceptance of alms, suppressing unsavoury and mysterious activities and modes of life, and recognising and physically marking falsity, than with the prevention of crimes against property.

There is, however, as noted by Minson (1985: 102–107), another general phase or aspect of this notion of police which becomes apparent with the emergence of the German science of police in the seventeenth and eighteenth centuries. It would be a mistake to view these later developments as essentially in contradiction with the objectives of earlier police regulations. The goal of the re-formation of the social order by the regulation of all the activities and relations within a political unit remains constant, except that later that goal comes to be interpreted through a new set of political priorities concerning, at its most general level, the welfare and happiness of the population. The object of police shifts from the conservation of the feudal estates or orders to the administration of the *population*, which entailed, according to Obrecht, the three tasks of the collection of information, the augmentation of wealth, and the institution of public happiness (Pasquino 1978: 49–50).

This latter notion of police falls within Foucault's definition of biopolitics as a 'political power which had assigned itself the task of administering life' (1979b: 139), in which the utilisation and fostering of human life becomes the object and mode of legitimation of political action. It also has strong resonances with Cunningham's interpretation of the Elizabethan industrial code, particularly the Statute of Artificers, as a comprehensive system of national administration of the population which implemented 'one great policy for regulating the lives and promoting the welfare of the working classes' (1912: 29).[5] In such a politics, the collection of information about the sum of human material within a political territory becomes germane to the art of political government. Hence, from the sixteenth century, a number of knowledge-

practices emerge as means of providing and organising such information, including census-taking, Political Arithmetick, and Political
Oeconomy. Police becomes no longer simply the condition of order in
a community but the prosperity, health, welfare, and security of the
totality of human life within that community, the population.

The emergence of the science of police in this particular form in
continental Europe in the seventeenth century certainly lends support
to Foucault's thesis that this period marked a fundamental transformation in the object and terrain of politics. Other developments, such as
those recorded by D.V. Glass (1973), including the proliferation of
census-taking and, later, the birth of vital statistics, as well as the controversies concerning the size and growth of the population, similarly
attest to the significance of the biopolitical domain during a long period.
However, because Foucault remained committed to a genealogical project
which sought to identify the conditions of emergence of a political
modernity, both in his lectures (e.g. 1979a) and in his histories (e.g.
1979b: 135–150), he was compelled to regard this shift in the constituents of police as an unambiguous break in the history of 'the West'.
This part of his thesis is extremely difficult to sustain. It is certainly true
that the formation of a moral and medical police of the population,
Foucault's biopolitics, marks an important departure from earlier
conceptions of government and police. It is more difficult to argue that
the police of the eighteenth century was continuous with the liberal and
post-liberal modes of government of the last two centuries. Similarly,
mercantilist policies towards the Poor cannot be made to refer forward
to the birth of a liberal–capitalist rationality concerning poor provision
and relief. As Minson suggests (1985: 104), the concern with the waste
of human beings which is characteristic of mercantilist policies towards
the Poor is not equivalent to the liberal critique of public charity as a
waste of (potentially productive) funds.

In the previous chapter, the Discourse of the Poor has been identified
as a region of the wider discursive field also occupied by Political
Oeconomy. It can now be noted that in its concern with the population
as a means of assembling the object of its discourse and evaluating the
merits of various policies and sectors (Tribe 1978: 90), Political
Oeconomy would appear to have more in common with its German contemporary, the science of police, than with the economics of Say and
Ricardo.[6] Moreover, the formation of the population as an object of
knowledge in the seventeenth and eighteenth centuries may be regarded
as a means of constructing a distinctive politico-moral discourse and not
an incipient economic discourse.

It is now possible to make intelligible the concerns with the suppression
of idleness, mendicancy, and, above all, the proper mode of setting the
Poor to work, in the epoch preceding that of industrial societies. But

first it is helpful to reflect upon the 'early' Foucault's suggestion that 'the house of confinement constitutes the densest symbol of that "police" which conceived itself as the civil equivalent of religion for the edification of the perfect city' (1965: 63). Foucault's analysis (1965: 46–55) itself points to the utopian character of the workhouse, arguing that labour acquired 'a certain force of moral enchantment', so much so that it became a general solution to all the problems associated with disorderly populations, as well as an infallible panacea and remedy for all forms of poverty.[7] This appealing suggestion certainly helps make intelligible the 'irrational' calculations of profitability by mercantilist workhouse projectors and the generality of the concern for 'setting the Poor to work', but it leaves open the problem of the conditions under which labour acquired this status. Why, we should ask, does the sequestration of the idle and the compulsion to labour become emblematic of the art of correct governing understood in terms of the prosperity, welfare, and security of the population, i.e. of good police? While it may be true that labour acquired a certain ethical transcendence, our discussion of police can be used to provide a more adequate understanding.

The emphasis on confinement continues the conservative dimension of police, not because it returns the body politic to its original shape but because it seeks to arrest disturbances to that body. Having immobilised the agents or symptoms of this disorder, it does not return them to their 'proper places' (of work, obedience, and residence) but attempts to duplicate an ideal moral–political order within the walls of the workhouse. Confinement can be placed in a long series of tactics in which the political ideal is held to be a happily-settled and properly-ordered kingdom or city, and in which the movements of persons without proper station or place of residence represent multiple sites of disorder, upheaval, and crime. In this regard, the house of confinement fulfils the function of the conservation of relations of domination and subordination characteristic of earlier police, but articulates it within the distributional character of mercantilist Political Oeconomy, concerned as it is with the augmentation of the patriarchal trading households of the nation.

Thus the workhouse is more than merely another instrument in the long battle against vagrancy. It may well aim to herd the vagrant micro-populations (the 'rogues, sturdy beggars, and vagabonds') off the streets and highways, but it also attempts to enhance the process of circulation by augmenting the trading households of the nation. The suppression of vagrancy combined three distinct actions: the forcible arrest of the mobility of the idle, the fraudulent, and the mysterious, typified by the putting of vagrants in stocks; the recoding of the idle within hierarchical relations of command and obedience by brandings and other inscriptions on the body as a token of the 'falsity of their deeds'; and the reinsertion of the idle within the social order by transporting them to their 'proper' place, usually of birth or residence. The workhouse, by contrast, manages to combine these three actions in a single moral–political space. It is able to demobilise the idle, recode their status, and reinsert them in a single movement which dispenses with the fuss and bother of putting the vagrant into the stocks, branding, and transportation, and at the same time contributes to the wealth of the nation by placing the idle Poor within the replica of the patriarchal household. In the workhouse, the idle Poor, with their irregular movements and their drain on the nation's wealth, are arrested, recoded, and reinserted not according to a nostalgic vision of their proper status and residence in a hierarchical political order but by the educative and disciplinary functions of a certain 'course of life', formed under patriarchal authority and organised around labour. The highest aspiration of the workhouse movement was thus different from that of the suppression of vagrancy. The mercantilist police of the Poor would no longer be haunted by the memory of an ancient order but would be linked to newly-formulated national goals. The ethical valuation of labour may have been utopian, but it was clearly rooted in everyday mercantilist concerns with increasing the numbers of the trading households in the nation, and converting the idle into the industrious Poor.

The workhouse, as a technique of this mercantilist police, thus went beyond the re-formation of the social order. In doing so, however, it became less a place for the reform of individuals than the site of the metamorphosis of the idle into the industrious, or dross into sterling, as Bentham might say. It was neither a protected workshop in which the Poor learned the skills for the supersession of their condition nor a reformatory in which they became normalised individuals, but a kind of switching mechanism. In it, the Poor would remain the Poor. That was their earthly lot. They would be transformed, but not as individuals so much as categories. The mercantilist workhouse, unlike later the prison, asylum, and reformatory, which were to be characterised by the regime of discipline described by Foucault (1977a), did not attempt to act on the 'soul' of the individual. It both gave rise to and was founded on the theory of associationism which sought an 'ideological' technique of power, a *semio-technique*, which would educate its objects in an orderly and respectful course of life by connecting mental representations of virtue, industry, and obedience with happiness, and vice, idleness, and insubordination with pain (Foucault 1977a: 93–103).

The workhouse aspired to absorb the idle and to harness them in the interests of the nation or, more concretely, in the interests of the national treasury. It formed a part of a series which included various public employment projects, farming out the Poor to private contractors, labour colonies, low wages, and the suppression of sporting activities, festivals, and taverns (George 1985: 275–286). In this sense the workhouse must be regarded as a single element in a configuration of 'complete, dispersed, but coherent' techniques (Foucault 1977a: 299), as but one axis of a movement of both 'institutionalisation' and 'disinstitutionalisation' in the seventeenth and eighteenth centuries (Minson 1985: 107). The workhouse, whether intentionally or not, was to operate in concert with a host of measures which made up a more or less calculated long-term strategy which used licensing and vagrancy laws, and the agency of the justices, to harass alehouses and taverns, to curtail the operations of fairgrounds, to prosecute travelling entertainers, gypsies, and minstrels, to withdraw access to commons and wastes, to restrict the use of sporting fields and areas, and to suppress gambling (George 1985: 275–278).

The interesting point about the mercantilist police of the Poor is that it is a strategy which is capable of emphasising either one of the two axes on which it operates. It is in this sense that we should read Defoe's proposal that the legislature should 'encourage' rather than confine the idle. The disinstitutionalised measures increase almost in exact proportion to the degree to which the utopian aspirations of the workhouse projectors come under scrutiny amidst accents of strident hostility (Coats 1976: 107). The shift to private contractors, especially to farming out the Poor, can also be viewed as a tactic which responds not only to the cost burden of poor relief but to the mercantilist vision of the patriarchal role of the heads of the nation's households in its political *oeconomy*. If the institutionalising aspect of this movement sought to increase the numbers of the industrious Poor, its complement was the distribution across the social body of a differentiated series of measures which sought to form the population in a fashion amenable to the goals of the state. The latter, however, would be relatively unrefined compared to those which would posit a private realm for the liberal governance which was to follow.

Nevertheless, all this may be at the base of the profound moral (r)evolution noted by Perkin (1969) and others (e.g. Malcomson 1973; Corrigan 1977: ch. 4) in which 'the English ceased to be one of the most aggressive, brutal, rowdy, riotous, cruel and bloodthirsty nations in the world and became one of the most inhibited, polite, orderly, tender-minded, prudish and hypocritical' (Perkin 1969: 280). In respect of eighteenth-century England, it is worth posing the question as to whether only a society with good *police* could leave the legacy of a *polite* society.

The problem of idleness located by the Discourse of the Poor corresponds to the particular mode of government formed in the epoch prior to the emergence of industrial capitalism. This police was neither the reformatory police of the period of the decline of the order of estates, nor the preventive police *force* of the liberal mode of government, although it shares with both the problem of securing the good order of the state. Where the earliest police were concerned with the conservation and re-formation of relations of servitude, obedience, and custom, its successor began to formulate new overarching objectives of establishing and maintaining national power and prosperity through the proper administration of the population. To do so, a utopian administrative space was invented for the transformation of the idle into the industrious, and to increase the number of the nation's productive households, the workhouse. While certainly the most dense instrument of industrial police, the workhouse formed only one node within a network of techniques and strategies projected on to the labouring population to promote work-discipline by increasing their motivation to follow a continuous and regular course of labour, and hence to liberate them from the 'taint of slothfulness' and make them profitable, above all to the nation. This form of police, and its objectives, which were embodied in the various solutions to the problem of idleness, had many features which can be described as non-capitalist, including the forms of labour it exhorted and compelled the Poor to do. This should not preclude us from regarding these great strategies of formation of the population as one of the central *preconditions* of capitalist social and property relations and a resource for the liberal revolution in government which sought to secure them.

The notion of labour in these discourses and in the practices of setting the Poor to work does distinguish this police from the later liberal – 'preventive', as Colquhoun, Bentham, and Chadwick would call it (see chapter eleven) – police. The industrial police of the end of the seventeenth century remained indifferent to the form of labour and may be, in Weber's terms, a version of 'irrational capitalism'. But even that phrase is perhaps a trifle anachronistic and unhelpful in making intelligible the practices which comprise this police. 'Setting the Poor to work' included enforced labour by public works, contracting poor relief recipients out to private employers, encouraging domestic manufactures, and establishing labour colonies and workhouses. It was of little concern to mercantilist policy whether such work was provided by the organs of the state or by 'private individuals'. The 'profitability' of the various measures could be calculated only by their degree of success in rendering members of the Poor self-sustaining, and in this way industrious bodies for the state.

From a genealogical perspective, the police of the Poor in the seventeenth and eighteenth centuries does make a fundamental contribution to the trajectory of what would later be called social policy. It does this by constituting the Poor as an object of observation, comparison, and information collection. Through such a process it begins to assess the modes of life of labourers and poor families in terms of the benefits or burdens they represent to the cause of national welfare. To regard the numbers of the Poor as representing national well-being, and to make this relation conditional upon a 'regular, industrious course of life' being practised among the Poor, is to take tentative steps in the direction of the delineation of a domain of personal conduct and familial and self-responsibility as crucial in the consideration of poor policy, and towards a redefinition of the relationship between state and patriarchy. However, the same framework which sought usefully to employ the Poor to link them to national goals meant that the Poor could never be abandoned to the vagaries of the labour market. The direction of the Elizabethan poor law to relieve and employ the Poor had established a bond between the landless and the legal–political order which would not be broken until the full deployment of this domain of personal responsibility. As Appleby has noted (1978: 150–153), the legislative provision for the able-bodied and the impotent provided the proximate context for the consideration of the Poor from the seventeenth century and brought the question of the idleness and distress of the Poor into protracted debate. The Discourse of the Poor could distinguish between different categories of Poor and different behaviours, customs, and habits of the Poor which were beneficial or detrimental to national goals. It could not rescind, however, either the desire to render the Poor useful to the nation or the implication that it was the duty of the rich, articulated through the national and local arms of the state, to see to it that the Poor were made to work and inserted into patriarchal relations.

Chapter four

Population, subsistence, poverty

Malthus' *Essay on the Principle of Population* (hereafter *Essay*), first published in 1798, stands at the intersection of many of the key themes of this study. In terms of the general problem of the transformation of modes of governance, it marks a definite break with the rationality characteristic of the Discourse of the Poor. In this respect, Malthus' doctrine brings to a conclusion a conception of population which had informed poor policy for nearly two centuries. Yet it is also one crucial site of the formulation of the first conception of poverty as a definite condition of individuals and groups as opposed to a conception of 'the Poor' as a given feature of the wise administration of the state and the establishment of police.

The principle of population figured prominently in the debates over the abolition of poor relief in the first decades of the nineteenth century which preceded the reforms of 1834. Despite the pedantic constructions of some intellectual historians, we shall show that Malthus' doctrine was crucial to the delineation of the objectives, if not the means, of the official strategy of 1834, the legislative centrepiece of liberal poor policy. More broadly, the principle of population prescribed a particular form of life and was able to define the spheres of responsibility of the state and of particular social categories. In this way, Malthus' doctrine became a central component in the formation of the objectives of liberal state-administrative and philanthropic practices. It is thus impossible to understand the classical liberal mode of government of poverty without understanding the Malthusian intervention and its consequences.

This chapter begins with the analysis of a text by Joseph Townsend which is often held to be a forerunner of the Malthusian doctrine. Such an analysis provides the means for highlighting the precise nature of Malthus' principle. The rest of the chapter examines the theoretical structure of Malthus' theory and its prescriptions for the poor and for poor policy. Chapter five will assess the complex relations between Malthus' intervention and poor-law debates and reform in the early nineteenth century.

Townsend, population, and poor laws

The first full-scale critique of the poor laws to employ the concept of population was not Malthus' *Essay* but Joseph Townsend's *A Dissertation on the Poor Laws by a Well-wisher of Mankind* (hereafter *Dissertation*), first published in 1787. It is necessary to understand the latter text if we are to grasp the way in which a theory of population could be drawn into the debates over the governance of the Poor at the end of the eighteenth century, and, indeed, to make clear the specific nature of Malthus' theoretical intervention. The purpose here is not to defend 'parson Malthus' against Marx's charge of plagiarism (1974: 578, 605–606), but to demonstrate that a definite break was made in Malthus' text with earlier conceptions of population and their application. First, let us briefly examine Polanyi's treatment of Townsend.

Polanyi's argument concerns the effects of a particular conception of the relation between population and subsistence on political discourse and action. In it, the *Dissertation* is said radically to have altered the grounds of political discourse: 'By approaching human existence from the animal side, Townsend by-passed the supposedly unavoidable question as to the foundations of government and in doing so introduced a new concept of law into human affairs, that of the laws of Nature' (1957: 114). This position is repeated in the foreword to a recent edition of the *Dissertation* which argues that Townsend was the first to introduce to social thought 'a biological model', 'a putative "Natural Law" ', to guide the reciprocal relations of classes (Montagu 1971: 13).

This is indeed the crux of the matter for Polanyi (1957: 111–115). The discovery of biological laws of the regulation of the population by the available food resources meant that 'the biological nature of man appeared as the given foundation of a society that was not of a political order' (115). This 'naturalism' justified poverty and indigence among the majority of the population by removing such items from the agenda of the state. Poverty was thus consigned to the ungovernable order of the *natural* by virtue of the fact that it was the poor who were the bearers of the operation of these laws through the mechanism of hunger.

Polanyi further argues that Townsend's naturalism was the basis of classical economic theory, instanced by 'Malthus' population law' and 'the law of diminishing returns as handled by Ricardo' (1957: 115, 123). Through political economy, this conception of the natural laws governing 'economic society' was to provide the intellectual foundations for the attack on the prevailing system of relief (123–129). In short, Polanyi proposes that the particular conception of population first vented by Townsend contained the premises of the theory and practice of liberal economic and poor policy in the early nineteenth century.

This obscure text is read as the originator of both biologistic theories of society and biological theory itself. On such a reading, it becomes not only an immediate precursor of Malthus' principle of population but also a forerunner of Darwin's theory of natural selection (Polanyi 1957: 113; Montagu 1971: 11–12). While expressing a certain incredulity at such claims, it is also necessary to limit them in order to restore the text to its rightful place among eighteenth-century polemics, and, more importantly, to appreciate the full significance of the Malthusian principle.

The *Dissertation* contains a series of loosely connected arguments against public assistance to the Poor, which, in its final half, discovers the problem of the ratio of population and food as a means of clinching its anti-relief ambitions. It commences with the paradox that 'poverty and wretchedness have increased in exact proportion to the efforts which have been made for the comfortable subsistence of the poor; and that wherever most is expanded for their support, there objects of distress are most abundant' (Townsend 1971: 20).

The reasons why this is the case, argues Townsend, have to do with the essential characteristics of the Poor themselves. The Poor have none of the motivations of the rich such as pride, honour, and ambition. They have 'only hunger which can spur and goad them on to labour; yet our laws have said they shall never hunger' (Townsend 1971: 23). Assistance to the Poor, by removing the spur of hunger, destroys the 'natural motive to labour and industry' (24). This natural stimulus is more effective than 'legal constraint' which is accompanied by 'too much trouble, violence and noise; creates ill will, and never can be productive of good and acceptable service' (23). The imperative to relieve the Poor therefore impedes the objective of setting them to work.

One of the primary themes of this tract, then, is that 'labour' is the result of a motive or 'spur' which is natural, namely hunger. In this respect, Townsend is at one with the mercantilist low-wage theory of industry. Labour is not a means for the creation of wealth, nor for the transcendence of poverty. Rather, it is the service rendered by the Poor to the community. Poor relief can be criticised not because it interrupts the production of wealth or nullifies the Poor's motives to overcome their poverty through labour, but because it fails to promote their 'cheerful compliance with the demands which the community is obliged to make on the most indigent of its members' and thereby destroys 'the harmony and beauty, the symmetry and order of that system, which God and nature have established in the world' (Townsend 1971: 36). He might have added that it destroys the proper police between ranks of the community.

Townsend's concept of nature does not depend on a distinction between biology and culture, but covers the providential order which is to be found in the world. Hence the sense of both 'nature' and 'labour' becomes clear when Townsend argues that the improvidence of the poor, far from being a source of disapprobation, is a law of nature which increases human happiness by providing those who 'fulfil the most servile, the most sordid, and the most ignoble offices in the community' (1971: 35). Labour refers to the most wretched occupations required by the community, and nature to that which ensures the proper functioning of the world. Improvidence is natural because by it the Poor constantly feel the spur of hunger and therefore are willing to accept the necessary roles of servants and labourers.

In the eighth of the text's fourteen sections, Townsend introduces a further argument against poor relief: that such relief encourages the increase of the numbers of people without a proportionate increase in food. This concept of the interdependence of food and numbers is first presented in the form of a fable drawn from events recounted by seafarers (Townsend 1971: 36–38). Polanyi (1957: 112–116) would have us grant much significance to this tale, claiming that Townsend 'deduced' his policy maxims against the poor laws from it and that it should be understood as a paradigm for the understanding of social relations in the emergent market society.

The story concerns a South Sea Island named, after its Spanish 'discoverer', Juan Fernandez. The Spanish were said to have placed a couple of goats on the island, which subsequently multiplied in conditions of plenty. The number of goats grew until they began to suffer hunger. Under these new conditions of relative scarcity, the weakest died and, for the rest, plenty was restored. Townsend concludes that, for the goats, there was a constant fluctuation between happiness and misery and that, except in periods of famine or human encroachment, their numbers were 'nearly balancing at all times their quantity of food' (1971: 37). A second event somewhat upsets this scene. Concerned that 'English privateers' were using this island for food provision, the Spanish attempted to destroy the population of goats by setting on shore a pair of greyhounds. The dogs likewise multiplied in conditions of plenty provided by the abundance of goats and, as a result, the number of goats diminished. However, certain of the goats were still able to escape the predations of the dogs on the craggy rocks of the island and a balance between the animal species was finally established. Now the moral of this tale can be told: 'The weakest of both species were among the first to pay the debt of nature; the active and most vigorous preserved their lives. It is the quantity of food which regulates the numbers of the human species' (38).

This tale is, quite obviously, open to a large number of interpretations. In order to draw out the moral that human numbers are regulated by the quantity of food, the text requires some means of jumping between a narrative concerning the balance of animal species and the relation of the human species to its food. This is effected by the notion of 'the savage state' in which the human species can be divided between the active and the indolent (Townsend 1971: 38). Where the pertinent distinction between the members of animal species is that of strong and weak, in the case of humans the distinction is made between the active and indolent or, to use the now more familiar terms, the industrious and the idle. The precariousness of subsistence in the savage state motivates the active to cattle-breeding, then to agriculture, and later to the full range of the division of labour (38–9). In the course of this process, the active acquire – and transmit – property and the indolent 'either starve or become servants to the rich' (38). The fluctuations between want and plenty, illustrated by the tale, are relevant to human society through the partial identity it posits of animal and savage states. These fluctuations can then be made into the nature which founds the progress of the division of labour, property, and population. This progress continues towards a final state where all fertile lands are cultivated to 'the highest pitch', and in which the multiplication of the human species can proceed no further (39).

It is clear that population growth does not drive this progress. It is merely one component of the greater progress of civilisation grounded in the precarious natural equilibrium of numbers and food, the agents of which are the industrious or active members of humanity. This natural balance gives rise to the bonds of servitude and duty in society which are hence also natural. The *Dissertation* presents a coherent conception of nature which can cover both the relation between population and food and that of masters and servants. Poor relief not only destroys the police which is established by the natural bonds of service. It also destroys the delicate *equilibrium* between numbers and food.

Townsend considers poor relief a type of communism, a 'permanent community of goods' which subverts the balance of numbers and food by increasing population without a proportionate increase in subsistence (1971: 38–42). If it were only temporary and occasional, a new equal division of property would be short-lived. Due to the natural division between the active and the indolent, 'things would soon return into their proper channel, order and subordination would again be restored' (40). Poor relief, since it is a permanent, legally enforced, community of goods, establishes an 'unnatural and forced' increase of people and thereby brings the nation to 'poverty and weakness' (41–42).

Poor relief encourages the Poor to marry and procreate without regard to the quantity of food available to enable their offspring to subsist (Townsend 1971: 43–44). Such an arrangement merely confirms the worst attributes of the Poor – after all, they are those whose condition is the cumulative effect of indolence and the associated characteristics of improvidence, prodigality, and vice (36). Poor relief will place an unnecessary burden on the active, industrious sector of the population, divert the 'occasional surplus of national wealth from the industrious to the lazy', increase the number of 'unprofitiable citizens', ultimately universalise misery, and increase general distress and death through want (40–41).

Not only, then, is poor relief a contravention of the natural bonds of harmony in society which are crucial to its police, but it also disturbs the difficult balance between population and food which, by distinguishing between the active and the indolent, underlies those bonds. The state of the Poor is doubly necessary: it provides members of the servile class and helps to maintain their proper attitudes; it also ensures, through the fear of not being able to feed one's future offspring, and the premature death of present members, that the advance of population will be kept within the limits of subsistence. The poor laws fail to attend to the requirements of the natural laws which, if obeyed, promote happiness. The 'wise legislator', a figure which pervades the *Dissertation* as it does other eighteenth-century oeconomic writings, will therefore act in accordance with nature and allow hunger to be a spur to relations of submission and to laborious occupation, and to maintain the delicate balance of population and subsistence.

In earlier chapters we identified a persistent theme in eighteenth-century political discourse which binds population to the happiness, wealth, and strength of a nation. The *Dissertation* remains firmly within such a discourse, in a way its successors would not. The linkage of population and collective good should not be taken to imply, however, that considerations of the availability of food resources are alien to eighteenth-century discussions of oeconomy, population, and the Poor.

In this regard it is instructive to examine an essay by Hume (1882: 381–443) in which he seeks to compare the populations of ancient and modern nations by recourse to arguments concerning the comparative wisdom of their institutions. Hume engages in this argument in order to refute Montesquieu's proposal, taken up by Wallace in 1753 (Smith 1951: 17–22), that the ancient world was more populous than the modern.[1] In the essay entitled 'Of the populousness of ancient nations', Hume argues that since no decline in the desire and power of human generation can be assumed and population is limited by the availability of subsistence, 'if every thing else be equal, it seems natural to expect that wherever there are most happiness and virtues, and the wisest institutions, there will be also the most people' (1882: 383–384).

Hume then compares the ancients and moderns through a range of institutional differences. While 'equality of property', 'liberty', and the 'small divisions of their states' are signs favourable to the populousness of ancient states, their more 'bloody and destructive wars' and 'factious and unsettled governments', their 'irregular and loose' police, and the 'more feeble' condition of their commerce and manufactures, all afford the view that the ancient state is less populous than the modern (Hume 1882: 413). Indeed, it is because modern institutions stimulate industry and manufactures that they undertake the most natural means of encouraging husbandry and subsistence by providing the labourer a 'ready market for his commodities, and a return of such goods as may contribute to his pleasures and enjoyment' (Hume 1882: 412). It is an index of the greater wisdom of modern institutions that they thus indirectly encourage an increase in subsistence and thereby bring into existence a greater population. For Hume, the growth of the means of subsistence is a necessary condition of the growth of population.

The principle that population can only increase to the limits set by the supply of the means of subsistence is the foundation of eighteenth-century discussions on populousness and is enunciated by Franklin, Mirabeau, James Steuart, Quesnay, and Wallace, as well as Townsend (Schumpeter 1954: 255–277). However, given Polanyi's insistence (1957: 111–112) on a cleavage between Townsend and Adam Smith on this matter, it would be well to examine the formulations on population to be found in the latter's *The Wealth of Nations*, the clearest of which is that:

> Every species of animals naturally multiplies in proportion to the means of subsistence, and no species can ever multiply beyond it. But in civilised society, it is only among the inferior ranks of people that the scantiness of subsistence can set limits to the further multiplication of the human species; and it can do so in no other way than by destroying a great part of the children which their fruitful marriages produce.
>
> (Smith 1976, 1: 97–98)

Against Polanyi's insistence on a break, it would be difficult to find a more succinct statement of the position enunciated in Townsend's *Dissertation*. Smith states the general rule applicable to all animal species, but he adds the proviso that in the human species the effect of population pressures falls on the lower ranks. Thus, in almost precisely the same terms as Townsend, Smith identifies the regulation of the growth of the population with the existence of the poor. He also employs the same conception of subsistence, in which food is given privilege over other items: 'Countries are populous, not in proportion to the number of people whom their produce can cloath and lodge, but in proportion to those whom it can feed' (Smith 1976, 1: 180).

On closer analysis, there is little to support Polanyi's claim that Townsend's conception of population marks a point of rupture with eighteenth-century political thought by introducing a hitherto absent naturalism. Townsend employs notions of population and subsistence which are found in Political Oeconomy, and argues in the same manner as Smith that there is a tendency for population and subsistence continually to re-establish an equilibrium by means of the want and misery of the numbers of the Poor, a position cogently detailed by Halévy (1928: 227–229).

What is different in Townsend is the use of such arguments to comment specifically on the effect of the social institution of state-enforced poor relief. It is here we can locate a divergence from Smith and other eighteenth-century writers on population. 'What encourages the progress of population and improvement, encourages that of real wealth and greatness', stated Smith (1976, 2: 566). Thus, where Smith had assumed that all conditions favourable to an increase in population implied an increase in wealth, Townsend can point to an institution which increases population without increasing the means of subsistence, 'real wealth', or 'greatness'. Robert Wallace in 1761 had already shown that a future society, with a community of goods and property, would remove the restraint upon procreation and therefore end in overcrowding and misery (Halévy 1928: 229; Schumpeter 1954: 256–257). Townsend changes the temporal co-ordinates of this possibility and suggests that the existing arrangements of the poor law are in fact the kind of permanent community of goods which have these effects in the present. What Wallace holds to be the defect of a communalist future, Townsend posits as operating in the here and now through a long-established set of legally-enforced practices.

Townsend's position is important because it inaugurates the possibility of bringing statements about population and subsistence to bear on matters concerning poor relief. However, this is done without disruption to the form of the existing conception of the relation of the two terms. This form is of an unstable, self-adjusting natural equilibrium, to which conditions such as hunger and misery are necessary. The possibility that there is a fundamental imbalance at the heart of the natural order, an insurmountable situation of scarcity, has not yet emerged.

The principle of population

Theory

In many places Malthus' *Essay* appears to employ and recapitulate these earlier arguments concerning population and subsistence. In the preface to the first edition, for example, it repeats a familiar eighteenth-century proposition: 'It is an obvious truth which has been taken notice of by many writers, that population must always be kept down to the means of subsistence' (Malthus 1798: iii). However, the identity of Malthus' principle with eighteenth-century discussions of the relation of population and subsistence is far from total. Where the latter had presupposed the existence of a natural equilibrium around which population and subsistence tended to fluctuate, Malthus introduces the possibility of a fundamental *disequilibrium* at the heart of the natural order. Where Townsend, for example, had located tendencies to overpopulation in the forced and unnatural disturbance of the fragile relation between population and subsistence brought about by the poor laws, Malthus was to find such tendencies in nature itself. The core of the Malthusian theory of population is its postulation of a constant, unalterable tendency towards overpopulation which is given by the comparative rates of increase of human population and its means of subsistence.

The pertinence of these different rates of growth is founded upon two primary anthropological invariants: 'that food is necessary to the existence of man' and 'that the passion between the sexes is necessary, and will remain nearly in its present state' (Malthus 1798: 11). The latter guarantees a near constant capacity for procreation, while the former is the material requisite for the maintenance of the products of this procreative capacity. For the *Essay*, any inquiry into the happiness of nations or the improvement of society and the perfectibility of mankind, such as those of Godwin or Condorcet, to which the first *Essay* was conceived as a reply, should be concerned with the effects of these two aspects of human material nature.

There are three steps in Malthus' theory. The initial stage assigns orders of magnitude to the rates of increase of population and subsistence. Population is held to have the *capacity* to increase in geometrical ratio while subsistence is said *actually* to increase in no more than arithmetrical ratio (Malthus 1798: 14). The effects of the difference between the two rates of increase is to establish an omnipresent *tendency* for population to outgrow the means of subsistence which is necessary for its support. Given that such a tendency can never be realised in the long run, the second stage is to argue that there must be some *check* or series of checks which limit the increase in population approximately to the level of the available food supplies. Having established such a tendency, and thereby deduced the existence of such checks, the final stage of the theory is an inquiry into the nature of the checks and a statement as to which check humankind ought to choose, if indeed choice is at all possible.

There are at least two different ways of classifying the checks. In the first *Essay* Malthus distinguishes between a *preventive* check which arises from 'a foresight of the difficulties attending the rearing of a family' and a *positive* check caused by the distresses of the lower classes in providing proper food and care for their children (1798: 61–63). This system of classification is apparently not exhaustive since Malthus adds, almost as an afterthought, a number of checks not covered by it. These are 'vicious customs with respect to women', presumably an oblique reference to techniques of birth control and abortion, 'great cities, unwholesome manufactures, luxury, pestilence and war' (99–100).

In the later editions of the *Essay* Malthus seeks to rationalise this system of classification by making the categories both mutually exclusive and exhaustive (Flew 1970: 23–24). Malthus now (1872: 8) holds the positive check to comprehend anything which shortens the 'natural duration of life', i.e. any cause of premature mortality, of which he mentions types of occupation, extreme poverty, diseases, epidemics, wars, and famines. However, birth control techniques have been shifted from the positive to the preventive check which now covers all restraints upon the birth-rate. The reworked category of the preventive check now includes not only the celibate restraint from marriage, as it had done before, but also 'promiscuous intercourse, unnatural passions, violations of the marriage bed, and improper arts to conceal the consequences of irregular connection'. This revamped classification is evidently intended to set the earlier distinction upon an ethically neutral footing (Flew 1970: 23).

However, there is another, evaluative and prescriptive mode of classification. In the first *Essay* Malthus concludes that all checks 'may be fairly resolved into misery and vice' (1798: 100). In all subsequent editions a third category, 'moral restraint', is added (e.g. Malthus 1872: 13). Despite this additional term, the check is not a new one, as may be thought, but simply covers the practice described as the preventive check in the first edition, that of a deferral of marriage after calculating its potential financial burdens. However, there has been some shift of ground. In the first *Essay* the practice of calculating a delay of marriage (for fear of not being able to support a family) must be resolved into a species of misery if it does not entail a resort to non-procreative forms of sexual satisfaction or birth control, which are, by Malthusian definition, species of vice. Later, however, this moral restraint becomes the means to ensure or at least maximise individual happiness.

This aspect of moral restraint will be examined shortly. There is, however, a central and simple dimension of this practice which, quite startlingly, seems not to have been noticed by most commentators on Malthus' theory (e.g. Glass 1953; Flew 1970; Winch 1987), or on his ideas about poverty (Poynter 1969: 144–151) or, indeed, on his ideas about the conditions of entry into marriage (MacFarlane 1986: 3–19). That is, the principal, if not sole, agents of moral restraint, are male. One commentator even goes so far as to claim that for Malthus:

> the proper means to the control of the natural increase consisted in the development and/or maintenance of institutions which conduced to 'moral restraint', to sufficient deferment of marriage on the part of women, until the age of 27 or 28.
>
> (Spengler 1973: no pagination; cf. Winch 1987: 39)

There is no textual support for such a view. There is no evidence that moral restraint is meant to be undertaken by women exclusively, and

77

little evidence that it was intended to extend to women at all, in the various editions of the *Essay*. The examples of moral restraint invariably examine the concerns of different classes of *men* in entering marriage. 'Men' and 'man' are used in such a fashion as to demonstrate their clear restriction to one sex. Very occasionally, Malthus uses the term 'person' and 'people', but when they are used to discuss calculations of the costs of marriage, particularly among the poor, these terms are restricted to males. Just as Charles Darwin exemplifies the calculative approach to marriage typical of the English in Alan MacFarlane's study (1986: 3–19), Darwin illustrates that it is males who are the actors in the Malthusian marriage stakes, and it is they who gamble on their capacity to be responsible for the support of their wives and their children.

Malthus defines moral restraint 'to mean a restraint from marriage from prudential motives, with a conduct strictly moral during the period of this restraint, and I have never intentionally deviated from this sense' (1872: 8). Here the agent exercising such a restraint is not specified in terms of sex. However, the agent is clearly male in those passages which illustrate the practice and the conditions under which it is liable to occur. In the first *Essay* Malthus argues that the preventive check 'appears to operate in some degree through all the ranks of society' (1798: 63). This proposition is then illustrated by examining why *men* of different ranks should engage in the practice. These ranks include men of the highest rank, men of liberal education, the sons of tradesmen and farmers, the labourer earning eighteen pence a day, and the servants living in gentlemen's families (63–69). The men of the highest rank, for example, are prevented from marrying 'by the idea of the expenses that they must retrench, and the fancied pleasures that they must deprive themselves of, on the supposition of having a family' (63).

While foregoing luxuries may appear to be a trivial consideration, this calculative attitude to marriage assumes much greater weight lower in the social hierarchy. A man of liberal education fears the descent of 'two or three steps' down the steep slope of social rank which would make him dependent upon the patronage of those who should be his equals (Malthus 1798: 64–65). Similarly, sons of tradesmen and farmers are well advised not to marry until they are settled into a business which enables them to support a family (66). When one descends the social scale even further these calculations come to involve matters of the utmost seriousness. At the bottom is

> The labourer who earns eighteen pence a day, and lives with some degree of comfort as a single man, will hesitate a little before he divides that pittance among four or five, which seems to be but just sufficient for one. Harder fare and harder labour he would submit to for the sake of living with the woman that he loves but he must

feel conscious, if he thinks at all, that, should he have a large family, and any ill luck whatever, no degree of frugality, no possible exertion of his manual strength, could preserve him from the heart-rending sensation of seeing his children starve, or of forfeiting his independence, and being obliged to the parish for their support.

(Malthus 1798: 67)

For a male earning a low wage, then, moral restraint arises from the fear that marriage would lead to a family of such a size as to present him with the alternative of watching his children starve or losing his 'independence' by being forced on to parochial relief.

The evidence that Malthus intends the practice of moral restraint to apply to men is not restricted to these passages. Although Malthus does suggest that both sexes may spend the early part of their lives in moral restraint (1872: 400), this position is inconsistent with the overall presumption of the male breadwinner which is well in evidence in the final version of the text. Thus he attempts to explain the 'double standard' (see Thomas 1958) by arguing that breaches of chastity rightly lead to greater disgrace for women because they cannot be expected to have sufficient means to support their own family. The results of female indiscretion therefore create the greater burden upon society (Malthus 1872: 279). If the point of moral restraint is to delay having a family until one can be sure of supporting its members, and women cannot be expected to provide that support, it is nonsense to imagine that the concept applies to women. For Malthus women should remain celibate outside marriage not because they calculate the financial burdens of procreation but because bastardy places a burden on the state. Malthus consistently understands marriage as the institutional form of the obligation of a man to support 'his' family (1872: 278–279, 403–404). Moral restraint becomes the only acceptable alternative for the male who fears he may be unable to fulfil this obligation. The implication for a female who has a child outside this marital obligation is, then, the fullest moral disapprobation of the society she has needlessly burdened.[2]

By definition, moral restraint is preferable to either vice or misery as a check upon the tendency of population to outstrip subsistence. For Malthus, it is only right that the conditions which encourage this restraint should be perpetuated. The failure to calculate correctly, or to do so at all, should be allowed to take its natural course.

If he cannot support his children, they must starve; and if he marry in the face of a fair probability that he shall not be able to support his children, he is guilty of all the evils which he brings upon himself, his wife and his offspring. It is clearly his interest, and will tend greatly to promote his happiness, to defer marrying, till by industry and economy he is in a capacity to support the children he may reasonably expect from his marriage.

(Malthus 1872: 404)

This passage demonstrates as clearly as any other that Malthus was bound to a position in which males remain the only effective agents of moral restraint. Moreover, it indicates the dependence of a man's wife, as well as children, on him not only as breadwinner but as calculator of his capacity to act as such. In the same passage Malthus had enunciated the maxim that 'the happiness of the whole is the result of the happiness of the individual' (1872: 404). On the present reading, the only agents who qualify as self-responsible individuals, as civil persons, are adult males. When Malthus' commentators claim that moral restraint meant 'the postponement of marriage until an individual had prospects of supporting a family' (Glass 1953: 28), they fail to realise that the individual in question is equivalent to the male head of household (Barker 1978). Wives and children thus constitute only segments of the whole whose happiness is determined for them by such individuals. Such a position would be entirely consistent with the common law doctrine of coverture and Blackstone's interpretation of it: that 'the very being or legal existence of a woman is suspended during the marriage, or at least is incorporated into that of her husband' (quoted in Corrigan and Sayer 1985: 36).[3]

It might be thought that this point about the male prerogative in entering, and his responsibilities in, marriage has long gone unacknowledged in commentary on Malthus since it would be unusual to find a comparable social and political theorist who did not make this traditional patriarchal assumption.[4] In Malthus, it is, however, more than an assumption. It is a part of the theorisation of the marriage contract, and its attendant obligations, which are held to be explicable in terms of the principle of population. It is crucial to understand the implications of this theorisation so that we may understand the *form of life* which Malthus assumed as natural, and to make intelligible the objective of his prescriptions for the poor and for the poor law. Malthus' explanation of the double standard certainly gives *that* debate a novel twist. Dr Johnson had regarded female chastity as paramount because 'upon that all the property in the world depends' and asserted that female adultery risks 'confusion of progeny' (quoted by Thomas 1958: 209). Malthus' ingenuity, by introducing considerations of relief, manages to adapt this model to those who are *without* property.

It should be noted that Malthus considers the use of contraceptive devices even within marriage as a form of vice. It was left to Francis Place in his *Illustrations and Proofs of the Principle of Population* to recommend that married persons 'avail themselves of such precautionary means as would, without being injurious to health, or destructive of female delicacy, prevent conception' (1821: 165). It could be argued that by such means a sufficient check might be given to the increase of population so that vice and misery could, to a large degree, be removed. Because Malthus' ethical stance refuses such a possibility, he is left with only one means, the encouragement of moral restraint, to stem the constant tendency to overpopulation and its accompanying vice and misery.

Policy

Moral restraint, or the delaying of marriage from prudential motives by adult males, accompanied by complete sexual abstinence, was to remain the central remedy to poverty throughout the six editions of the *Essay* Malthus saw published. His arguments against the poor laws, however, and his 'palliatives' to poverty display quite a degree of variation. Despite this variation, it must be insisted that the form of life of the poor continued to be the major focus of the Malthusian prescriptions.

As Poynter notices, the first *Essay* begins with the general claim 'that no distribution of money could raise the general standard of comfort among the poor' (1969: 152). Money given to the poor might provide some stimulus to agricultural production, but this would be more than offset by the spur that 'fancied riches' would give to population. Redistribution to individuals would mean general lowering of the condition of the (more numerous) lower classes and, indeed, the nation, further compounded by the 'strong and immediate check to productive industry' (Malthus 1798: 78).

These criticisms can be directly applied to the poor laws (Malthus 1798: 83–90). They increase population without increasing the food for its support, and therefore create the poor they maintain. They depress the condition of the industrious by diverting provisions to the idle and unproductive, thus raising their cost.

To these arguments are added others which have no discernible relation to issues of population growth or the cost of provisions. It is the tendency of these laws to eradicate the 'spirit of independence' fortunately still alive among the peasantry (1798: 84–86). The settlement laws, which authorise the practice of prosecuting men whose families could become chargeable and pregnant women, form a 'set of grating, inconvenient and tyrannical laws . . . contradictory to all ideas of freedom' and obstructing the market of labour (92).

There is thus an uneven mixture of arguments and assertions, some of which posit a basis in the 'scientific' principle of population, others concerned with the moral effects of poor relief upon the spirit of the lower classes, and still others dealing with general political problems of freedom and tyranny. One commentator is thereby led to conclude:

'The *Essay* became not a reasoned case against poor relief, but a farrago of all available abolitionist arguments' (Poynter 1969: 155). Perhaps so. However, it is also clear that the diversity of the criticisms of the poor laws is not so much unified by the consequences of an immanent logic of population growth but by the aims of promoting modes of conduct most conducive to human happiness defined, of course, against a fundamental insufficiency of nature, a fundamental horizon of poverty.

In the later editions of the *Essay* Malthus arrives at the bald position that all relief to the poor is simply a waste which does not stimulate production. The poor laws depress the general condition of the labouring poor by raising the price of provisions and lowering the real price of labour (Malthus 1872: 303–304). However, despite these 'economic' arguments, the main thrust of the continued opposition to poor relief is that its provision contravenes the commandment to a form of ascetic existence for the poor. He states that:

> The labouring poor, to use a vulgar expression, seem always to live from hand to mouth. Their present wants employ their whole attention, and they seldom think of the future. Even when they have the opportunity of saving they seldom exercise it; but all that they earn beyond their present necessities goes generally speaking to the ale-house. The poor-laws may therefore be said to diminish both the power and the will to save among the common people, and thus to weaken one of the strongest incentives of sobriety and industry, and consequently to happiness. The mass of happiness among the common people cannot be diminished when one of the strongest checks to idleness and dissipation is thus removed; and positive institutions which render dependent poverty so general, weaken that disgrace which for the best and most humane reasons ought to be attached to it.
>
> (Malthus 1872: 304)

Moral restraint thus encapsulates the premises of a broader calculative attitude towards life which imposes a certain worldly asceticism on the poor. They must also engage in the foresight which is embodied in the will to save against the possibility of distress. The poor laws attack the moral character of the poor's existence, and encourage its worst tendencies. It is their status as rational, virtuous beings, able to better their own condition and take responsibility for themselves, which relief calls into question.

The Malthusian state is therefore not a paternal one, caring for those in need and providing for the wants of its members as its children. But this does not mean that it has ceased to be a patriarchal one, in so far as it seeks to enforce relations of subordination within the family. The state is to do this through a certain pedagogy, if by that is understood the creation of the institutional conditions which allow the lessons of nature to be taught. To govern is to render as natural a specific form of life necessary for the survival of those in poverty, one which at base turns on the economic responsibility of husbands and the dependency of wives. It is a form of life which attaches the propertyless man to wage-labour, to what we might call capitalism, and attaches the poor woman to submission to what we might call patriarchy.

By the second edition the proposal for abolition had been developed. 'In the moral government of the world', Malthus argued, 'it seems necessary, that the sins of the fathers should be visited upon the children' (1803: 544). He therefore proposed that no legitimate child born one year after a proclaimed date (or two years after that date for an illegitimate one) should ever be entitled to parish assistance. After this time, private charity, provided it was discriminating in its objects and encouraged prudence and foresight, could be depended upon to assist cases of genuine need and want.

Nevertheless, there did remain a realm of possible intervention for the state in keeping with its pedagogic role, and that was as a provider of a national system of education. A key objective of this system in respect of the poor would be 'to infuse into them a portion of that knowledge and foresight' which secures the operation of moral restraint, so that

> In addition to the usual subjects of instruction . . . I should be disposed to lay considerable stress on the frequent explanation of the real state of the lower classes of society as affected by the principle of popula-tion, and their consequent dependence on themselves for the chief part of their happiness or misery.
>
> (Malthus 1872: 437)

It was no longer a matter for national government to establish police, to ensure proper relations between the ranks in society, between men and women, between parents and children. If nature itself taught that a certain form of self-reliant life was best suited to our happiness, the state could fulfil its duty only by the replication of nature's lessons.

The economic and demographic arguments against relief to the poor are secondary to the complaint that such relief is contrary to the disciplined, prudential, and industrious mode of conduct which is appropriate to the poor population, and whose principal agents are adult males. Malthus' palliatives for poverty, and his position on the effects of the poor laws on population growth, fluctuate around the persistent claims that poor relief destroys the spirit of independence and industry of the poor, weakens their willingness to save, removes the restraint from improvident marriage, and fails to discriminate between the proper and improper objects of charitable benevolence. It is clear, then, that the principle of population embodies a rationality capable of specifying a form of life for the poor. The Malthusian intervention must figure prominently in accounting for the additional virtues demanded of the poor in the nineteenth century. They were not only to be docile, industrious, and sober, as in the previous century, but also to be frugal in domestic economy, avoid pauperism at all costs, practice proper restraint from unconsidered marriage and improvident breeding, join a friendly society, and make regular deposits of savings in a savings bank (Poynter 1969: xviii–xix).

Matters of marriage and procreation, both within and outside the context of the poor laws and the treatment of the poor, had been among matters of state in England long before Malthus' intervention and the debate over the poor law and the reform which followed. The positions of the husband and the wife had been specified and treated in law and other state practices in quite distinct ways, as they are by Malthus. Nevertheless, the examination of Malthus' position gives added insight into the consequences of the marriage contract and procreation for the poor, and their differences for poor men and women. It also indicates the transformation that was occurring in the relations between patriarchy, the household, and the state.

Marriage had long been a point of overlap between the interests of the Church and the state, especially given its location in that elementary unit of Erastianism, the parish (Corrigan and Sayer 1985: 22–23). From 1200, marriage banns first had to be read and the ceremony held in public, usually at the parish door. Only marriages contracted in *facie ecclesiae* were recognised in common law. Marriages had to be recorded in parish registers from 1538, and the publication of banns or purchase of a licence, two witnesses, and registration were compulsory after 1753. Moreover, the common law doctrine of coverture rendered the wife civilly dead. Until the late nineteenth and early twentieth century, she could neither own property nor make contracts in her own right. All her property belonged to her husband. Her chattels were for his absolute use and disposal and her real property for his use for the duration of the marriage, or, if children were born, for life (Pateman 1988: 90–100, 119–120; Corrigan and Sayer 1985: 36).

Malthus' concerns about marriage, however, were for those who were propertyless, and it is here that the insights we can gain from reading him are greatest. Marriage makes the poor man a breadwinner, i.e. one who is economically responsible for his family. Moreover, it renders the poor woman a dependant in the fullest sense of the term, so that her future existence and those of her children depend on this man, and her fate is tied to his fortune. For Malthus, marriage implied an absolute limitation on the responsibility of the state for *all* wives and their children. While Malthus' suggestion that every marriage include a sermon on the evils of matrimony without adequate means was greeted with ridicule by his critics (Poynter 1969: 157), it would have been little more than a further extension of the state concern over this contract. As it was, those intending to marry would have to notify three successive weekly meetings of the Poor Law Board of Guardians in the 1840s and 1850s (Corrigan and Sayer 1985: 23).

The matter of bastardy also had implications for poor law. Bastardy had long carried legal impedimenta, with the whipping of female and, less often, male, offenders from Tudor times (Corrigan and Sayer 1985: 22). An Act of James I authorised the Justices to imprison 'a lewd woman who shall have a bastard which may be chargeable to the parish' (Henriques 1979: 16). Under the laws of settlement, pregnant women would be dumped over the parish border, and forced marriages, with the putative father shackled to the church door, were arranged, particularly if he came from another parish. Women were urged to name a father who could be made to provide security to indemnify the parish against relief costs for the child, and men charged as fathers at Quarter Sessions risked imprisonment. While Malthus railed against the tyranny of overseers who practised such methods, the implication of his position is that, in the absence of a man who has contracted by marriage to support her and her child, that is, to be their breadwinner, the mother and her illegitimate child are rightly the subjects of social disgrace and are at the complete mercy of the society on which they are a burden. Neither state nor community has responsibility for their assistance. Society may offer them some occasional or charitable relief, but this would stem more from Christian charity than any fundamental obligation to do so.

The government of poverty is no longer about creating a good police through strengthening patriarchal relations of authority and subordination within the nation's households. It is about removing the institutional barriers to the natural laws which teach propertyless men the obligations attendant upon their own private exercise of patriarchal authority. It is about the dire consequences for those who place themselves under the protection of that authority if men should fail to meet these obligations. If for Blackstone the wife places herself under the 'wing, protection, and cover' of her husband, for Malthus the poor wife must be left exposed if that cover is lifted or is threadbare. The Malthusian prescription for the poor is about allowing those laws of nature to operate which bind the poor man to the yoke of wage-labour and the poor woman to the yoke of conjugal dependence.

The emergence of an administrative rationality to educe such a form of life is a later theme of this book. In contrast to Max Weber, who showed how a methodical conduct of life arose from Christian asceticism (Hennis 1983: 135–180), we shall examine the emergence of a rationality which was capable of not only formulating a way of living for the poor as a targeted group but also producing the institutional strategies which would promote it. It is not a question of social actors undertaking a life style consistent with a conscious set of beliefs, but rather of strategies for the establishment of the (material, social, institutional) conditions which promote a form of life for categories of social agent. The paradox of the first liberal mode of government is that it should make such investment in the institution of what it held to be the order of nature.

Chapter five

The Malthusian effect

In assessing the impact of the *Essay* upon its contemporaries, and its relation to poor-law reform in particular, we must abandon a model in which ideas are first generated by individual creation, then are transmitted to other individuals and to groups, and finally are applied to institutions and practices. In other words we must abandon an analytic framework which presupposes an opposition between the weight of institutions, laws, and established social practices and the intersubjective agency of ideas, the problematic of *influence*. If we are to 'rethink the dispersion of history' beyond the quasi-causality and vagueness of this notion, as Foucault suggests (1972: 21), then what are we to do in the case of Malthus?

This chapter is conceived as at least a partial answer to the problem of analysing the significance and effectivity of Malthus' *Essay* without relying on the 'too magical' support of the notion of influence (Foucault 1972: 21). In the last chapter we considered Malthus' writings on population as a significant *break* with eighteenth century conceptions of population and subsistence, and their implications for policy, and sought to specify and delimit the nature of that break. Here I would like to regard Malthusianism as an *intervention* into a complex field of discussion and debate, in which economic, moral, theological, governmental, and practical themes, arguments, and concepts cross and intermingle with diverse effects. Malthusianism, to use a term which allows some dissociation between author and doctrine, is treated as an intervention which structures that field of which it is an instance.

While the major concern in this chapter is with the relation of this intervention to the reform of the poor laws in 1834, it will first show that Malthusianism did structure philanthropic debate over relief, and articulate discourse more generally, in the decades after its publication. It will then seek to specify the relation between the aims of Malthusianism and the consequences of the poor-law reform of 1834. This argument suggests a fundamental kinship between the Malthusian policy and the new administration of relief. Taken together, these first two arguments imply a significant relation between Malthusianism and poor-law reform. Finally, arguments which seek to deny such a relationship under the rubric of notions of 'influence' will be addressed.

Malthus, philanthropy, opinion

There is a little-noticed aspect of Malthus' thought which has implications for the reception of his abolitionist conclusions by that sector, Christian philanthropy, from which may have been expected at least some opposition to his sombre thesis. This aspect concerns the theological arguments which so preoccupied Malthus that he devoted the final two chapters of the first *Essay* (1798: 348–396) to its resolution. These arguments take the form of a theodicy, of an attempted reconciliation of the facts of evil with the existence of a (benevolent, omniscient, and omnipotent) God. In Malthus' particular case, of course, a central component of his theodicy was bound to show how the evils associated with the principle of population are consistent with the existence of such a being. It must address the existence of natural laws of the growth of population and subsistence which permanently produce poverty and its attendant vice and misery. Nevertheless, it is not so much the intellectual success of Malthus' theological arguments which is at stake here, but the practical success of his doctrines in the arena of Christian philanthropy.

In the first *Essay* human, material existence is conceived as providing the 'various impressions and excitements' which, acting according to general laws, awaken 'Mind' – a concept which covers both intellectual and spiritual attributes – from the 'sluggish existence . . . the torpor and corruption of the chaotic matter, in which he [i.e. 'man'] may be said to be born' (Malthus 1798: 352–354). It is from such a mighty teleology that Malthus infers the 'animating touches of the Divinity'. The production of Mind from matter is thus understood as God's plan. According to this plan, the principle of population functions to deprive humankind of such security from material want as would lead it back to this original indolence and away from the course which produces Mind.

The 'impressions and excitements' which so arouse Mind include:

1 the wants of the body (Malthus 1798: 356–359);
2 the constancy of the operation of general laws, in particular that of the pressure of population upon the means of subsistence (361–371); and
3 the sorrows of life, moral evil, the infinite variety of nature, and the obscurity involved in metaphysical subjects (372–381).

The last group gives rise to such 'higher' human characteristics as social sympathy, moral excellence, and a developed intellect. However, it is the first two which are of greatest interest, for they accomplish the fundamental transformation of matter into Mind in Malthus' system.

The wants of the body, specifically its need for nourishment, are crucial because 'the supreme Being has ordained, that the earth shall not produce food in great quantities, till much preparatory labour and ingenuity has been exercised upon its surface' (Malthus 1798: 360). God has therefore designed the natural order so that the difficulty of attaining subsistence gives rise to an heroic labour caught in an unremitting battle with a niggardly earth. Labour becomes a form of the deferral of gratification, the renunciation of the immediate pleasures of an inherently indolent human nature in favour of the exertions which provide some tenuous security against want and ultimately raise matter into Mind. Although not explicitly drawn, moral restraint could be similarly conceived as the renunciation of constant sexual passion which leads to moral and spiritual attributes of Mind.

The principle of population underlines how tenuous is the security against want (Malthus 1798: 361–363). As a general law, the principle ensures that the wants of the body never receive a lasting satisfaction and makes the insufficiency of nature constant no matter the degree of past exertion and labour. Moreover, the generality of such a law endows humans with a reason. This can be conceived as the recognition of the constancy of the laws of nature and the certainty that the same effect follows the same cause (362). The condemnation of humanity to perpetual labour by the laws of population becomes a divine plan for the awakening of this faculty, among the achievements of which are the conquering of sexual passion in the practice of procreative prudence. The principle of population, and the evil it produces, are therefore the material basis for an industrious approach to life which is conducive to the development of the moral virtue and intellectual attainment, from which Mind is fashioned.

The chapters containing the theodicy in this form are excised from later editions. However, even in the final form of the *Essay*, Malthus argues that natural and moral evil function negatively as 'instruments employed by the Deity in admonishing us to avoid any conduct not suited to our being', and positively, to provide the experiences which lead to 'all the advantages and extended enjoyments which distinguish civilised life' and 'the conduct most favourable to the happiness of man' (1872: 390). In this formulation, the evil founded on material existence provides the experience which leads to rational behaviour conceived as a calculus of happiness. The evil attendant upon the principle of population is thus the force which promotes civilising conduct and institutions.

Malthus' position can justifiably be called a 'theology of scarcity' (LeMahieu 1979: 467–474). It is significant, from the point of view of philanthropy, that Malthus' argument sought a theological basis to explain (away) the existence of the evils attendant upon the principle of population and hence provide, if not a theological justification, a Christian apologia for the abolition of poor relief and the right to assistance. The fact that the attempt to develop a theology of scarcity was retained despite subsequent changes in the format of the *Essay* emphasises its significance, notwithstanding the possibility that Malthus may have tempered his line either due to pragmatic deference to criticism from Church authorities (Pullen 1981: 39) or to the positive intellectual influence of William Paley (Harvey-Phillips 1984: 605–607). Whatever the case, the capacity of the principle of population to provide arguments by which poverty and its attendant evils could be theologically justified constituted one of the major tactical weapons which philanthropy would use as it became absorbed in the movement for the abolition of poor relief.

The Malthusian ethic is at once pessimistic and triumphalist. It posits a God who endows his creatures with the constant sexual passion and inherent indolence of their material nature and subjects them to such natural laws as inevitably result in distress. But this God also leaves his creatures the option of overcoming the evils produced by this material nature. Procreative prudence and unremitting exertion are part of their transformation into reasonable, responsible, and virtuous beings. Thus the Malthusian God subjects humans to the scarcity and indolence inscribed in material nature so that they may transcend it, maximise their happiness, and minimise misery. The Malthusian ethic amounts to a life and death choice for the poor: to obey or to transgress the dictates of the laws which are an essential part of divine providence, to choose a particular ascetic form of life or to perish.

The final half of the eighteenth century witnessed a large number of philanthropic and humanitarian reforms to the national system of poor-law administration inaugurated under the Elizabethan legislation of 1597–1601 (Cowherd 1977: 2–10; Webb and Webb 1963a: 271–276, 342–344). Under the impetus of Jonas Hanway, laws were enacted in 1761 and 1767 protecting pauper infants in workhouses and encouraging apprenticeship of pauper children (2 George III. c. 22 and 7 George III. c. 39). In 1782 'Gilbert's Act' (22 George III. c. 83) was passed enabling the union of parishes for administrative purposes, and effectively repealing Knatchbull's 'workhouse test' Act of 1723 by encouraging outdoor relief and promoting the employment of salaried officers. In 1793 other legislation encouraged and protected mutual assistance or friendly societies, and in 1795 the law of settlement was partially repealed. The latter allowed that no one should be removed until chargeable upon the rates with the exceptions of 'rogues and vagabonds', 'idle and disorderly persons', and, odiously, pregnant, unmarried women (Webb and Webb 1963a: 343–344; Poynter 1969: 3–7).

The final decade of the century witnessed the climax of this period of reform under the leadership in Parliament of William Pitt. The tempo of the debate had been quickened during the years following the French Revolution, no doubt fuelled by fears of that event inspiring an English uprising, but also by the conjunction of the requirements of national wartime mobilisation after 1793 with rising prices of provisions, bad harvests, and consequent famine and rural revolt in the final years of the century (Poynter 1969: 45–48). Pitt proposed a large number of reforms of the poor laws including schools of industry to educate poor children, rewards for large families, the advance of credit to the poor, and the granting of relief to people with some property (Poynter 1969: 62–65; Webb and Webb 1963b: 34–39). His reforms became the key field of struggle over poor policy during the next decade. For example, Sir F.M. Eden printed Pitt's Bill among the appendices to his three volume *The State of the Poor* (1797) in order to reject it both on principles derived from Adam Smith and on fears about the institutional treatment and education of pauper children (1797, 1: 479–484). Similarly, in February 1797 Jeremy Bentham wrote his *Observations on the Poor Bill* in the midst of devising his own Pauper Plan (1843: 8). It was a devastating, if disingenuous, criticism both of the clauses, which he termed the *supplemental-wages* clause, *the extra children* clause, the *opulence relief* clause, and the *cow money* clause, the last of which received particularly biting invective, and the drafting of Pitt's proposals, which became influential through circulation in manuscript form (Poynter 1969: 68). By contrast, the Society for Bettering the Condition and Increasing the Comforts of the Poor (SBCP), established in 1796, took on the specific aim of assisting in the enactment of the provisions of this bill and overcoming opposition to them (Cowherd 1977: 14–17).

At the end of the eighteenth century the respective positions of philanthropy and Adamite natural-law theory such as that of Eden were constituted by opposing and irreconcilable dogmatisms based on the acceptance or rejection of public relief. The philanthropic position of the SBCP may be stated in the words of its founding member, Thomas Bernard, who defined the role of the parish officer as 'the guardian and protector of the poor' whose role, in terms which owe their framing to eighteenth-century conceptions, is 'to provide employment for those who can work and relief and support for those who cannot', to assist the young in gaining a livelihood, and 'to enable the aged to close their labours and their life in peace and comfort' (quoted by Cowherd 1977: 15).

Philanthropic notions in favour of a comprehensive parochial assistance were founded upon an adherence to contemporary principles of Christian benevolence and notions of the obligation of the rich attendant upon the rights of property which I shall discuss in the next chapter. On the other hand Eden (Poynter 1969: 111–116; Cowherd 1977: 16–18) derived his opposition to the relief of the poor from the wage-fund thesis attributed to Adam Smith. This held that all compulsory payments to the poor came from the employers' fund available for the payment of wages and the employment of additional workers. Moreover, Eden's adherence to Smith's 'system of natural liberty' can be instanced by his argument that parish employment diverted the 'capital stock' of the natión from its 'natural' channels, hindered the accumulation of that stock, and provided undue competition with existing manufactures and employments (e.g. 1797, 1: 467–468). Such a theory, as long as it remained premised upon arguments deduced from the Adamite system of natural liberty, remained powerless to engage with a philanthropic movement founded on entirely different a priori principles derived, in the last instance, from an interpretation of the duties of Christian benevolence.

Malthus' doctrine differed in one crucial respect from these natural-law arguments. From its earliest formulations, it sought to address the religious and other moral arguments in favour of public poor relief. As well as elaborating what it claimed to be a scientific principle, it engaged in theological arguments about the existence of the evils attendant on poverty. It sought to develop a veritable cosmology in which philanthropic objections to abolitionism might be met and in which a theological justification for the denial of a public system of relief could be produced. In this manner Malthus' position sought to redefine the role of the Church in respect of charitable endeavour by a radical reassertion of the primacy of its responsibility for the administration of benevolence, the like of which had not been seen since the confiscation of the ecclesiastical endowments in the sixteenth century. Malthus' doctrine not only marks the point of the elaboration of a new kind of rationality towards poverty and matters of poor policy, but also the point of intellectual co-optation of Christian charity as an instrument of that rationality.

In various editions of the *Essay*, there are specific arguments that the principle of population is part of a divine plan for the production of the faculties of reason and virtue and the industry, civilisation, and cultivation of the Earth they imply. If it is accepted that all these effects of the principle are necessary to human happiness, and that the pressure of population upon the means of subsistence perpetually places some segment of humanity in a state of want, it follows that poverty is not only essential to the formation of reason but also to the constitution of human happiness. The followers of this line could thus argue that the principle of population has, surreptitiously and without scientific recognition, led humankind to the practice of what has been long understood as proper conduct, exemplified in moral restraint, unremitting labour, self-discipline, self-reliance, independence, and foresight. In simple terms, the Malthusian position resonated with a set of connotations for Protestant theology, especially for the preacher who saw salvation in a strictly disciplined conduct of life. The life of the poor man had become an everyday struggle in which the only escape from starvation for himself and the members of his family (besides the degradation and dependency of poor relief) was constant industry, a prudential approach to procreation, and the foresight to accumulate savings. When the evangelicals objected that the principle of population was refuted by the commandment to increase and multiply, Malthus was to reply that the express command of God 'is given in subordination to those great and uniform laws of nature, which he had previously established; and we are forbidden both by reason and religion to expect that these will be changed in order to enable us to execute more readily any particular precept' (quoted by Cowherd 1977: 33).

The evangelicals came to accept that the principle of population was indeed a providential discipline for the labouring poor, as evidenced by the changes in opinion on Malthus in *The Christian Observer* and the publication of a major theological work in 1816 by John Bird Sumner, who would become a bishop, a member of the Poor Law Commission of 1832–4, and later Archbishop of Canterbury. This was a *Treatise on the Records of Creation and the Moral Attributes of The Creator*. In it, the existence of various ranks in society is justified because it creates the best conditions for the development of the faculties and exercise of virtue. This includes the lower classes who have no choice but to live in 'cheerful equanimity under hardships no discontent can remove or alleviate' (quoted by Poynter 1969: 229). Poverty itself exemplifies that life is a state of discipline in which the faculties are exerted and 'moral character formed, tried and confirmed previously to their entering upon a future and higher state of existence' (quoted by Cowherd 1977: 39). Although he could demur at Malthus' continual stress on the 'evil' of the law of population, and insist that the ratios were hypothetical and not the ordinance of God, Sumner's view of the beneficence of population was even less equivocal than Malthus' (Poynter 1969: 229–231). Scarcity led to property, which led to the ranks, each with their own 'separate probation' before God. Population pressure led to economy, exertion, universal industry, and men striving as breadwinners. It fostered exchanges and European expansion, and would eventually Christianise and civilise barbarism. The principle had become the great missionary.

The debate in the *Observer* displayed a tendency towards acquiescence with all Malthus' views regarding poverty (Cowherd 1977: 38–41). By 1807, it had capitulated to the principle of population while dissenting from its implications for poor relief. In 1812, it held that Malthus was not inconsistent with Providence and accepted his position that the poor laws aggravated the condition they were supposed to relieve. By 1816, it dubbed Malthus an 'enlightened philanthropist' and deemed moral restraint a better solution to poverty than compulsory charity, praising voluntary abstinence as a great virtue. Finally, as an index of how far humanitarian Anglicanism had come by 1817, it now concluded: 'Providence has constituted society upon such a model which renders a certain degree of poverty and dependence in a great number of its members essential to its healthy condition' (quoted by Cowherd 1977: 40). Its statement on the elements of poor policy of the same year was taken along Malthusian lines, advocating general education to exalt the character of the poor, provident banks to better the condition, and Christian charity for the relief of temporary distress.

By the end of the second decade of the nineteenth century, the acceptance of Malthus was by no means limited, among philanthropic groups, to those of Established Church and Tory religious persuasion. Although some Quakers rejected Malthus' view that increased misery arose from a redundant population, the Dissenters' magazine, *The Philanthropist*, from its first issue in 1811 followed the line on Christian charity and the poor laws identified with the author of the *Essay* (Cowherd 1977: 41–43). It is certainly the case that Malthusianism 'severely inhibited the charitable impulses of some simple and benevolent men', including one who conceived of planting vegetables for the poor but, after reading Malthus, instead planted potatoes for livestock, and foresaw that they could be fed to men during the next scarcity brought about by the poor laws (Poynter 1969: 227–228).

The devout were at first shocked by what they took to be exclusion of God from the moral government of the world (Jarrold 1806), and reasserted God's benevolence against impious speculative systems (Leslie 1807), or, like the Rector Ingram, thought that 'virtue and intelligence have a very powerful influence in preventing, or alleviating, misery' (1808: 8). But that so many of the devout felt compelled to stand up against what they first saw as blasphemy and irreligion, and that there were so few who resiled from its drastic conclusions only a decade later, demonstrates clearly the success of Malthusianism as an intervention into philanthropic debate, and its critical role in structuring the terms in which that debate was to be held.

The period of high Malthusianism in matters of poor policy was, undoubtedly, the second decade of the nineteenth century, some fifteen years before the critical reform of the poor laws in 1834. Outside the philanthropic sphere it had become widely accepted, among the Whig-liberal intellectual leadership voiced in the *Edinburgh Review* from the early years of the century and – much to the discomfort, one supposes, of Southey and Coleridge – even among some voices in the Tory *Quarterly Review* when, in 1817, the poor laws were again under parliamentary discussion (Cowherd 1977: 41–46; Spengler 1973; Poynter 1969: 172–174, 251–254).

The 1817 *Report from the Select Committee on the Poor Laws*, said to have been mainly the work of Frankland Lewis, who would become the first chairman of the Poor Law Commission in 1834, wrote the science of population into its findings (Poynter 1969: 245–48). It summoned up all the common moral and economic arguments against the poor laws with a caveat on the impracticality of abolition. It argued that compulsory relief morally degraded those dependent on it and thus led to an increase of pauperism and relief expenditure. Further, it viewed the object of setting the poor to work as beyond the capacity of the poor laws and recommended a check on expenditure by the abolition of outdoor relief and the use of the workhouse as an effective deterrent. Significantly, in keeping with the Malthusian remedy of moral restraint, it proposed the abolition of allowances apportioned to family size (Cowherd 1977: 57–59). Despite the inaction of the Tory government, which must be viewed partially as a result of the difficulty in translating the Report into clear and comprehensive principles of relief, it placed the radical reorganisation of the poor laws on the *parliamentary* agenda for the first time. What was virtually unthinkable at the time of Pitt's Bill had become the major parliamentary statement on relief at the end of the Napoleonic Wars. This alone signals the significance of Malthusianism in the quest for poor law reform. By the end of the decade, certain amendments to the poor laws had been made with the twin objects of curtailing expenditure and restoring the independence of the labouring poor (in the so-called 'Select Vestry Act' of 1819) (Cowherd 1977: 75–78). These amendments sought to restrict the benevolence of the justices and the direct democracy of the ratepayers assembled in vestry in order to increase the power of the largest property owners and ratepayers who were thought to be able to effect the proper discrimination 'between the deserving and idle, extravagant and profligate poor'.

If one takes into account the massive shift in articulate opinion evidenced in the intellectual and philanthropic journals of the first two decades of the nineteenth century, one is forced to conclude that Malthusian abolitionism played a central role in structuring debate over the poor laws and hence placing their fundamental reorganisation on philanthropic, intellectual, and parliamentary agendas. The hegemony of abolitionism is further evidenced by both the conclusions of the Report of 1817 and the absence of any significant oppositional position. That Malthusian abolitionism was not translated into legislation and the reform of relief practice may be due not to its failure to convince and mobilise support, for it won converts in every quarter of the ruling classes, nor to the strength of its opponents, of whom all but a few eventually acceded to its policy prescriptions, but to the immanent limitations of its logic. The abolition of the poor law could thus become a laudable and necessary goal which was unrealisable. The logic which deliberately eschewed the legislative and administrative framework of poor relief could hardly conceive of the legal and administrative means to its dissolution.

Malthusianism should be understood as more than a simple 'influence' upon poor-law debate in the first decades of the nineteenth century. It must be understood as an intervention which had its greatest triumph in the area one would least expect, that of Christian benevolence. Malthusianism was both the cause and symptom of the transformation of philanthropy. Indeed, by the 1820s, and in the writings of those such as the Reverend Thomas Chalmers, philanthropy had become Malthusian. In its success at attaining such an identity, this doctrine had succeeded in co-opting the opposition, among the governing forces, before the battle, which the Radicals of 1832 were to wage, had even begun.

Relief practice

Let us now turn to the crucial question of the affinity between Malthus' doctrine and the reform of the poor laws embodied in the 1834 Poor Law Amendment Act and the subsequent administration of the New Poor Law. This question is crucial to one of the overarching ambitions of our study, to understand the relationship between the conceptualisation of poverty in nascent economic discourse and the forms of administration characteristic of the state in the liberal mode of government. It is also critical to the assessment of the effectiveness of the Malthusian intervention in the debate about poverty and poor relief, and to the intelligibility of liberal policies concerning poverty throughout the nineteenth century. An investigation of the relation between this discourse and liberal administrative practices brings to the fore a mostly unacknowledged dimension of those practices, i.e. they constitute able-bodied *men* as economically responsible for themselves, their wives, and children by depriving this group of assistance outside the deterrent institution of the workhouse.

The interconnection of the Malthusian doctrine with the poor law and its administration can be examined in two ways: first, by investigating the pertinent aspects of the actual operation of the New Poor Law for the remainder of the century; and second, by addressing arguments formulated within the problematic of influence which seek to sever the relation between intervention and reform. With regard to the first, this study argues that there exists a fundamental affinity between the Malthusian remedy for the poor, organised around the advocacy of moral restraint, and the institutional configuration of relief, with its distinctive mode of discrimination of proper objects, practised under the new administration. In respect of the second, it is concluded that the case against a Malthusian influence is weak and that, while the New Poor Law is evidently different from strict abolitionism, its objectives were the same. These positions revive the views expressed by Malthus' contemporaries and nineteenth-century scholars with the added inflection that both the Malthusian strategy and the operation of the new administration implied differential treatment of the poor according to their sex.

It would follow from the Malthusian prescription for the poor that if a poor law could be devised which was educative in self-reliance, encouraged reproductive prudence and the foresight of savings, and found some means of discriminating between the proper and improper objects of relief, then the Malthusian programme towards the poor might be realised without the necessity of the compete abolition of the existing system. In the specific sense of failing to abolish all forms of public expenditure on the poor, that is of failing to create a Malthusian utopia, the law so devised may be judged contrary to the letter of Malthus' aims. In the general sense of creating a Malthusian universe of possibilities for the poor by different means, this poor law would be perfectly consistent with them.

A poor law which fulfilled these criteria was devised in the pages of the *1834 Report from the Commissioners for Inquiry into the Poor Laws* (Checkland and Checkland 1974) and implemented in the Poor Law Amendment Act of 1834. In the insightful study of Karel Williams (1981), the post-1834 poor law is shown to achieve what was the key Malthusian goal, the abolition of relief to able-bodied males and those who were constituted as their dependants. The possibility of using poor relief to maintain or contribute to the maintenance of himself, his wife, and their children would be denied to the able-bodied poor adult male for almost the whole of the next century. Similarly, the chances of a woman who was separated from her husband or her child(ren)'s father receiving relief outside the 'less-eligible' – on which more later – conditions of the workhouse were negligible.

Williams' analysis circumscribes the objects and forms of relief practice before and after the 1834 reform. Such a concern allows a consideration of the relation of this reform to the Malthusian remedy for the evils accompanying the condition of poverty. Using the scant official statistics on relief in the thirty years before 1834, Williams finds that 'these resources independently show extensive assistance to the able-bodied in all four [surveyed] years' and that 'in the last thirty years of the old poor law before 1834, able-bodied men were consistently included among the classes obtaining relief' (1981: 51). In direct and dramatic contrast he finds that after 1834 'a line of exclusion' was drawn against relief to able-bodied men and those construed as their natural economic dependants (69–75).

These conclusions are of great interest not only in terms of the numbers of specific classes of paupers receiving relief but also in terms of the forms of relief granted under the two administrative regimes. The contrasts that can be drawn between these two regimes clearly demonstrate the effect of three decades of debate within a Malthusian framework. The Abstracts of Returns for 1802–3 show that 11.4 per cent of the total population received some form of poor relief and that four out of five of these were able-bodied adults and their children (Williams 1981: Table 4.2, cols vi and ix, 149–150). This relief took the form first of child allowances to the low-paid, which were nearly universal in 1824 and commonplace in 1832. Second, the same group also had received 'wages out of the rates' in half of all districts in agricultural counties, and a quarter of industrial counties in 1824, but this has declined to marginality by 1832 (Williams 1981: Table 4.3, 151). The majority of districts (55 per cent) continued to provide one or both forms of relief to the low-paid in 1832 on the eve of the poor-law reform. Moreover, 92 per cent of urban areas provided either money relief or work to the jobless in 1832 (Table 4.2, 151). Paupers were typically relieved outdoors, with only 8 per cent of the pauper host of 1802–3 receiving permanent indoor relief in 'workhouses or houses of industry' (Williams 1981: Table 4.2, col. ix, 150).[1]

After the 1830s, all this changed. Williams shows a massive shift away from this practice of granting relief to the unemployed, the underemployed, and their dependants. At no time between 1839 and 1845 did the numbers of able-bodied men 'in want of work' receiving outdoor relief rise above 3.3 per cent of the total number of paupers (Williams 1981: Table 4.9, col. v, 181). Only once after 1850 did this figure rise above 1 per cent and that was at a time when the unemployment rate among certain trade unions was 11.9 per cent in 1858 (Williams 1981: Table 4.10, cols ii and iii, 182). This saga of the steady relative and absolute decline of the relief of the able-bodied male continues through the rest of the century. In these decades the absolute numbers in this category rarely go beyond a few thousand and often plunge into the hundreds (Williams 1981: Table 4.10, col i, and Table 4.11, col i, 182–183).

If able-bodied males were to be systematically expunged from outdoor relief after 1834, so too were their wives and children whether or not they still, or had ever, lived with them. On the one hand, the death of the breadwinner was evidently regarded as a legitimate reason to provide out-relief for women and children. They formed about one fifth of the pauper host for the rest of the century and more than a third of all widows (aged 20–45) were relieved by the poor law until the 1870s (Williams 1981: Table 4.20, cols iv and v, 199). However, the category of 'widows with dependent children' was so defined that separated or unmarried women with dependent children rarely received out-relief (Williams 1981: 196). Moreover, under the 1834 Act, the full economic consequences of illegitimacy were placed upon the mother. No longer would she be imprisoned but her right to sue the putative father would be effectively withdrawn, and no money recovered from him by the parish would be paid over to her (Henriques 1979: 41). Whereas a substantial minority of all widows and their children were relieved under the New Poor Law, the fate of all other categories of women with children was to be offered relief only in the 'less-eligible' conditions of the workhouse. The poor law was in the business of moral discrimination on grounds which were pure Malthusianism.

To summarise, the granting of relief to able-bodied males and their families was widespread and accounted for the majority of those receiving out-relief prior to the Poor Law Amendment Act of 1834. The poor – whether through low wages or lack of employment – received money doles, work, child allowances, or had their wages supplemented from the rates. After 1834, the body of the pauper host was composed of the aged and the infirm, widows with dependent children and a growing number classed as insane.[2] Able-bodied men were not relieved in significant numbers, nor were those who were considered to be their rightful dependants. Separated women and their children were still regarded as the responsibility of their husbands. The only category of women who were compelled to take full economic responsibility for their children were those who had failed to secure a marriage contract with the fathers of their children. From the viewpoint of the New Poor Law, marriage for the female poor was about contracting economic dependency for oneself and one's children, which only concluded on the husband's death. Hence the wives of able-bodied men, and separated women with children, and the children of these women, were excluded from out-relief. Because unmarried mothers had failed to contract a male breadwinner, their shame was to be even greater but the material effect, of exclusion from out-relief, was the same. The basic point is that despite the fluctuations in a developing capitalist economy, the male wage-labourer was virtually excluded from all state-administered relief, as were those he had contracted in marriage as his economic dependants, as well as those not covered by such a contract, under the compulsory acceptance of the workhouse test.

The core of the Malthusian strategy was articulated around the notion of moral restraint. It sought to construct adult males as breadwinners, i.e. as agents responsible for the subsistence of themselves, their wives, and their children. The objective of Malthusian abolitionism was to remove the barriers for the operation of this agency as a natural condition. In like manner, the operation of the New Poor Law in the second half of the nineteenth century established the institutional conditions by which adult males and those they had contracted as their dependants would have no legitimate claims for subsistence except inside the deterrent institution of the workhouse. The New Poor Law thus can be understood as a kind of state-run Malthusian charity which establishes a domain of economic responsibility of both the state and of adult male individuals. It uses a means of discrimination between proper and improper objects of relief centred on the workhouse. It thus reveals the full force of the Malthusian attack on relief as 'indiscriminate' by producing the means of discrimination which effectively excludes the majority of the earlier users of poor relief. Moreover, the categories excluded from out-relief are such that it seems probable that this exclusion could only be legitimised in Malthusian terms, i.e. as a sanction against those who have failed to practise moral restraint, those who have been made their dependants, those whose existence is the result of this failure, and those who are subject to no relations of responsibility and dependency as established in the marriage contract.

Malthus and the New Poor Law

Having established this correlation between Malthusian discourse and the operation of relief practice after the 1834 reform, their relationship will now be approached from another angle, that of 'influence' and arguments *against* a Malthusian influence on the formation of the new law and administrative regime. The term 'influence' is directly appropriated from the debates on Malthus and the New Poor Law undertaken by historians of ideas. While remaining fully cognisant of the uncertain status of this term, the rest of the chapter addresses key arguments of intellectual history in order to show the weakness of the anti-Malthusian-influence case.

The question of the relation of the *Essay* to the reform embodied in the Poor Law Amendment Act of 1834 has been extensively canvassed in the literature on his work. The opinion of contemporaries was summed up by Bishop Otter in the following sentence (1836: xvi): 'There is scarcely any other instance in the history of the world of so important a revolution effected in public opinion, within the compass of a single life and by a single mind.' This statement echoes that of Whitbread who, in reference to the poor law in a speech in Parliament as early as 1807, claimed that it was Malthus who had first 'ventured to surmise that the system was radically defective and vicious' (Webb and Webb 1963b: 24). In his *Memoir* Otter identified the *Essay* with the 1834 Act in these terms:

> But this act is founded upon the basis of Mr Malthus' work. The Essay of Population and the Poor Law Amendment Bill, will stand or fall together. They have the same friends and the same enemies, and the relations they bear to each other, of theory and practice, are admirably calculated to afford mutual illumination and support.
>
> (Otter 1836: xix)

The position that the *Essay* was overwhelmingly influential on that ill-defined entity, public opinion, and on the poor policy of the New Poor Law, was also taken by Malthus' intellectual biographer, Bonar (1885: 304–305), who suggested that Malthus fathered not only the New Poor Law but also the latter-day Charity Organisation Societies. In summary, nineteenth-century contemporaries and scholars of Malthus were convinced that the degree of influence of the *Essay* upon the reform of the poor law was of the highest order and that the vehicle of this influence was a profound transformation of public opinion towards questions of poor relief. This received view is repeated in the writings of twentieth-century historians of social policy, notably Webb and Webb (1963b: 21–25), and commentators on the *Essay* such as Smith (1951: 296–297).

This view has more recently been cast into doubt by the arguments of Grampp (1974: 302–3). He argues that the received opinion is supported by two provisions of the 1834 Act, the abolition of family allowances and the separation of the sexes in the workhouses. Both of these measures are deemed by Grampp to be consistent with the Malthusian objectives of encouraging marital prudence and checking early marriages (303). However, he continues, there are three pieces of evidence which weaken any demonstration that Malthus was influential upon the 1834 Act: first, the prime architects of the policy, Nassau Senior and Edwin Chadwick, did not believe there was a population problem and therefore could not have believed they were solving such a problem; second, the Act failed to eliminate the principle of the right to relief, the feature Malthus is said to have held most objectionable; and third, Malthus was not consulted by the Poor Law Commission.

The first and second of these assertions merit serious attention. The last, since virtually anything may be inferred from it, will be allowed to pass.

The first objection to a Malthusian influence relies on the presumption that Malthus believed that there was an actual or imminent problem of overpopulation in Britain at the time he was writing. It should be recalled, however, that the principle of population asserts no more than that there exists a *capacity* for population increase of a greater order than that of the means of subsistence. Therefore, in terms of the principle itself, it would be wrong to assume that population was actually increasing faster than subsistence in Britain in the early nineteenth century, or anywhere else for that matter. The mature Malthusian position on the actual rate of increase of the population of Britain, illustrated in his discussions of the census figures of 1801, 1811, and 1821, tends towards circumspection and even obscurity rather than dogmatism and alarm. While, as would be expected, Malthus claims that this material is 'striking proof' of his principle (1872: 215), he is careful to note the decline of birth, marriage and mortality rates as exemplifying the 'increasing healthiness of the country' (219). One of the most significant aspects of Malthus' later views was the argument that the increase in population was due to 'the greatly increased power of production, both in agriculture and manufactures' (215). Thus Malthus thought that the population increase of contemporary Britain was fundamentally sound. He held that it was increasing production, and accompanying increases in resources and the demand for labour, and not mass procreative imprudence, which accounted for the actual increase in population (215). This position would be consistent with the movement of Malthus' thought on matters of economic development towards a view which understands manufacturing production, as well as agricultural expansion, as a potential contributor to the happiness and welfare of those at the base of the social pyramid (Gilbert 1980: 83-96).

The argument that the fact that Senior and Chadwick did not believe there was a population problem undermines evidence of a Malthusian influence on the reformed poor law is, therefore, not pertinent. Malthus did not believe in any imminent disaster of overpopulation. He was even equivocal as to whether overpopulation was the prime cause of distress, a point conceded by Poynter in his argument against Malthusian influence (1969: 326). As we have just noted, he eventually acceded to the beneficial nature of the course of English economic development. It is important, however, to consider Senior's entry into the debate on the *Essay* since not only was he a co-author of the *1834 Report* which projected the reform, but he also provided the first academic resistance to Malthus' principle of population and attempted to enunciate an alternative theory of population. This was first contained in two lectures delivered at Oxford University in 1828 (Senior 1829), in an ensuing correspondence with Malthus in 1829 (Senior 1829), and in his *Outline of the Science of Political Economy* (Senior 1938).

Senior makes two striking modifications to the doctrine: he discards the different ratios, claiming that all animals and plants are capable of increase at a geometrical rate (Senior 1829: 7), and claims that 'there is a natural tendency for subsistence to increase in a greater ratio than population' (49). The first modification is rhetorically very strong since it appears to do away with the natural basis of the constancy of population pressure. However, its effectiveness is weakened since Senior admits that the law of diminishing returns makes the increase of food production more difficult than that of population (12-13).

The second modification relies on a change of the sense of the word 'tendency'. Where Malthus had employed the term to refer to an ever-present cause which, if left unchecked, would lead to a specific result, Senior (1938: 47) uses it to denote the actual movement of things to a certain state. Thus, for Senior, the means of subsistence become proportionately more abundant in the 'natural tendency to rise from barbarism to civilisation' (1829: 49). This is the sense of his proposition that there is a natural tendency for subsistence to increase in greater ratio than population. Moreover, among the contributory factors to this tendency are Malthusian ones depending on the constitution of economic agents as rational calculators of the effects of marital delay upon future luxury consumption and the rise or fall of social status (Senior 1829: 25–27).

In general, Senior's population theory implies that the course of development of the economy is necessarily to the benefit of the labouring class. He is, unequivocally, an advocate of industrial production and the types of consumption it makes possible for this class. He argues that such production creates the reserves against potential famine and the subsequent desire for luxury means a shift from positive to preventive checks (Senior 1829: 27–36). Nevertheless, this position entails a reformulation, rather than a rejection, of Malthusian policy towards the labouring poor. For Senior (1829: 87–90) policy should place as much emphasis upon promoting production (of subsistence) as preventing the too rapid increase of population. In fact, in Senior's view the responsibility for the former falls on the higher orders just as much as the (Malthusian) responsibility for the latter falls on the lower. This position supplements rather than negates the Malthusian remedy for poverty in a world of perpetual scarcity. Hence the key economist associated with the 1834 reform maintained a position which, although it implied a shift away from Malthus' ambivalence to the powers of production increase, retained his core prescription for the propertyless poor. Senior's critique does not so much do away with the Malthusian principle of population as maintain it in relation to a modified view of the capacity of production.

The other argument against a Malthusian influence is that the right of relief is not eliminated by the New Poor Law. Put another way, this is equivalent to the claim that since Malthus was 'consistent in his abolitionism', and the Poor Law Commission explicitly rejected abolitionism, then it was 'at best heretical by the master's standards' (Poynter 1969: 326). In making this argument, others (e.g. Himmelfarb 1984: 156) have noted Malthus' testimony to the Select Commission on Emigration in 1827 to the effect that those born after a certain time should be refused parish assistance. To such arguments, we must reply that it is incontestable that the 1834 Act did not deny the *right* to relief in principle, but it placed such strict conditions on it for certain categories of paupers (e.g. the workhouse test, the principle of the 'less-eligible' conditions for those on relief) as to render it practically nonexistent. It is also true that Malthus devoted considerable effort in arguing for a formal renunciation of that right and combating objections to this disavowal (e.g. 1872: 430; 490–507), and was destined to remain committed to abolition rather than reform.

However, it must be said that all these arguments simply miss the fundamental point. To imagine that Malthus' fundamental objective was the elimination of rights misrecognises the nature of those rights. The 'rights of the Poor' under the old poor law were for very limited and specific forms of provision for highly circumscribed social categories and can in no way be construed as universal human rights. It is not the elimination of ancient rights which is at stake in Malthus' social pronouncements as much as the inculcation of 'moral restraint' and the promotion of a sphere of personal responsibility. The 1834 reform is clearly more limited than the complete abolitionism of doctrinaire Malthusianism. Yet the refusal of the right to relief in the former, like the virtual elimination of relief to able-bodied males and those construed as their natural dependants in the latter, serves the same ends. A rationality, no matter how crude, capable of formulating a mode of life for the propertyless is generated by the debates on population and the poor laws which engaged with the basic propositions of Malthus' *Essay* in the first third of the nineteenth century. This mode of life was conducive to, among other things, the generalisation of wage-labour among a particular sector of the population, as will be shown in chapter nine. The *1834 Poor Law Report* and the subsequent Poor Law Amendment Act employed definite administrative means, which were not Malthusian, to institute the conditions of a form of life based on a male civil individual capable of rationally calculating the costs of gaining a wife and the potential economic burdens represented by children. Once a man contracts to become a husband and therefore a father, he assumes full responsibility for his wife's and children's fates. This is the classical meaning of the term *breadwinner*.

Therefore, it can be concluded, the central objectives of the reformed poor law remained starkly Malthusian even if its administrative means were fabricated from other sources. The *1834 Report* criticised the existing poor law in terms which underline its Malthusian perspective when it argued that

> We have seen that one of the objects attempted by the present administration of the Poor Laws is to repeal *pro tanto* that law of nature by which the effects of each man's improvidence or mis-conduct are borne by himself and his family. The effect of that attempt has been to repeal *pro tanto* the law by which each man and his family enjoy the benefit of his own prudence and virtue.
>
> (Checkland and Checkland 1974: 156)

The strategic objective of the poor law after 1834, like that of the *Essay on Population*, was to create the conditions necessary for the operation of what it took to be the natural laws of family life. It went so far as to list among the four classes of effects of the proposed administrative regime the explicit Malthusian rationale of 'the diminution of improvident and wretched marriages; thus arresting the increase in population' (Checkland and Checkland 1974: 349–351). The *1834 Report* and ensuing law and administration may have had, as their ultimate objective, the conversion of paupers into 'independent labourers' (e.g. Checkland and Checkland 1974: 341). However, this end could not be accomplished without making the (potential or actual) independent labourer the sole responsible agent of the welfare of *his* wife and children. When it did effectively abolish relief to able-bodied men and their families, the New Poor Law revealed its Malthusian aims.

Chapter six

From morality to economy?

It is easy to accept that the formulation of state policy in terms of an explicit economic rationality is an historically specific phenomenon. It is more difficult to grasp what this economic understanding of the role of the state is supposed to have succeeded. One story, which runs through many accounts of the capitalist order, is written in terms of a fundamental shift from an ethical framework of state policy to an economic one. In this and following chapters (seven and eight) this historical schema will be examined, and subsequently displaced, as a way of organising the analyses of the emergence of a definite conception of poverty, the application of political economy to poor policy, and the place and function of moral statements within the context of governmental transformation.

The historical schema

It is tempting to adopt a certain historical schema which postulates a shift from an ethical to an economic framework for political action, social arrangements, law, and policy. One of the fullest and best examples of this schema is that made by R.H. Tawney who locates a transformation in the 'moral and religious environment' which 'sets its stamp on the individual' (1938: 26–27). This transformation entails a shift from a view of society as composed of unequal classes contributing towards a common end to one in which society is a self-adjusting mechanism founded on economic needs and motives. The imagery by which Tawney conceives this transformation connotes a loss of control over certain activities. On the one hand, he posits a religious ethic which 'represses economic appetites' and which treats and judges economic activity as a species of moral conduct (26–27, 35–48). On the other, he finds an 'individualism' which views economic conduct as 'dependent upon impersonal and almost automatic forces' (27). Tawney's schema is discontinuist, with the differences between its two poles regarded as a 'chasm'. The opening up of this chasm, for Tawney, becomes evident as the 'spontaneous, doctrineless individualism' propounded by Smith, but which had already become the 'rule of English public life' a century before, especially exemplified by the 'new medicine for poverty' initiated by the Puritans and manifested in their attitudes towards the enclosure movement and the poor laws (Tawney 1938: 252, 151–170).

Such a schema is tempting because it provides a framework with which to grasp the transformations in poor policies and doctrines of poverty we have been charting in the present study. However, it is the confirmation of something similar to it in a wide range of historical discussion which makes this schema all the more compelling. What is most striking is its very ubiquity, its countless variations on a single theme, its almost surreptitious dominion over a whole domain of historical interpretation. Tawney's discussion, however, serves to illustrate a number of the fundamental features of this schema which merit serious attention:

1 the representation of the transformation of cognitive frameworks for social policy as a shift from a moral to an economic framework;
2 the claim that this shift is a profoundly discontinuist one; and
3 the assertion that this shift involves a loss of political and, more generally, human control over vital matters of the provision of subsistence and the organisation of work.

These are all features which Polanyi finds in the discussion of pauperism. He asserts that 'The problem of poverty centred around two closely related subjects: pauperism and political economy. Though we will deal with their impact on modern consciousness separately, they formed part of one indivisible whole: the discovery of society' (Polanyi 1957: 103). Polanyi assumes something of the same order as Tawney's moral environment in charting the emergence of this 'modern consciousness'. He seeks to follow the integration of the knowledge of society 'with man's spiritual universe' (Polanyi 1957: 84). However, where Tawney posits a pre-modern, functionalist conception of society, Polanyi places the problems of pauperism and the intellectual dominance of political economy in an historical configuration which leads to the *discovery* of society itself. He finds that, driven by the extension of the market to labour, 'the mind of man turned towards his community with a new anguish of concern: the revolution . . . shifted the vision of men towards their own collective being as if they had overlooked its presence before' (84). This revolution, that of the generalisation of market relations, underlies for Polanyi the emergence of a conception of the social totality as one governed by its own laws, the first instance of which was to be found in the naturalistic interpretations of political economy (111–129).

Polanyi is less concerned with the forms of consciousness which precede the practical and intellectual effects of the irruption of economic logic than is Tawney. Nevertheless his characterisation of pre-modern consciousness and practices hints that they may be conceptualised in terms of a moral universe. Thus the discussions which culminate in Smith's *Wealth of Nations* are said to be undertaken within a politico-moral framework and the Tudor labour and poor legislation is regarded as forming 'a national organisation of labour based on the principles of regulation and paternalism' (Polanyi 1957: 111–112, 87). He contrasts this form of consciousness with one in which the discovery of the natural laws of the economy comes to be the source of 'moral law' and 'political obligation' (112).

Indeed, the transition from a politico-moral to an economic conception of the role of social policy can be said to underlie the conflict Polanyi intuits in debates over pauperism and the 'Speenhamland' system of poor relief (1957: 78–85). This system of relief is viewed as the last-ditch efforts of rural paternalists to maintain a protected organisation of labour under the pressure of the extension of the market to labour. Accordingly, it is the clash of these two contradictory forces which provides for Polanyi the basis of the problem of pauperism which would lead to the discovery of the natural laws of the economy by classical political economy.

There are thus interesting parallels and disjunctions between the understanding of the developments of the terrain of political discourse advanced by Polanyi and Tawney. Both would appear to be committed to dividing discourses on state policy in terms of a hypothetical schema of a transition from morally- to economically-grounded frameworks. However, where Tawney is concerned with the articulation of this transition through religious values, Polanyi is concerned with its articulation at a political level. So while Tawney emphasises the restriction of market activity by an ethics derived from relgion, Polanyi regards the *paternalist* system of labour organisation as the means of prevention of the commodification of labour (1957: 86–89). This latter disjunction has important consequences for historical interpretation, not the least of which is that the system of regulation which Polanyi claims to be an obstacle to the formation of a labour-market is that which Tawney takes to illustrate the creeping individualism of the new Puritan ethic. The notion of paternalism will also provide a key to understanding this schema, and we shall return to it shortly.

More recently, this schema has received a fillip from the distinguished social historian, E.P. Thompson (1971), in the context of a discussion of conflicts over bread prices in the eighteenth century. The reputation of the author, as well as the clarity and literary qualities of the exposition of its interpretive significance, will probably mean that his concept of a 'moral economy' will ensure the intellectual survival of this schema for some time to come. It is not surprising, then, that the concept is a general theme in a recent history of the 'idea of poverty' (Himmelfarb

1984). It *is* surprising that this history uses it in a way which subverts its critical value.

Compared to the intricacies of Polanyi's analysis, Thompson's conceptual armoury is relatively straightforward. Indeed, taken out of the context of the empirical social history it sustains it appears rather too neat, simple, and general. Thompson argues (1971: 79) that in the eighteenth century there existed a 'popular consensus' among the poor which found support in the paternalist traditions of the authorities. This consensus was 'grounded upon a consistent traditional view of social norms and obligations, of the proper economic functions of the several parties within the community which, taken together, can be said to con-stitute the moral economy of the poor' (79). This concept of a moral economy is thus remarkably similar to the functional view of the social organism found by Tawney. However, where the latter discovers the existence of such a moral formation at the decline of the Middle Ages, Thompson relocates it to the eighteenth century. Despite the temporal shift, the resonances between these English social historians of different generations are strong.

In shifting this moral economy forward in time, Thompson has unwittingly created a parallel with Polanyi. Where the latter finds a paternalist tradition in poor and labour legislation dating from the sixteenth century, Thompson (1971: 79–88) discovers a 'bread-nexus' of rich and poor encoded in paternalist regulations concerning the marketing and manufacture of grain and bread. For him, the moral economy of the poor is derived from a 'traditional platonic ideal' of the processes of trade and production of this most necessary of subsistence items.

Thompson provides an account of the other side of this 'chasm' which is very similar to that of Tawney and Polanyi. Again, one encounters the now familiar figures of the dominance of the self-regulating market and its intellectual mouthpiece, political economy, and the general problem of the morally unwarranted extension of market practices (Thompson 1971: 89–94). Thompson takes Adam Smith and his theories as the model of this new intellectual disposition which he characterises as 'de-moralised' and 'disinfested of moral imperatives' (89–90). The parallels between the de-moralised political economy of Thompson and Polanyi's self-regulating market, which gives rise to the natural laws of the economy as the foundation of moral and political judgements, are evident. Parallel concepts are deployed in both cases to conceive the processes and effects of the commodification of the two different spheres, labour and grain.

The notion of a 'moral economy of the poor' is used extensively in Gertrude Himmelfarb's *The Idea of Poverty* (1984), an intellectual history of poverty, according to its subtitle, in 'England in the early industrial age'. Despite its close reading of the literature on poverty, this study fails to address problems of the historical transformation of ideas and the way in which a reading of the archive on poverty can be organised. It uses the notion of a moral economy in an *ad hoc* fashion which suppresses the questions of transformation and organisation which the term, however inadequately, attempted to address. Furthermore, the effect of its employment in this text is to lend weight to the classical liberal supposition of the inherent contentiousness of public poor relief.

These problems may not be apparent from a superficial reading of the text. Indeed, the title of the relevant part, 'The Redefinition of Poverty: from Moral Philosophy to Political Economy', would appear to reproduce the critical intent of the notion of the moral economy and the schema of which it is a component. The transformation implied by that title is not, however, in evidence in the text. It constitutes a 'moral economy of the poor' in the eighteenth century by suggesting,

> But if poverty was natural, so was the relief of poverty: private, voluntary charity as enjoined by the sacred tenets of religion (reaffirmed by Methodism) and by the 'social affections' innate in every man (reaffirmed by the moral philosophers); and public, compulsory relief as prescribed by the poor laws (and modified but also reaffirmed in the course of the century). Although both forms of relief varied enormously, from time to time, from one parish to another, from one individual or group to another, the principle remained. And that principle, more than the principle of a just wage or just price, was part of the 'moral economy of the poor'.
>
> (Himmelfarb 1984: 41)

This is a highly ambiguous statement of the concept. It affirms that this moral economy covers the complete framework of the relief of poverty in the eighteenth century. Yet, on closer reading, it is only 'voluntary charity' which receives justification from either religion or moral philosophy. Here, public poor relief is merely 'prescribed' as natural by legislation. If that were the case, how can this last form of relief correspond to a moral economy? Clearly it cannot.

Why should this moral economy not extend to encompass the legitimation of poor relief? If we are to employ such a concept and then withdraw its application from such a key area, then surely we are bound to provide an explanation. Himmelfarb's text is silent on this crucial issue which her ambivalence over the ethical legitimacy of public relief creates. This silence inevitably gives the impression that the public relief of poverty is, by its very nature, morally contentious. This, of course, is exactly the stance which liberal discourse would consistently take in matters of poor policy.

This impression is borne out by Himmelfarb's analysis of the debates on the poor laws. She argues that while 'private charity continued to flourish', 'the locus of moral responsibility' had shifted to the state and it was this shift 'which made the debate over the poor laws so agonising' (Himmelfarb 1984: 5). Himmelfarb does not ask why this should be the case. She merely assumes the public nature of this relief as a natural reason for controversy. It is not surprising, then, that she discovers that the morality of poor relief versus that of voluntary charity is the corner-stone of contemporary controversies (6).

In contrast to previous writings such as those detailed above, this creates the effect of a moral continuity of the debates concerning poor policy. Even when political economy enters the polemical fray, there remained 'something like a moral consensus, a common view of what was moral and immoral, and, more importantly of the primacy of morality in the formulation of the social problem and in the making of social policy' (Himmelfarb 1984: 12). This consensus meant that 'the main objective of public policy was to enhance the moral integrity of the inde-pendent laborer by preserving his independence and preventing his pauperization' (12). This passage allows us to understand the crucial con-flation of forms of discourse by which this text undermines the critical value of the schema. The effect of this conflation, whether intentional or not, is to remove the specific characterisation of classical political economy as a form of discourse which subjugates the discussion of the ethical legitimacy of relief to an economic rationality. Himmelfarb's argu-ment appropriates Thompson's concept but fails to recognise that it indicates a schema which presupposes that it is possible to distinguish between two distinct places accorded to moral statements in a discourse. The first place is one in which morality is construed in a 'foundationalist' manner (Minson 1985: 6–7, 149), i.e. as an order of statements which claims the privilege of being able to evaluate, and even derive and organise, other types of statement.[1] The second is one in which moral statements are held to be derivative of other, more fundamental orders of consideration, e.g. in the case of political economy, the natural laws regulating production, exchange, and distribution.

For Himmelfarb no such distinction of the place of moral statements in a discourse is possible. It would appear that after noticing the plethora of moral statements concerning the poor in classical political economy, she simply assumes a foundationalist morality. However, the existence or frequency of moral statements in a particular discourse is not what is at issue in this schema. This schema does not imply that moral statements are completely absent from statements of poor policy constituted within economic discourse. What is at issue is whether their place in the order of statements undergoes a decisive transformation from a foundationalist one to one in which moral statements about poverty are derived from the newly-discovered region of the economic.

A further issue concerning the suppositions of this schema is its employment of the notion of paternalism, a term favoured most by Polanyi but common to a whole range of historical, legal, and philosophical reflection. Carole Pateman (1988: 32) points out that the term has long been common in philosophers' debates about whether the entry into contracts can be regulated by law in such a way as to prevent harm to individuals. She also notes that many legal writers oppose status to contract in a manner which recalls Maine, and employ the term to describe the use of the law to restrict the freedom of contract, hedging contracts about with considerations of status. It should also be noted that the debate over paternalism reappears among post-war historians of the welfare state. For example, while Asa Briggs was confident that the Second World War made 'all residual paternalism seem utterly inadequate and increasingly archaic' (1961: 257), T.H. Marshall still agonised a decade later as to whether, for the 'consumer' of welfare, 'the authoritarian, or paternal, character of welfare must do him injury . . .by limiting his scope for the exercise of choice, and by weakening his initiative and self-reliance' (1972: 25).

Given that these debates are all germane to the issue of the transformation of patriarchy, Pateman finds it strange that feminist theorists 'have had little or nothing to say about paternalism and its relation to patriarchy' (1988: 32). If patriarchy is identified with paternalism, and the liberal economic governance was opposed to the 'paternalist', patriarchalist dimension of the mercantilist police of the Poor, then the liberal break could be construed as a break with patriarchy. The organisation of social life and governance around the father as head of household, which indeed was found to be a feature of eighteenth-century conceptions of oeconomy and the wise administration of the state, would be swept away by the freedom of the individual to enter contracts and for the poor to better their own condition. Himmelfarb's moral economy to enhance the individual would be a break with patriarchy, while Tawney's moral environment which sought to 'repress economic appetites' and judge economic activity in moral terms, or Thompson's 'bread-nexus' of rich and poor, would imply a patriarchal subject with particular powers and prerogatives. At bottom, then, or as we should say, at the level of its governing statements, such a schema implies that the choice is between a patriarchal restriction on capitalism or a capitalist restriction of patriarchy. While such a choice would mean that we have only to decide the lesser of the two evils, it is ultimately a false one. As we have already demonstrated, the Malthusian dimension of the reformed poor law, the very centrepiece of liberal policy, entails both a *rejection* of the old paternalist patriarchalism embodied in the Elizabethan command to provide for and relieve the Poor, and an *enforcement* of patriarchal relations of economic responsibility and dependence within poor families.

The liberal break in poor policy is not with, but within, forms of familial relations, forms of patriarchy. The patriarch of the household has given way to the male breadwinner, the wage-labourer.

The right to subsistence

Did the emergence of a poor policy governed by political economy displace one governed by a moral economy? Did this moral economy presuppose traditional rights of the poor to relief and work, and even to subsistence? A final support for such a schema can be found in Halévy's claim that since the sixteenth century 'there had been in England a kind of *state socialism* which recognised the magistrate's right to define the rate of wages, define by legal disposition the conditions of apprenticeship, and finally allowed to the indigent . . . the protection of society' (1928: 205, emphasis added). Such a state socialism, Halévy continues, consisted not only in the paternal regulation of labour but in a right to assistance, which was variously interpreted as a right to subsistence or a right to work, which was maintained and flourished even as this regulation was repealed (225). In sum, could it be said that there was moral economy, which guaranteed a right to assistance for the poor, and was ultimately a species of paternalism or state socialism? The full consequence of this schema is an elision of concepts of a moral economy, paternalism, state socialism, and a right to assistance. Let us proceed to disentangle this.

Two preliminary points must be made. First, the language of rights immediately evokes an essentially humanist framework in which rights are interpreted as universal and applicable to a transhistorical human entity. Second, such a moral economy could be said to exist if and only if the practices and debate on such issues were primarily derived from and legitimated by a foundationalist morality of such universal human rights. Rights would have to take such a form in order to fulfil the requirement of a moral economy that moral evaluation is given priority over the particularistic and one-sided claims of other spheres.

Let us put the case clearly. Based on our analysis of seventeenth- and eighteenth-century literature, the Discourse of the Poor does not conform to the characteristics of such a moral economy. Such a discourse is not characterised by a foundationalist morality. Nor does it bear witness to the legal recognition of universal human rights or a system of state socialism.

It is true that moral statements have a place in this discourse in determining the options available in the classification of 'the numbers of the Poor'. However, these statements are not foundational. Arguments concerning the moral character of the Poor and the duties of the rich are not privileged in relation to other statements within this discourse. In fact, what makes these moral judgements pertinent is that this discourse seeks to locate the 'numbers of the Poor' in terms of the wealth, strength, and greatness of the nation. If any statements can be said to be foundational of the Discourse of the Poor, it is those which formulate national policy issues of the administration of the population in terms of the augmentation of the prosperity, power, and order of the state, i.e. of good police. It is because 'work' is the crucial means by which the numbers of the Poor are linked to the goals of state policy that the questions of whether the Poor are idle or industrious, and whether the Poor ought be provided for, are of interest.

It is these goals which lead to the definition of the obligations and rights of both the Poor and the sovereign. The moral obligation of the Poor to work and of the sovereign to provide work hence emerge in the context of the proper police of the nation. Arguments over the regulation of wages might appeal to principles of justice, for example, but only in connection with considerations of national expediency and well-being (Furniss 1957: 157). The rights of the Poor, however interpreted, were just that. They were not the rights of all citizens, and hence could not be understood as a prevision of social or even social*ist* rights, as T.H. Marshall claims (1983: 252). If the Poor were to be provided with employment and relieved within the poor laws, it was because these laws sought to harness the Poor for the nation. Moreover, these same national goals required that the Poor had a duty, so far as they were able, to engage in employments which were profitable to the nation (George 1985: 216–222). The poor law was not about the national administration and local enforcement of social rights, but about the specification of particular, limited rights and duties of a definite category, the Poor. The only characteristic of the putative moral economy which is in evidence in the Discourse of the Poor is its paternalism. The patriarchalism of the household is evident in conceptions of state administration, in the workhouse movement, and in discussions of disciplining the Poor and of their place in the natural relations between the ranks. However, such a paternalism was not based on forms of public ownership and control of social resources, or on a conception of universal rights to an optimum, or even minimum, standard of life, and hence cannot be considered a species of socialism. The liberal break was with the paternalism of household patriarchalism, but not also with a state socialism, a moral economy, or a human right to work and subsistence.

There were, nevertheless, several morally founded attempts at justifying poor relief in the late eighteenth century, but these do not seem to be conceived as elaborations of an older paternalist tradition. The analysis of these arguments should not assume a model in which they become expressions of the ancient legitimating principles of the poor laws which later came under attack from modernisers wishing to abolish or curtail poor relief. Indeed, it was only when abolitionists had begun to elaborate a moral rationale *against* poor relief, that a foundationalist morality emerged which addressed and evaluated issues of the poor and their relief and provision.

There were three proximate conditions for the problematisation of the poor laws in the second half of the eighteenth century, which were in operation before the general agrarian crisis and feared political crisis of the final decade: the disillusion with the project of setting the Poor to work; the emergence of contributory alternatives; and the example of philanthropic endeavours.

The implicit faith in setting the Poor to work was constitutive of the arguments about the poor laws and the proper means of relief from the seventeenth century onwards. Even opponents of make-work schemes like Defoe did not reject the principles on which they were based but simply contested the current need for them. By the end of the eighteenth century, however, the widespread failure of the institutional form of the workhouse to fulfil its elementary goals of profitable employment and the suppression of beggary and vagrancy formed the basis of a pervasive disenchantment (Webb and Webb 1963a: 134–144).

The workhouse, which had once been seen as a place for the habituation of the Poor to the ways of patriarchal discipline and an industrious life, was now viewed as a scourge on the body politic (Webb and Webb 1963a: 141–144). For the likes of Jonas Hanway, it was a source of physical and moral disease and degeneration, prone to excessively high death-rates and the visitations of epidemics. It was said to corrupt the morals of the youth brought up in it, making the males unsuitable for outdoor occupations and leading the females into prostitution, and to confine the old and infirm without sympathy among strangers. To cap it all, workhouse manufactures were found to be unprofitable to such a degree that the cost of maintaining these institutions would constantly increase.

These charges are symptomatic of the fact that the old solutions, and perhaps the old problems, were no longer appropriate to the question of poor policy. Such charges would seem to have led to the passing of Gilbert's Act of 1782, which encouraged outdoor relief for the able-bodied by establishing 'unions of parishes of reformed workhouses in which the aged, the sick and the infirm, together with their dependent children, and all the orphans, might be humanely provided for' (Webb and Webb 1963a: 110). The reformed institutions would expressly exclude those inhabitants which had been the key objects of the late seventeenth-century workhouse movement, the able-bodied Poor. The able-bodied were now to receive out-relief until they could find or be given employment. As A.W. Coats has pointed out (1976: 110), this measure represents a major shift in poor policy towards out-relief for the able-bodied and away from the institutional form advocated by earlier poor-law commentators and enshrined in earlier legislation such as the Workhouse Test Act of 1723.

Co-terminous with the decline of the institutional make-work schemes was the emergence of 'contributory alternatives' to the poor law (Poynter 1969: 35–39). The significance of these alternatives does not lie solely in the fact that there now existed a body of opinion which maintained that make-work schemes could be replaced by an entirely different approach to the poor. Rather, the contributory schemes sought to redefine the position regarding the rights and obligations of the poor. Such contributory alternatives included the annuity plan of Francis Maseres of 1772, the insurance proposals of Acland of 1786, as well as the actual practice of the mutual assistance or 'friendly societies' which had begun to proliferate among labourers in this period (Poynter 1969: 35–39; Eden 1928: 67–68, 75–77). Acland's scheme, for example, was to transform the poor law into a national friendly society, with the poor contributing to a national club which would provide for them in infirmity and old age. The principle involved in all these proposals is an interesting one because it introduces the future into the calculations the poor must make about their subsistence. Not only would the poor rate be reduced or abolished but the poor would be encouraged to be industrious and frugal in their present efforts in order to provide for themselves in the future.

The use of the future to govern conduct in the present brings the question of the non-able-bodied into the centre of the debate over the legitimacy of the poor laws. Earlier critics of the poor laws had recognised a right to relief of those distressed by age and sickness. For the most part, the relief of the 'impotent Poor' had been insulated from controversies concerning the provision of work and relief for the able-bodied, which had turned on the problem of idleness. The advocates of contributory schemes, however, claimed that the expectation of future relief had the effect of lessening work-effect and frugality in the present. If the decline of the workhouse had left the situation of the able-bodied unresolved, the rise of the contributory alternatives brought the non-able-bodied into the mainstream of controversy over the legitimacy of relief for the first time.

Nevertheless, the *coup de grâce* delivered against the poor law was an entirely ethical one which had as its context the philanthropy which, through subscriptions, had established charity schools for poor children, as well as hospitals and almshouses and the multitude of benevolent societies (Himmelfarb 1984: 35–37; Owen 1964: 11–96). Here, the categories of 'the Poor' are not simply confounded, or the techniques of the workhouse left in disarray, but a wholly new set of considerations is introduced into the debate over the legitimacy of the poor laws, i.e. the effects of different forms of relief upon the relations between rich and poor. Hence the Reverend Thomas Alcock argued in 1752 that as 'Force tends to destroy Charity in the Giver, so does it Gratitude in the Receiver' (quoted by Poynter 1969: 40). A nation is happy where its inhabitants live in mutual love and dependence, continued Alcock, and 'the several Ranks of Kings and Subjects, Masters and Servants, Parents and children, High and Low, Rich and Poor, are attached to each other by the reciprocal good offices of Kindness and Gratitude' (40). Like Joseph Townsend, Alcock criticised public relief as degrading the moral police between rich and poor, while charity was held to reaffirm this commonality. Public relief, it was said, fails to produce the attributes of benevolence, respect, and gratitude which are essential to the constitution of the social affections. As Alcock said, the rich 'harden their hearts' and the poor, because they believe they have a right to relief, 'labour less and spend more' (41). The ultimate consequence, Alcock warned, was to create more poor: 'The very law that provides for the Poor, makes Poor' (41).

At the end of the eighteenth century, Eden presented the case against the existing system of poor relief which effectively summed up all the lines of argument we meet in the literature of the time. The 'legal provision for the Poor', he argued (Eden 1928: 92–93), by providing security for the poor in all circumstances, removes the 'emulative spirit of exertion' which can only arise from the want of necessities and the taste for 'superfluities' on the part of the labouring poor. Further, the security from want under the poor law encourages the poor to engage in debauchery and mothers to leave their children to the discretion of the parish officers (94). Thus, Eden suggested, an ample provision for the poor will show 'a tendency to increase the number of those wanting relief'. If this argument was proto-Malthusian, the next twist in Eden's case was very similar to those who argued for voluntary charity. He argued that 'the certainty of a legal provision weakens the principles of natural affection, and destroys the strongest ties of society by rendering the exercise of domestic and social virtues less necessary' (96–97). Finally, he turned to issues of maladministration. The poor rates 'will unavoidably be burdensome and unequal' and their distribution 'will ever be the source of partiality and peculation' (97).

For Eden and his contemporaries, this maladministration is symptomatic of a deeper malaise which stems from the corruption of those natural ties of society which are expressed in domestic and social duties. The reason that the poor laws are imperfect in their execution and the right to relief impracticable to satisfy is that such laws and rights rest on a mistaken principle. 'The old laws', said Eden, 'for "the eschewing of idleness" and "setting the Poor on work" were framed on the mistaken principle that, with the incitements of civilisation before them, the people must be compelled to follow their own interest' (1928: 92). There

117

could be no right of the poor to be supplied with employment when able to work and relieved when incapacitated.

With Alcock and Eden, then, we discover, first, arguments concerning poor relief which have as their foundation the moral relations which exist between the various parties to society, and second, references to rights of the poor. However, a foundational morality of the right of subsistence is invoked to contest the legitimacy of the poor law, decide favourably on the merits of voluntary charity over those of poor relief, and to deny the existence of such a right. It is significant that a right of subsistence derived from moral philosophy is not widely elaborated, even as a 'traditional platonic ideal', as E.P. Thompson would have it, before these eighteenth-century attacks on the law. Indeed, the earliest example of the assertion of such a right and the explication of its moral grounds that we can discover is by R. Woodward, Bishop of Cloyne, in *An Argument in Support of the Right of the Relief of the Poor in the Kingdom of Ireland* of 1768. This text is referred to in the above discussion by Eden (1928: 86–87). Its argument was one of several, including those of Paley in 1786, Ruggles in 1793, and Sherer in 1797, which sought a justification of the poor law in a moral philosophy which held that the right to relief was a corollary to the right to property (Poynter 1967: 34).

Woodward argued that the exclusive property in the common heritage of mankind can only be justified by the consent of those who enact laws excluding the poor from any share in the land or use of the beasts of the field to provide for their subsistence (Eden 1928: 86). The argument therefore rests on a conception of natural justice which ought to be guaranteed by the legislature. By such a justice the subsistence of the poor must be provided for. The classic statement of this position, however, is perhaps that of William Paley, who insisted:

> The poor have a claim founded in the law of nature which may be thus explained. All things were originally common. No one being able to produce a charter from heaven, had any better title to a particular possession than his next neighbour. There were reasons of mankind's agreeing upon a separation of this common fund; and God for these reasons is presumed to have ratified it. But this separation was made and consented to, upon the expectation and condition, that every one should have left a sufficiency for his subsistence, or the means of procuring it: and as no fixed laws for the regulation of property can be so contrived, as to provide for the relief of every case and distress which may arise; these cases and distresses, when their right and share in the common stock was given up or taken from them, were supposed to be left to the voluntary bounty of those, who might be acquainted with the exigencies of their situation, and in the way of affording assistance. And therefore, when the partition of

property is rigidly maintained against the claims of indigence and distress, it is maintained in opposition to the intention of those who made it, and to *his*, who is the Supreme proprietor of every thing, . and who has filled the world with plenteousness for the sustenation and comfort of all who he sends into it.

(Paley 1794: 246–247)

Here, then, is a moral economy of poor relief stated in full intellectual rigour. The right to subsistence of the poor and the duty of the rich to provide that subsistence are founded upon the rights of humankind in a state of nature in which all things were originally held in common. If natural reason, backed by divine will, decreed the establishment of a partition of this commonwealth, it did so on the condition that everyone would receive sufficient for subsistence. Moreover, to ensure that all would receive what was theirs, there was implanted in each human breast 'pity' as a 'remedy for those inequalities and distresses which God foresaw that many must be exposed to, under every general rule for the distribution of property' (Paley 1794: 245). But what if this pity fails to provide that subsistence which is everyone's divinely willed natural right? Paley is ambiguous on this crucial matter. In the above passage, he mentions only the original 'voluntary bounty' of those acquainted with the individual case of distress. Yet he plainly supports the objectives of the poor laws to provide 'relief of the impotent, and the protection and encouragement of the industrious poor' (241). Moreover, in his opening remarks on the poor laws he states: 'The care of the poor ought to be the principal object of all laws, for this plain reason, that the rich are able to take care of themselves' (241).

It is interesting that both Eden (1928: 86–87) in his interpretation of Woodward, and Poynter (1969: 34–35) in his commentary on Paley, argue that such statements merely established a right to relief and a duty of charity but not the specific means by which the right was to be satisfied and the duty fulfilled. Hence they both leave open, some two centuries apart, the possibility that this foundational morality of poor relief is consistent with the rejection of the legal form of relief. However, this rejection of social assistance would be internally inconsistent for a simple reason. If the rights of the rich are protected by the legal enforcement of property, then should not those of the poor be enforced in the same (i.e. legal) fashion. If the protection of property is not left to moral sympathies of the poor to the rich, then why should the protection of subsistence be left to the pity of the rich for the poor? If the poor have no right upon the rich to subsistence, then why, as Samuel Taylor Coleridge clearly saw in 1820, should the poor recognise the right of property? The starving labourers could say:

You disclaim all connexion with me: I have no claims upon you? I can then have no duties toward you, and this pistol shall put me in possession of your wealth. You may leave a law behind you which will hang me, but what man who saw assured starvation before him, ever feared hanging?

(quoted by Colmer 1959: 146)

In the writings of the divines at the end of the eighteenth century, as in the Tory defenders of the 'agricultural interest' of the early nineteenth century, there are the constituents of a moral economy of poor relief. This is clear. However, it is equally clear that such a moral economy did not form the grounds on which public poor relief was legitimated in the seventeenth and eighteenth centuries. The grounds for the evaluation of poor relief did not refer primarily to the requisites of a benevolent, paternalistic conception of the moral obligations of the rich or the state and the rights of the poor. Rather, the evaluation of systems of relief, and of the relations between rich and poor, was made in terms of the requisites of a police understood as the establishment and maintenance of national power and prosperity through the proper administration of the population and the augmentation of the nation's patriarchal trading households.

We can conclude it is only with the breakdown of this police at the end of the eighteenth century that poor relief becomes the object of moral legitimation and critique. Critics and defenders of the poor laws began to cast their arguments as moral problems only after a number of breaches had been made in the police of the Poor instituted under the Tudor monarchy, including the exhaustion of the goal of setting the Poor to work, the emergence of the contributory alternatives, and the emergence of an opposition between 'voluntary charity' and 'compulsory legal provision'. There is little evidence of the existence of a moral economy which provided the foundations of the police in which the Poor were constituted as an object of knowledge and governance in the two centuries prior to the emergence of industrial capitalism. Rather, this moral economy first arose in a debate over the comparative effects of forms of relief at a time in which the edifice of this police had begun to collapse.

The schema of an historical transition from a moral to an economic framework for the understanding of poverty and poor policy is a chimerical one. On the one hand, there does not lie a veritable arcadia of rich and poor bound together by paternal benevolence, but rather a system of police in which the numbers of the Poor make up a crucial sector of that population which represents the wealth and strength of the nation. On the other hand, in the form of Malthusianism, one discovers not the rejection of ethical themes and concepts but their emplacement in subordinate relations to what we might call the *bioeconomic* laws of population and subsistence.

It is now possible to show how these Malthusian laws came to be embodied in economic discourse and its applications for poverty and poor policy. To do this it is necessary to formulate a new hypothesis. It may be stated thus: the opposition between moral and economic conceptions of poverty is a result of the transformation in modes of government it seeks to explain. The liberal transformation of police displaces oeconomic governance within patriarchalist households, and the state as household, with a legally specified 'private' sphere of the family constituted by patriarchal relations of responsibility and economic dependency, which is located at the intersection of the two axes of morality and economy. But this image of two equal, intersecting axes is not sufficient. For the ethical sphere acts as a foil to the economic rationalisation of poverty and is displaced on to the entirely different domain of 'the personal', which had been previously only hinted at.

In order to understand the specific character of the emergence of economic rationality and its implications for issues of poverty, it is first necessary to address the status of a text which is often held to be representative of that emergence, Adam Smith's *An Inquiry into the Nature and Causes of the Wealth of Nations*.

Chapter seven

The moral economy of Adam Smith

If one were to follow the lead of recent scholarship in the history of ideas, one would, with little hesitation, regard the contribution of Adam Smith to poor policy as negligible. Two collections, published near the bicentenary of Smith's most famous work, do not contain among their forty-four essays a single one directly dealing with the poor (Skinner and Wilson 1975; Wilson and Skinner 1976). Similarly, a recent four-volume collection of 150 critical assessments of Smith (Cunningham 1984) contains only one piece on the poor (Rimlinger 1984) and one on social welfare policy (Gee 1984).

It might be supposed that such neglect corresponds to the relative insignificance of such issues for Smith's political and economic writings or his moral philosophy. Indeed, in his celebrated *An Inquiry into the Nature and Causes of the Wealth of Nations*, there is only one reference to any aspect of poor policy and that is to the laws of settlement and not to the poor laws proper. After a lengthy disquisition on this matter, Smith concludes:

> To remove a man who has committed no misdemeanour from the parish where he chuses [sic] to reside, is an evident violation of natural liberty and justice . . . . There is scarce a poor man in England of forty years of age, I will venture to say, who has not in some part of his life felt himself to be most cruelly oppressed by this ill-contrived law of settlements.

> (Smith 1976, 1: 65)

Smith argues that the law of settlements is perhaps the greatest disorder of 'any in the police of England' since it obstructs the 'free circulation of labour' and leads to grossly unequal wages in places not far distant from one another (1976, 1: 152–159). He claims that this is due to the reluctance of labourers, particularly those with families, to pursue employment in places for which they do not hold a certificate of settlement (156).

There is nothing in this discussion which could be used as evidence of a general condemnation of the poor laws by Smith. It is germane, in this context, to examine the index of J.R. McCulloch's edition of the *Wealth of Nations* (1889: 658). This edition was first published in 1828 and includes a biography, introductory discourse, footnotes, and supplemental dissertations by McCulloch, that 'intransigent disciple' of Ricardo, as Halévy dubbed him (1928: 343). In its index, there are three-quarters of a column of references to the poor law, poor rates, and poor policies, only one of which refers to Smith's text, the remainder being the additions of the editor. This obscure bibliographical fact may be read as illustrative of the different degrees of preoccupation with the poor laws in the writings of Smith and in those of his self-proclaimed followers. The elementary point to be made as a preface to this discussion of the *Wealth of Nations* is that, whatever its importance in the history of economic thought, this book simply did not make a direct contribution to a debate on poor policy in the fashion of Malthus's *Essay*. This, however, does not mean that it would not be invoked to justify criticisms of the existing system of poor relief.

Neither does it follow that Smith and his *Wealth of Nations* must be relegated to a minor role in this study. Smith's advocacy of a 'system of natural liberty' implies a distinctive perspective on the *labouring* Poor, their status and their just reward, especially in the 'progressive state of society'. Smith's understanding of the Poor, in many respects continuous with other eighteenth-century discourses, introduces enough pliancy within established formulations to make possible a new mode of understanding by those who sought to apply Smith's work to the question of poor policy.

The key to Smith's perspective on 'the Poor' can be found in the principles which underlie his notions of exchange and the division of labour and can be best illustrated by his discussion of wages. Before doing this, however, the general character of the investigation which is embodied in the *Wealth of Nations* must be considered. Here it will be addressed in terms of the general theme of the formation of economic discourse, and our concern with the distinction between economic and ethical foundations of state policy.

The nature of the *Wealth of Nations*

Is the *Wealth of Nations*, then, the birthplace of economic science as the nineteenth-century political economists believed, or does it belong to another kind of discourse different from that of classical political economy? This is a complex question which has been thoroughly dealt with by Tribe (1981: 121–152; 1978: 100–145). Nevertheless, it is important to grasp, in a non-recurrent fashion, the general nature of its investigations. The resolution of such an issue is vital to understanding the nature of Smith's contribution to the debate on the poor in the eighteenth century.

At the beginning of the nineteenth century, Jean-Baptiste Say was to remark that hitherto there had been a confusion over the constitution of the various domains of the 'science of politics' and 'political economy', so that

> For a long time the science of *politics*, in strictness limited to the investigation of the principles which lay the foundation of the social order, was confounded with *political economy*, which unfolds the manner in which wealth is produced, distributed, and consumed. Wealth, nevertheless, is essentially independent of political organisation.
>
> (Say 1880: xv)

What appeared to Say as a confusion, however, is a primary condition of eighteenth-century Political Oeconomy (Tribe 1978: 80–109). As we have already seen, 'oeconomy' is not a theoretical object constituted through mechanisms of production and distribution separate from the political order. It is an *art*, as Sir James Steuart said in 1767 (1966: 15), or a technique, as we might say, practised, first, by the head of a household and, second, by the heads of states. It is a notion which is bound very closely to a householding metaphor of the relation of the sovereign to the members of the state. In his *An Inquiry into the Principles of Political Oeconomy*, which predates Smith's text by nine years, Steuart defines oeconomy as the 'art of providing for all the wants of a family, with prudence and frugality' (1966, 1: 15–16). Political oeconomy, he continues, is to the state what oeconomy is in a family, but with several essential differences. In the state, all are children, there are no servants as in the household. Further, while the head of the family establishes his own plan of oeconomy, the statesman must respect the workings of a political oeconomy already formed from a thousand circumstances. The statesman must practice oeconomy as if the nation were a watch, making sure that it is touched with none but the gentlest hand, but in the knowledge that it is precisely its delicate workings which require constant attention (Hirschman 1977: 86–87). He 'is neither to establish what oeconomy he pleases, or, in the exercise of his sublime authority, to overturn at will the established laws of it, let him be the most despotic monarch upon earth' (Steuart 1966, 1: 16).

The object of political inquiry is thus to assist the statesman in the art of political oeconomy by informing him of 'the spirit, manners, habits, and customs of the people' so that he might secure the subsistence of all inhabitants. When Steuart writes of the established laws of oeconomy of the state, he is not referring to the self-regulating functioning of a region to which the political order must submit, i.e. *the* economy, but to the particular means which, taking into account the circumstances of the state, are established for the provision of the wants of its members.

Oeconomy was thus a branch of the art of government and sometimes coupled with police as a central aspect of legislation. In her *Instructions*, the Empress Catherine distinguished between the domestic oeconomy of the state concerned with the 'expenses, revenues, and publick management of the finances . . . otherwise termed direction of the Exchequer' and its political oeconomy which 'comprehends the whole body of the people and affairs and distinct knowledge of their situation, their ranks and their occupations' (quoted by Hume 1981: 35). The jurist Blackstone, in his *Commentaries on the Laws of England*, stated that oeconomy, together with police, was that aspect of legislation concerned with 'the due regulation and domestic order of the kingdom, whereby the individuals of the State, like members of a well governed community, are bound to conform their general behaviour to the rules of propriety . . . to be decent, industrious and inoffensive in their respective stations' (1830, 4: 162). For the eighteenth century, then, Political Oeconomy was not a discourse about the autonomous reality of the economy, but about the art of conducting the wise administration of the things and subjects in a state. The arguments of Political Oeconomy are constructed by means of a polity composed of households, governed by the patriarchal figures(s) of the sovereign and/or statesman.

This is significant for the reading of the *Wealth of Nations*. While the interpretation of this text as the birthplace of modern economic science is based on a reading of the first two books made by classical political economy, its final three books, dealing with the 'different progress of opulence in different nations', 'systems of political oeconomy', and the 'revenue and expenses of the sovereign or commonwealth', make explicit the political and legislative framework of its investigations, as many commentators have noted. Dugald Stewart, at the end of the eighteenth century, called it a perfect and comprehensive account of 'the general principles of any branch of legislation' (1966: 56). Polanyi saw the analysis of wealth as conducted within a definite political framework (1957: 111).

In introducing the fourth book, Smith states that Political Oeconomy, 'considered as a branch of the science of a statesman or legislator', has two objects: to enable the people to provide a plentiful revenue or subsistence for themselves, and to provide sufficient revenue for the public services (1976, 1: 428). Significantly, the McCulloch edition footnotes this definition with its own alternative:

> Political economy is now most commonly defined as 'the science of the laws which regulate the production, distribution, and consumption of those articles or products that have exchangeable value, and

are, at the same time, necessary, useful, or agreeable to man'. When thus understood, it obviously embraces most of the investigations into which Dr Smith has entered in his "Inquiry into the Nature and Causes of the Wealth of Nations".

(Smith 1889: 187n)

From the vantage point of the consideration of discursive form, the obviousness claimed by McCulloch's footnote disappears. Indeed, the definition of political economy McCulloch gives is evidently not that of Smith and does not specify the way in which the *Wealth of Nations* is constituted. This does not mean that there are not important differences between it and other texts in Political Oeconomy such as Steuart's, or that certain formulations in it mark a partial cleavage with this discursive form. It does alert us, nevertheless, to the dangers of a recurrential reading of this particular text. Moreover, to read the text as an inquiry into a branch of legislation concerned with one region of the proper administration of the state has important consequences for the implications which may be drawn from it concerning the poor and poor policy.[1]

Before detailing such implications, there is another problem concerning the nature of the *Wealth of Nations* which must be addressed, i.e. its relation to ethical questions. There have been two contradictory images of its relation to the 'moral economy'. For E.P. Thompson (1971: 88–91), it is the model (or, rather, 'anti-model') of the new political economy, and as such opposed to the old paternalistic moral economy.

The image, in many respects a conventional one, has, however, not gone uncontested. Others regard the *Wealth of Nations* in the light of the presuppositions enunciated earlier in Smith's *Theory of Moral Sentiments* and thus as grounded in a moral economy consisting of 'an aggregate of calculating sympathetic individuals' (Tribe 1981: 140–141), or as a part of a 'larger moral philosophy' (Himmelfarb 1984: 48), or as embodying the principles of the 'dignity of man' as a 'moral being, who is, as such, a member of the civic order of family, state, and the great Society of mankind' (Polanyi 1957: 112).

These commentators present an image of the *Wealth of Nations* which stands in opposition to the view of it as the site of the discovery of a theoretical conception of the economy as an independent and determinate sphere, i.e. of the discovery of the 'hidden hand' of the market which vitiates normative conceptions of humanity. They present the possibility, which we shall now explore, that not only is this text best characterised within the political–legal investigations of Political Oeconomy, but also that, far from eschewing moral considerations in favour of a purified economic rationality, its 'economic' concerns are treated within a particular moral philosophy which reproduces many conventional patriarchal assumptions.

Exchange and the division of labour

Smith's account of the origin and progress of the division of labour embodies a particular ethical framework which arises from a philosophy of human nature.

> The division of labour, from which so many advantages are derived, is not originally the effect of any human wisdom, which foresees and intends the general opulence to which it gives occasion. It is the necessary, though very slow and gradual consequence of a certain propensity in human nature which has in view no such extensive utility; the propensity to truck, barter, and exchange one thing for another.
> (Smith 1976, 1: 25)

Exchange is thus presented as a universal attribute of rational individuals and the cause, rather than the effect, of the division of labour. The exchanges which these individuals undertake are not made to secure a general welfare but are expressions of self-love or self-interest: 'It is not from the benevolence of the butcher, the brewer, or the baker, that we expect our dinner, but from their regard to their own interest' (Smith 1976, 1: 26–27). Even beggars, who depend on benevolence and not self-interest for their means of subsistence, must still barter items and exchange money they are given to procure their necessities.

The division of labour for Smith thus rests on the supposition of a society of independent, rational individuals made interdependent by their propensity to exchange. It is a division between certain persons rather than between firms or enterprises. The one substantive illustration of the division of labour, that of the pin factory (Smith 1976, 1: 14–15), makes this quite clear. The example of the pin factory illustrates the breakdown of handwork manufacture into more specialised tasks. It describes, as Tribe shows (1978: 104), neither the division of labour between enterprises in a capitalist economy nor the integration of specific tasks and means of production into a unified production process at the level of the firm. The pin factory illustrates a conception of the division of labour as a division which arises between self-interested individuals and not as a feature of capitalist industrial organisation.

This propensity to exchange is a natural attribute of those individuals who provide the basis of the Adamite 'economy'. But is this a 'moral economy', one grounded upon a specific moral philosophy, or is there still a possibility that it is constituted by theories of the production and distribution of wealth? Moreover, who exactly is included in this economy of exchange? To answer this, it is necessary to examine Smith's theory of value.

Halévy suggests (1928: 92) that for Smith exchange not only differentiates between tasks but reconciles the interests of individuals as both producers and consumers. This is because – as Foucault showed (1970: 221–226) – what is represented in exchange is not simply the value an object has for its purchaser and the way in which the object fulfils his or his family's needs, but the relative difficulty and effort, the toil and trouble, the expenditure and dissipation of life energies, which went into its production. Hence:

> The real price of every thing, what every thing really costs to the man who wants to acquire it, is the toil and trouble of acquiring it. What every thing is really worth to the man who has acquired it, and who wants to dispose of it or exchange it for something else, is the toil and trouble which it can save to himself, and which can impose upon other people. What is bought with money or with goods is purchased by labour as much as what we acquire by the toil of our own body.
>
> (Smith 1976, 1: 47)

From the perspective afforded by Ricardian (or, later, Marxian) political economy, Smith here appears to confuse two forms of value, the one which is the embodiment of a quantity of labour and the one which is the estimation made by individuals of the utility of an object, exchange-value and use-value (cf Foucault 1970: 253). However, in Adamite exchange both forms of value are united by the calculations of *men*. These men are the subjects who exchange the effort of acquiring something with the equivalent effort made by another to acquire some other item of need or want. In utilitarian parlance the exchange is between the pain of acquisition by labour and the pleasure of the satisfaction of wants afforded by what is thereby bought (Halévy 1928: 93).

Therefore, there is no disjunction between value as embodying labour and value as subjective estimation in the *Wealth of Nations*. Labour measures value because it can 'command', through the representation of wants made by calculating subjects, equal quantities of labour. Moreover, it is in this process of exchange, in which these subjects calculate their self-interest, that allowances can be made for the severity, hardship, dexterity, ingenuity, skill, and talent required to perform the several species of labour. Such adjustments are made 'not by any accurate measure, but by the higgling [sic] and bargaining of the market, according to that rough sort of equality which, though not exact, is sufficient for carrying on the business of common life' (Smith 1976, 1: 49).

It is the calculations of male individuals in exchange which thus guarantee the equivalence between the relative amounts of effort embodied in each thing exchanged and which provide the basis for the estimation of value made in the 'higgling' and bargaining of the market. But why should these calculations take such a form? And why should it be men who undertake them?

The answers, for Smith, are so evident that he does not spell them out. They are these: the calculations made by sympathetic, male individuals in exchanging their products embody a tacit ethical code which, without anyone realising it, secures a kind of primitive justice and equity. This ethical code is a natural component of exchange and can be instanced by the state of humankind before the 'accumulation of stock and the appropriation of land' (Smith 1976, 1: 65). In this rude state, the individual producer, like a self-employed tradesman, receives the 'whole produce of his labour':

> If among a nation of hunters, for example, it usually costs twice the labour to kill a beaver which it does to kill a deer, one beaver should naturally exchange for or be worth two deer. It is natural that what is usually the produce of two days or two hours labour, should be worth double of what is usually the produce of one day's or one hour's labour.
>
> (Smith 1976, 1: 65)

In this, the earliest state in the 'progress of opulence', the self-interested calculations made in exchange establish an implicit principle of fairness or equity. The beaver/deer example illustrates the kind of elementary natural justice which is established in the exchanges of humankind. Under this system of natural justice, it is right that an individual receives the equivalent amount of labour in return for his own effort. Transactions in which this does not occur thus should be called 'extortion' or 'plunder' rather than exchange. Hence, Smith can recommend his 'system of natural liberty', in which exchange is allowed to operate as free from restriction as possible, because there is this fundamental morality which inheres in men's natural propensity to exchange and pursue their self-interest.

Smith, however, recognises that the conditions under which the labourer receives the full produce of his labour now no longer hold. The equivalence of effort and reward only applies to a time before the development of the institution of property. Nevertheless, the ethical framework which is implied in Smith's account of exchange and the division of labour to which it gives rise is maintained in his discussion of the reward for labour under conditions in which stock has been accumulated and land partitioned.

It may be concluded that, in opposition to E.P. Thompson's suggestion, the discussion of economic matters in the *Wealth of Nations* is not an amoral one but rather is founded upon a definite moral philosophy. This philosophy is not, it is true, a paternalistic one of the putative rights and obligations of the different orders which constitute the body politic. Instead it appeals to principles of natural justice and equity which inhere in the human propensity to exchange. But these principles, while post-paternalistic, are not post-patriarchal. Smith's moral framework is one which is immanent to the relations between autonomous male individuals in their exchanges with one another. Smith's definition of civil individuality as the ability to enter into exchange ignores the question of whether women may enter into such exchanges, whether they constitute rational subjects, and assumes their existence only as an afterthought when considering the conditions of the male labourer. The male poor were to be granted civil individuality by virtue of their entry into exchange by their labour. The figure of the labourer would be irredeemably male, and the whole question of his conjugal and familial rights remains outside the sphere of exchange and only enters into question as the problem of the level of subsistence necessary for the reproduction and maintenance of the labouring population. Therefore, the framework of Smith's discussions can be justly called a 'moral economy of exchange', one which, however, rests upon a implicit order of patriarchal domination of men over women.

The liberal reward for labour

Smith's chapter on wages (1976, 1: 82–104) bears only a passing resemblance to later discussions of wages by political economists such as Ricardo (1951, 1: 91–109). From the perspective of the latter's concern with 'the laws by which wages are regulated', Smith's discussion is extremely wide-ranging. Only by the selective isolation of certain passages can his discussion be read as a contribution to such an object of analysis.

What unity there is in Smith's treatment of wages is given by his explicit moral, political, and legal concerns. The general problems addressed in it are, first, the juridical issue of the various circumstances and conditions under which labourers and masters enter into the wage contract, and, secondly, the political and moral issues of what ought to be the reward for labour.

The chapter on wages opens with a reiteration of the dictum, which depends on the moral economy in which diverse interests of calculating subjects are harmonised in exchange, that 'the produce of labour constitutes the natural recompense or wages of labour' (Smith 1976, 1: 82). The discussion then restricts this equivalence of product with reward to two different cases. The first is the 'original state of things' prior to the appropriation of land and accumulation of capital stock; the second is the 'single independent workman' with sufficient stock to purchase the materials of work and to maintain himself (82–83). Under the conditions of landed property and ownership of stock, and in the absence of sufficient of either for the maintenance of the labourer, this natural reward is subject to two 'deductions', rent and profit. The natural wages of labour are thereby divided three ways.

None of this, however, allows the text to comment on the actual rate of wages. When it deals with the problem of 'the common wages of labour' it does not attempt to provide an account of a mechanism of distribution of the total product between various economic classes but examines the varying circumstances of the wage-contract between masters and workers. The question of rent drops out of the analysis altogether at this point.

> What are the common wages of labour depends every where upon the contract usually made between those two parties, whose interests are by no means the same. The workmen desire to get as much, the masters to give as little as possible. The former are disposed to combine in order to raise, the latter in order to lower the wages of labour.
>
> (Smith 1976, 1: 83)

The moral economy, which ensures the natural equivalence of efforts and rewards, and which harmonises individual interests in exchange, is absent from Smith's discussion of the circumstances which influence the level of wages. In its place is not a theoretically determinant conception of the distribution of the social product but, as a first order of consideration, the problem of combination. Thus, Smith suggests that while there is a prohibition by parliament on the combination of workmen, 'masters are always and every where in a sort of tacit, but constant and uniform combination, not to raise wages above their actual rate' (1976, 1: 84).

This political circumstance of the wage-contract is only the first of a series of considerations germane to the fixing of wage levels in Smith's discussion. The second is the practical and moral issue of the maintenance and reproduction of workmen.

> A man must always live by his work, and his wages must at least be sufficient to maintain him. They must even upon most occasions be somewhat more; otherwise it would be impossible for him to bring up a family, and the race of workmen could not last beyond the first generation.
>
> (Smith 1976, 1: 85)

Almost as an afterthought, the subject of the exchange of labour is thus revealed as having a double identity. The workman is both labourer and head of household. But this latter consideration does not enter the discourse in a theoretically determinate fashion. It is simply another factor in the fixing of wage levels. In classical political economy and Marxism, wages are theoretically determined by the cost or value of the means of subsistence which, in a particular society and in the course of the historical relations between employers and employees, come to be necessary for the maintenance of the labourer and his family. However, the above statement by Smith is in no way equivalent to such a theoretical position. It merely describes the minimum level of wages necessary for the subsistence of the labouring class. In fact, the crucial question of reproduction is left completely indeterminate and the lowest wage-rate becomes that 'which is consistent with common humanity' (Smith 1976, 1: 86). The problem of reproduction, which would warrant attention to the relations between workmen, their wives, and their children, is glossed over by Smith as the problem of the humane rate of wages.

It is only now, after the question of maintenance has been raised, that the text turns to the consideration of the wages fund. However, it does not do so in the context of an attempted theoretical specification of the regulation of wages, but by offering another order of consideration of the circumstances of the contract. Smith argues (1976, 1: 86) that there are certain circumstances which sometimes give the labourers an advantage, and enable them to raise their wages above the maintenance/reproduction rate. These circumstances are ones in which there is a scarcity of hands and competition between masters leads to a breakdown of their tacit combination. This happy set of circumstances cannot occur except in a state in which there is a growth in the funds for maintenance of labourers, the 'progressive state' of society.

Hence, Smith infers that the demand for labourers can only increase in proportion to the increase in 'the funds which are destined for the payment of wages' (1976, 1: 86). The employment of the word 'destined' here illustrates the place of these considerations on wages. Smith is not dealing with the mechanism by which such funds are distributed. Rather, he assumes that distribution as their destiny. The circumstances of the wage-contract thus includes the size of the fund so destined. Moreover, the size of this fund varies under the different states of society – progressive, stationary, and declining – so that:

> It is in the progressive state, while the society is advancing to the further acquisition, rather than when it has acquired its full complement of riches, that the condition of the labouring poor, of the great body of the people, seems to be the happiest and the most comfortable. It is hard in the stationary, and most miserable in the declining state. The progressive state is in reality the cheerful and hearty state to all the different orders of the society. The stationary is dull; the declining, melancholy.
>
> (Smith 1976, 1: 99)

The level of wages of the workmen, and the happiness of the labouring class, are thus dependent on the growth of the riches of the nation and whether the funds for the maintenance of the labourers are progressive, stationary, or declining. The different states of society, or of the growth of the wages fund, which amounts to the same thing, provide a third order of consideration of the circumstances under which masters and labourers enter into contract.

In the course of the discussion of these circumstances the *Wealth of Nations* enunciates various maxims which resemble those of classical political economy, concerning the relation between the demand for labour and the fluctuations in the wages fund, and notions of wages as maintenance and reproduction of the labouring class. These maxims can certainly be read as suggestions of an incipient economic theory of wages. Yet, however they are interpreted, their place in this text is located within a wide-ranging discussion of the various circumstances of the wage-contract between masters and labourers and not as the product of a theory of distribution. Smith here initiates what may be considered the modern critique of the wage-contract by examining the inequalities between the parties to the contract, and how extra-contractual circumstances determine its nature. He does not, however, view the wage-contract as the means by which particular forms of domination between employer (and his agents) and employee are secured, nor does he understand, as Marx would do, that this domination is crucial to the exploitation of the labourer. For Smith, the wage-contract is the path to civil status for the propertyless male labourer, and happiness for all the poor.

When these different orders of consideration are taken into account, the text concludes its discussion of wages by first resurrecting the moral economy and then returning to the typical eighteenth-century question about the effects of high wages on 'population' and 'industry'. First, Smith poses the problem, 'Is this improvement in the circumstances of the lower ranks of the people to be regarded as an advantage or as an inconveniency to society?' (1976, 1: 96). In replying it becomes evident that the progressive state is not an end in itself but the means by which the principle of equity, which was general in the primitive state of humankind, comes to be re-inscribed as a central theme in the arguments about the wage-contract. He postulates that

> What improves the circumstances of the greater part of mankind can never be regarded as an inconveniency to the whole. No society can surely be flourishing and happy, of which the far greater part of the members are poor and miserable. It is but equity, besides, that they who feed, cloath and lodge the whole body of the people, should have such a share of the produce of their own labour as to be themselves tolerably well fed, cloathed and lodged.
>
> (Smith 1976, 1: 96)

In this and following passages, the moral economy, in which the natural reward for labour is founded upon the propensity of individuals to

133

exchange in proportion to the effort in acquiring goods, is reasserted by making considerations of equity and natural justice pertinent to the discussion of wages. The justification of the progressive state, so favourable to the labourers in their wage-bargaining with the masters, is ultimately grounded on the principles of exchange in the moral economy. According to Smith, the labourers ought to be free to exchange their only property, their labour, for the highest possible reward so that they might maximise their happiness and that of their families. The progressive state, because it best ensures such an eventuality, is to be favoured as the most just and equitable state.

To cap the discussion of wages, Smith returns to the characteristic eighteenth-century theme of the effects of high or low wages on population and industry. The scene has been set, however, for a general disposition in favour of a 'liberal reward' for labour by making collective happiness and equity the principles by which the prosperity of nations is judged. High wages are argued for as a factor in the augmentation of population which is unconditionally understood as good: 'The most decisive mark of the prosperity of any country is the increase in the number of its inhabitants' (Smith 1976, 1: 87–88). High wages expand the numbers of present consumers and future workers and thereby increase the wealth of the nation (98–100). But how does this occur? Why do high wages make the workmen more likely to marry and procreate? What is the nature of the relations which these rational individuals enter into with the women who partner them in procreation and raise their children? He does not ask such questions, simply assuming that the supply of labourers will follow demand represented by high wages. Smith's text may be concerned to enunciate an anti-paternalist conception of the place of the worker in political oeconomy, but he simply assumes that the worker, as a full civil individual, will be head of a patriarchal domestic oeconomy. The labourer is both civil individual and household head.

Smith then concludes his discussion by turning to the theme of industry:

> The liberal reward of labour, as it encourages the propagation, so it increases the industry of the common people. The wages of labour are the encouragement of industry, which, like every other human quality, improves in proportion to the encouragement it receives. A plentiful subsistence increases the bodily strength of the labourer, and the comfortable hope of bettering his condition and of ending his days perhaps in ease and plenty, animates him to exert that strength to the utmost. Where wages are high, accordingly, we shall always find the workmen most active, diligent and expeditious, than where they are low.
>
> (Smith 1976, 1: 99)

'The Poor' are no longer merely regarded as constituting the numbers which, by judicious policies, can be made to represent the wealth and strength of the nation. Instead, the problem of 'the Poor' has been replaced by that of the labourers who ought be treated, like all other groups, as rational subjects of exchange. They are not a special aspect of the wise administration of the state but individuals who, like all other property-owners, pursue their self-interest and seek to better their condition, and that of their families, by the only means at their disposal, their only property, their labour.

From such a perspective Smith is able to dispel the criticisms of the labouring Poor found in other eighteenth-century writings. As owners of labour, which they naturally exchange for the highest reward, they seek to preserve and protect the sole means of subsistence at their disposal. Thus if they are found to be idle two or three days in the week, this is not due to their inherent sloth but to the excessive application required by piecework on the other days (Smith 1976, 1: 99–100). As a remedy to this, Smith eschews the proposal to reduce wages and urges 'masters to listen to the dictates of reason and humanity' and moderate their demands so that workers might work regularly, be most productive, and preserve their health and life-span (100).

The moral economy of exchange is a novel inflection in eighteenth-century debates concerning the Poor. 'The Poor' enter into and are transformed by the moral economy, not by virtue of a right to subsistence, but as bearers of labour and as subjects capable of making a wage-contract. In the *Wealth of Nations* one could speak of a right to an equitable return for labour. In the primitive state of humankind, every man receives the full produce of labour in exchange. A system of natural right and justice is implicit in the propensity to exchange. In civilised society, in which property in land is protected by civil government and in which a 'capital stock' has been built up as the result of previous labours, the poor can no longer expect to receive the full produce of their labours. On the other side of this restriction on natural rights, however, this class of men ought to be at liberty to sell their only property, their labour, for the most liberal reward. Thus the poor, who have no land or stock to work on, can most benefit from the expenditure of their labour if there are no restrictions placed by civil government on their capacity to acquire the highest wages they can command. Hence, as we saw at the start of this chapter, the *Wealth of Nations* can be found to be opposed to those regulations restricting 'the free circulation of labour', and to be silent on all positive aspects of the provision and employment of the poor. Moreover, the moral economy means that different states of society can be evaluated according to the degree to which they contribute to the happiness of the mass of people. The existing division of labour exists for the sake of the happiness of and justice for 'the common people'. For it alone makes possible the progressive state in which a liberal reward for labour can be provided, in which a degree of equity for the workmen is attained, and by which the happiness of all the people – men, women, and children – can be secured.

The lessons of the *Wealth of Nations* for poor policy are not principally economic ones. They are moral and political ones. As a moral science, Smith's political discourse transforms 'the Poor' in a fashion which makes them equivalent to all other participants in exchange, as subjects with a capacity to calculate their self-interest, as labourers. Those who constitute the 'race of workmen' are no longer simply among the objects of the wise administration of the population. Due to their relation to the sphere of exchange, they possess interests which are both represented and capable of being harmonised. In the *Wealth of Nations* the poor as the workers are active participants in the social and political order, a position unthinkable under the old system of police.

For Smith the poor make this entry on to the socio-political stage only on the condition that they exchange their only property, their labour, for its optimum reward. As will be shown in the next chapter, this solicitous disposition towards the labouring population is reworked by the following generation of the *Wealth of Nations'* readers so that the rights of the poor are narrowly circumscribed by this domain of the sale of labour. This text itself is, nevertheless, symptomatic of the new-found status of the poor attendant upon the dissolution, or at least incipient transformation, of the old police. It remained for its self-proclaimed followers to place the moral condition of the labourer within the context of biological laws of reproduction and economic laws governing production and distribution.

Contrary to first impressions, the *Wealth of Nations* does contain an implicit policy regarding the poor. The major plank of such a policy would be the encouragement of a 'progressive state' of society of which the poor would be the principal beneficiaries. Beyond this, and beyond moves to permit the unrestricted movement of labour, it is extremely difficult to translate this policy into practice. For one thing, in the Adamite moral economy, the poor are addressed either as bearers of labour, or as members of families headed by labourers, a position which expressly excludes consideration of those poor who are unable or unwilling to work or who are outside such families. For another, Smith does not recommend any measures which could be taken in a declining or stationary state of society to alleviate the distress of the labouring poor. He does not, moreover, offer his readers advice as to the course of action they could take during a situation of generalised scarcity or in protracted economic crisis. The former condition, however, was precisely that which the self-proclaimed followers of Adam Smith had to face in the final decade of the eighteenth century. The latter condition might be more familiar to his present-day students.

Chapter eight

The condition of poverty

For Adam Smith, the poor man's labour enabled him to enter into exchange with the same civil status as masters and landlords, that of property-owner. Smith had entrusted the natural progress of the division of labour and the removal of restrictions on the movement and sale of labour with the mission of securing a liberal reward and happiness for the poor and, even more importantly, establishing their stake in civil society. His concept of exchange is a democratic, if patriarchal, one, opening the possibility for a mutuality between rationally calculating male individuals of all stations in society. The following generation were not given the opportunity to be so sanguine about the 'progress of opulence' or solicitous towards the needs and problems of the labouring poor. The war years of the 1790s, in particular, were years of agrarian crisis and of widespread rural distress, of inadequate harvests and massive increases in grain prices. This decade was also one of an unprecedented intellectual fecundity in theories, schemes, and practical solutions to such distress and, more generally, in matters of the provision for, and relief of, the poor. Indeed, it is possible that this decade witnessed the *discovery*, or even the *invention*, of a concept of poverty, if by this is meant a movement beyond the old notion of 'the Poor' as a permanent mass which must be properly administered by the state to the notion of a particular condition of individuals and groups determined by bioeconomic forces and movements of population, subsistence, and capital.

This chapter shows how poverty was produced and appropriated in various writings and projects from the end of the eighteenth century and how it came to be inscribed in the premises of the new political economy. The first section undertakes a survey of discussions of the poor and poor policy at this time and shows the shift which had occurred between these discussions and Smith's moral economy of exchange. The second section analyses the pertinent aspects of a key text of classical political economy, David Ricardo's *Principles of Political Economy and Taxation* (1951: 1), to demonstrate the place of poverty in the formation of economic discourse.

The invention of poverty

The last decade of the eighteenth century was a peculiar combination of an outpouring of literature on poverty on the one hand, and legislative inaction and absence of reform on the other. During this decade we witness not only the publication of Malthus' *Essay*, which we have already shown to be vital to the formation of the liberal poor policy some forty years later, but also Eden's massive three-volume survey of the poor (1797), which included both a history of the poor and poor laws over seven centuries and an investigation into the 'diet, dress, fuel and habitation of the labouring classes'. This same decade saw the formulation of Jeremy Bentham's elaborate scheme of Pauper Management (discussed in chapter ten) and many other practical projects and local initiatives. These include: the practice of granting allowances to make up for the insufficiency of wages, which would be condemned in the *1834 Poor Law Report* (discussed in chapter nine); the founding of philanthropic societies such as the Society for Bettering and Increasing the Comforts of the Poor; Count Rumford's plans, especially his dietaries, which may have the dubious honour of having popularised the notion that soup was the appropriate food for the poor; and policies of allotments of land and the provision of cows from the recommendations of David Davies to the clauses of Pitt's Bill to, a little later, the schemes of Arthur Young (Poynter 1969: 45–106; Webb and Webb 1963a: 168–189; Hammond and Hammond 1913: 123–165; Owen 1964: 104–109). Nevertheless this fertile intellectual and practical environment failed to produce a single major piece of legislative reform. The rejection of the two legislative initiatives of the decade, Samuel Whitbread's minimum-wage legislation and Pitt's ill-drafted and labyrinthine Poor Bill, signals the parliamentary paralysis of both the Tory government 'formed to defend all the old traditions, even the old abuses' against Jacobinism, and the Whig opposition, 'now become so weak and unpopular' and fallen into 'profound discredit' (Halévy 1961: 18, 172).

One should be careful not to interpret all this productivity with respect to the poor merely as the result of the current agrarian crisis and rural distress and discontent. Doubtless this was the context which placed the matter of the poor on the intellectual and political agenda with a renewed urgency. Yet the crisis should not be thought to have determined the form in which the discussion took place and the implications which were to be drawn from it. After all, agrarian crises throughout the eighteenth century had led to no more than the familiar response to food riots, the attempt to regulate the trade and marketing of grain (E.P. Thompson 1971: 77–135). Even during the years of the mid-1790s, and again at the turn of the century, there were conspiratorial theories of scarcity, denouncing the role of middlemen speculating in the market and urging the government to take action against the now well-worn enemies of 'forestalling', 'regrating' and 'engrossing' (Poynter 1969: 45–46). Others demanded price regulation, and the rioters of 1795, during what Hammond and Hammond call the 'revolt of the housewives', chose to fix prices rather than plunder the shops over which they gained control (1978: 76–77). What was different this time was that rural scarcity brought into question the poor laws and the various means of poor relief. Why this should be so is due no doubt to the severity of the distress, and to the fear among the governing classes of popular discontent engendered by the events in France. Yet it is also the case that the ensemble of Tudor legislation, and its administration, had reached a stalemate. This was in part due to the disarray of existing practices of relief and forms of discourse which followed developments in philanthropy and in contributory schemes. It was also due in part to widespread complaints about the diversity, localism, and maladministration of relief, and the burden of the rates, although there was no unanimity on this last point. It should also be noted that the intellectual framework provided by Adam Smith, which had gradually gained ground in political debate at the end of the eighteenth century, and was even mouthed by the Tory reaction as an excuse for its failure to act, provided very little in the way of intellectual tools for the intricacies of the poor laws, but much in the way of easy-to-repeat generalisations.

Indeed, the most profound effects of the advocacy of positions derived from readings of the *Wealth of Nations* were negative ones. Chief among these was the riposte they delivered to the demand for wage regulation which culminated in the bill of brewer, Samuel Whitbread, of 1795–6. In *The Case of the Labourers in Husbandry*, published in 1795, Davies had argued for wage regulation by fixing wages to family size and the price of grain. His proposal had received considerable discussion in the *Annals of Agriculture* (Hammond and Hammond 1978: 86–96; Poynter 1969: 49–52). The *Annals* had even published an advertisement in November 1795 setting out a table for the fixing of wages according to the price of wheat, which had been placed in a Norwich newspaper by local day labourers with the intent of petitioning Parliament. This intent was perhaps quashed by the Treason and Sedition Acts passed in the same month (Hammond and Hammond 1978: 90–91). The gentry were quick to point out that regulating wages by the price of wheat did not address the more fundamental problem that the scarcity of wheat would be unchanged no matter how high wages were raised (Poynter 1969: 50). It was further suggested that, because regulation would entail an equalisation of wages, and was incompatible with piecework, it would remove the discretion of the employer to assess the quality and worth of the labourer. The philanthropist Bernard argued that regulation would ignore *moral* worth and equalise wage-rates between the idle and the industrious.

These objections did not stop the proposal being brought before Parliament in the form of Whitbread's Bill. Nevertheless, the tide was turned against the bill when, immediately after the motion for its second reading had been seconded, Pitt arose and made a speech which 'dazzled the House' (Hammond and Hammond 1978: 93). He challenged Whitbread's picture of the relative movement of wages and prices, praised the beneficence of the propertied during the distress, attacked the law of settlements, and foreshadowed a reform which would restore the poor laws to their original intent. He also invoked the principles of Adam Smith, referring to instances where 'interferences had shackled industry', and asserted the principle that 'trade, industry and barter would always find their own level, and be impeded by regulations which violated their natural operation, and deranged their proper effect' (quoted by Poynter 1969: 58).[1]

In terms of the formation of an object of knowledge and delineation of fields of governance, the ramifications of the readings of the *Wealth of Nations* were more intricate and of more enduring significance. In the interpretation of the implications of the status of the poor in the social order after Smith, several different conceptual elaborations arise. The first may be instanced by Edmund Burke's objections to the term 'the labouring Poor'. In his *Thoughts and Details on Scarcity*, written in November 1795 to Pitt in the midst of the minimum-wage campaign, Burke railed:

Nothing can be so base and so wicked as the political canting language, 'The *Labouring* poor'. Let compassion be shown in action . . . but let there be no lamentation of their condition. It is not relief to their miserable circumstances; it is only an insult to their miserable understandings . . . Patience, labour, sobriety, frugality, and religion, should be recommended to them; all the rest is downright '*fraud*'.
(Burke 1826, 7: 377)

In the next year, Burke was led to elaborate on his charge against this 'foolish, puling jargon'. He continued his polemic in his third *Letter on a Regicide Peace*:

We have heard many plans for the relief of the 'labouring poor' . . . . Hitherto the name of the poor (in the sense in which it is used to excite compassion) has not been used for those who can, but for those who cannot, labour – for the sick and infirm, the orphan infancy, for languishing and decrepit age; but when we affect to pity, as poor, those who must labour or the world cannot exist, we are trifling with the condition of mankind. It is the common doom of man that he must eat by the sweat of his body, of the sweat of his mind.
(Burke 1826, 8: 368)

These passages sound discordant coming from an author pausing from his counter-revolutionary campaign, renowned as a passionate defender of patriarchal traditions, the great Whig orator of the 1780s who found solace against the Revolution in the 1790s in Pitt's party. We must immediately agree with Halévy who highlights Burke as the 'first to interpret political economy as a purely conservative orthodoxy' (1928: 230). What Burke objects to in both these passages are the connotations of the term 'poor' when it is applied to the condition of the labouring classes. There is absolutely no doubt that he rejects Smith's solicitous attitude towards the poor. Yet it does follow from Adamite moral economy that if the propertyless masses are recognised as participants in the order of exchange by virtue of their labour, then their condition is not one to be lamented or pitied.

For Burke, the labouring population represents not so much rational actors in exchange, as bearers of the 'common doom', who must be urged to face difficult labour as their lot. The surplus of the rich, so necessary to the circulation of national wealth, would make no significant difference to the condition of the labourers. Instead the small rise in wages created by any regulation administered by the justices would result in the destruction of farmers' and traders' property, and end in generalised want, wretchedness, and beggary. This is not only because the wages fund is limited, but also because there are varieties of wages, depending, for instance, on the difference between the normal work of men and the lesser work of women, children, and the aged, which had to be taken into account. The wage-contract for Burke was not opposed to the moral police between rich and poor. Rather, he might have said that the contract fixed the statuses of the members of the labouring classes. The 'zealots of the sect of regulation' ignored the interest, habit, and tacit conventions of a thousand circumstances, which produced a 'tact' that regulated those relations which laws and magistrates could not. The contract had become the epitome of patriarchal relations of mutual dependence, and therefore interest, between employer and labourer (Burke 1826, 7: 383–390; Halévy 1928: 230–232; Poynter 1969: 54–55).

For Smith, the labourers should be at liberty to sell their labour. They ought be freed from the yoke of settlement restrictions and saved the obstructions to an equitable and just wage presented by the combinations of manufacturers and merchants. For Burke, the corollary to this proposition was that the state and the rich should be free from juridically defined obligations to the labourers. This class was a proper object of neither public nor private forms of relief and the Christian obligation of charity could be called upon only to attend those worthy of the name 'poor', i.e. the sick, the aged, and those burdened with too many children (1826, 7: 390–391). Arthur Young found him thunderously rambling 'about the absurdity of regulating labour and the mischief of our poor laws' (Hammond 1978: 88). While much can be made of the 'Tory socialism' and its support among Radicals and trade unionists in the 1830s (E.P. Thompson 1968: 377–380), it is well to recall how Burke was able to turn the tenets of economic liberalism to the conservation of the proper moral relations between classes.

Almost contemporaneous with, but in many ways opposed to, Burke's rather didactic pronouncements on the labouring poor was Frederick Morton Eden's careful history in which the labouring population and the poor are understood as coincident. He argues that the 'growth of civilisation' and development of commerce led to the introduction of a new class, described as 'the Poor', who are 'freemen' who, for whatever reason, have become unable to work and are thereby obliged to seek charitable support (Eden 1797, 1: 56–57). By contrast those who remained in a 'state of servitude' could not be properly designated 'the Poor' since they would always have recourse to their masters for their maintenance. Eden concludes that it is

> To the introduction of manufactures, and the consequent emancipation of those who were dismissed by their masters, and those also who ran away from them with the adventurous project of trying their fortunes in the lottery of trade, I ascribe the introduction of a new class of men, henceforth described by the Legislature under the denomination of the *Poor*; by which term, I conceive, they meant to signify freemen, who, being either incapacitated by sickness, or old age, or prevented by other causes from getting work, were obliged to have recourse to the assistance of the charitable for subsistence.
>
> (Eden 1797, 1: 57)

'The Poor', then, are identical with those who have no means of production of their subsistence other than by the sale of their labour and who, when unable to labour, are at the mercy of others to provide for them. For Eden, the benefits of economic liberty were great, and the enclosure and improvement of wastes and commons should be applauded as part of the 'improving' state of society but it is true that 'the decrease in villeinage seems necessarily to have been the era of the origin of the Poor. Manufactures and commerce are the two parents of our national Poor' (Eden 1797, 1: 60–1; quoted by Marx 1974, 1: 676n). Although Marx acknowledges Eden as 'the only disciple of Adam Smith during the eighteenth century that produced any work of importance' (578), he ponders the 'stoical peace of mind' with which Eden, 'philanthropist and tory to boot', recounts the expropriation of the people from the fifteenth century, the 'most shameless violation of the "sacred rights of property" ' (680). The same point about 'Tory liberalism' made in regard to Burke could be applied to Eden. The latter's regard for the poor, however, is more surely in the sanguine camp of Smith than that of the polemicist of reaction.

Eden's account is indeed remarkable, and its scholarly weight has meant a wide use by those who would draw conclusions which were contrary to his. His history of the emergence of a class of 'freemen' is referred to extensively in Marx's genealogy of capitalism in Part 8 of *Capital*, and anticipates it on many of its essential points (1974, 1: 667–712). His household budgets, together with those of David Davies, form the backbone of Hammond and Hammond's picture of the condition of the agricultural labourer at the time (1978: 66–86). The reason for Eden's double identity as an apologist whose researches fire the critical imagination may be that he identifies what for Smith's policy had remained essentially a blank space, i.e. the space in which the poor are no longer able to exchange their labour in propitious circumstances. If Smith had left the welfare of the poor to the rights of labour in a progressive state, and Burkean quietism had wished to abolish the labourers' poverty with the stroke of a pen, Eden was prepared to confront the historicity of 'the Poor' in relation to the emergence of the conditions of formally free labour. It is this perspective which rendered his solutions to the poor laws less radical than those of Burke, the putative conservative. Although he opposed the principles of public poor relief, and was able to marshal as many arguments against the 'legal provision for the Poor' as anyone before Malthus, Eden remained cautious about the prospects of its abolition and sought to recommend alternatives which presented the labourer with the greatest prospect of exercising the rights to use and sell his labour to his greatest advantage. Eden was thus particularly taken with issues of domestic economy, and indeed maintained that his budgets endorsed the contributory alternative of the labourers themselves, the friendly societies (cf Poynter 1969: 111–117).

There emerges, in the debate over the labouring poor in the final decade of the eighteenth century, a new object fundamentally different from the one constructed in the Discourse of the Poor. In this earlier discourse, 'the Poor' was an object to be described, classified, and appropriately governed because it comprised the greatest numbers of the state which must be wisely administered. If Burke was now able to seek to dissociate the labourers from the poor and Eden to give historical content to the 'labouring Poor', it is because 'the Poor' was no longer a given object of taxonomic knowledge and correct governance. *Poverty*, a condition which was distinct from its bearers, had become a site of theoretical and historical argument and conceptual elaboration.

In fact, Smith had done more than introduce the poor as participants in the social order when he defended their rights as labourers. By positing a dynamic of the 'natural progress of opulence' of nations which was dependent on the state of the division of labour, the possibility had been

opened of an understanding of the role of poverty in the course of civilisation. Even Malthus, whose principles of population had located poverty
in the interplay of the natural processes of the propagation of the species
and the growth of subsistence, lamented the absence of the history of
this part of humanity:

> The histories of mankind that we possess, are histories only of the
> higher classes. We have but few accounts that can be depended upon
> of the manners and customs of that [lower] part of mankind . . . .
> A satisfactory history of this kind, of one people, and of one period,
> would require the constant and minute attention of an observing mind
> during a long life. Some of the objects of enquiry would be, in what
> proportion to the number of adults was the number of marriages.
> Therefore to what extent vicious customs prevailed in consequence
> of the restraints upon matrimony: what was the comparative mortality
> among the children of the most distressed part of the community, and
> those who lived rather more at their ease: what were the variations
> in the real price of labour: and what were the observable differences
> in the state of the lower classes of society, with respect to the ease
> and happiness, at different times during a certain period.
>
> (Malthus 1798: 32–33)

If labourers were subject to history, it would follow that the relation
between labour and poverty would no longer be fixed but would depend
on the state of the development of the division of labour, the real price
of labour, the customs of the labouring classes, and the rates at which
they propagate. What is happening in these writings is that 'the Poor',
that plebeian mass which must be utilised correctly by the governors
of the state, has given way to 'poverty', which is no longer a category
of humankind but a condition with specific causes and functions and
definite relations to labour, population, and subsistence. Nevertheless,
the immensity of this conceptual innovation may be obstructed from view
by the fact that, at the moment of its emergence, it was naturalised by
the relations of population and subsistence and made necessary, via its
participation in labour, to the progress of civilisation.

This new concept of poverty can be shown to be at work in many
different political and intellectual frameworks. Let us demonstrate its
flexibility by addressing only two more. The first is the much quoted
argument by a magistrate of London, Patrick Colquhoun, who is also
credited with establishing a Chamber of Commerce in Glasgow and constituting the science of police on a new footing. It illustrates how, in
the first decade of the nineteenth century, it was possible to conceive
of the condition of poverty.

Without a large proportion of poverty, there could be no riches, since riches are the offspring of labour, while labour can only result from a state of poverty. Poverty is that state and condition in society where the individual has no surplus labour in store, or, in other words, no property or means of subsistence but what is derived from the constant exercise of industry in the various occupations of life. Poverty is therefore a most necessary component of society without which nations and communities could not exist in a state of civilisation. It is the lot of man. It is the source of wealth, since without poverty there could be no riches, no refinement, no comfort, and no benefit to those who may be possessed of wealth, in as much as without a large proportion of poverty surplus labour could never be rendered productive in procuring either the conveniences or luxuries of life.

(Colquhoun 1806: 7)

This argument should not be confused with the eighteenth-century position that low wages made 'the Poor' more industrious. The earlier argument has a strictly limited function. Low wages were conceived as one of the many means by which the numbers of the Poor could be made to contribute to the aims of national policy. Here, the question is not of wage levels but of a condition which is general to the great body of people. Moreover, this condition forms the basis of the development of civilisation and is originally inscribed in the natural state of humankind. All the accompaniments of civilisation derive from this original state of humankind in poverty: poverty is the origin of history and necessary for the maintenance of the civilisation which is its end. Hence civilisation is the result of a dialectic of poverty and labour which arises from a natural order constituted by a fundamental scarcity.

Colquhoun's argument is a sketch for the Whig-liberal position which was to be filled in by Chadwick, Senior, Kay, and others, and came to be embodied in the revolution of poor policy of the 1830s. But it is not the only way in which the concept of poverty, once constituted, can be used. Witness the case of S.T. Coleridge. His annotations to Malthus' 1803 *Essay* had formed the basis of Southey's venomous review, although his contempt for the effect of the poor laws was as great as any held by the abolitionists. In his *Lay Sermons* Coleridge blasts the poor laws as forming 'a subject, which I should not undertake without trembling, had I the space of a whole volume to allot to it', as 'impossible to exaggerate their pernicious tendency and consequences', and as 'an enormous mischief [which] is *undeniably* the offspring of the Commercial System' (1972, 6: 221–222). Following Burke he commented on the term 'the Labouring Poor' in a *Morning Post* article in February 1800, and reiterated his stance on 'an ominous but too appropriate change in our phraseology' in the 1817 sermon (207, 207n). However, unlike Burke, Coleridge's position was placed in a wider social critique which was fundamentally hostile to the maxims of political economy, its replacement òf the hoping, suffering individual by 'economic man', and the 'overbalance of the commercial spirit', which was responsible for obscuring the crucial distinction between *persons* and *things*, on which 'law, human and divine is grounded' (169–170, 218–220; cf Colmer 1959: 129–145, and Corrigan 1977: Appendix 3). He railed against the poor law because in three-quarters of agricultural districts rates are paid 'to healthy, robust, and (O sorrow and shame!) *industrious, hard-working* Paupers in lieu of Wages' (222). Poverty may be natural, as the economists asserted, but it should never be the permanent lot of the individual. So he noted in 1831:

> Poverty, whatever can justify the designation of 'the poor', ought to be a transitional state to which no man ought to admit himself to belong, tho' he may find himself *in* it because he is passing *thro'* it, in the effort to leave it. Poor men we must always have, till the Redemption is fulfilled, but *The Poor*, as consisting of the same Individuals! O this is a sore accusation against society.
>
> (quoted by Colmer 1959: 143)

Coleridge's writings are undoubtedly possessed of a broader vision of the moral rights and duties of the state, evidenced in his continued concern for its educative role, than virtually any others encountered in this study. But it is the same fundamental transformation which had allowed Eden to link the poor to the history of manufactures and commerce, and Burke to turn poverty into a matter of semantics, which is found in these passages. If a Malthus or a Colquhoun could naturalise poverty by economic laws and make it necessary to Smith's progress of opulence, Coleridge could call on a higher 'Spirit of the State' which required breaking hold of such laws and necessities. A space had opened, within the changing forms of governance, in which the condition of poverty could be debated, its causes argued over and assessed, its place and functions analysed, and its moral implications sought. The closed, classificatory knowledge of the Poor, with all its moral rigidity, had given way to a terrain which could accommodate both the moral 'responsibilisation' of the labourer for poverty, and the state for poverty. The Poor had hitherto remained an eternal referent of governance. Poverty, despite the tenets of the naturalisers, is the breaking of the nexus between deprivation, want, and suffering, and this referent. This is indeed an epoch-making moment.

We should note in passing that the moral economy of exchange marks another possibility, one which leads away from a liberal mode of government. It was now possible to ask some quite different questions. If poverty is a historical condition, as Smith implied and Eden showed, and if it exists in definite relations to the fluctuations of wages and prices, to forms of labour and the living conditions of the labouring population, then would it not be possible to extend the trajectory of that history towards a finality in which this poverty, not just of individuals as Coleridge had foreseen, but of classes and nations, would be overcome? Moreover, what is there which now stands against a return, although at our present higher stage in the progress of society, to that original state of natural justice by the abolition of property? Would it not be possible, then, to reclaim that natural justice by which the labourer was granted the rights to the full reward for the produce of his labour? These questions indeed formed one possible axis along which discourses on poverty would develop which was initially realised in William Godwin's *Political Justice* of 1793 (1971) and the writings of Owen (e.g. 1818), and later in those of the seriously misnamed 'Ricardian' socialists, Hodgskin (1825, 1827, 1832; Halévy 1956), Bray (1839), and William Thompson (1824). This is a chapter which must be written at a later time.

Nevertheless, the formation of the liberal discourse on poverty in the early nineteenth century closed off the possibility of such a transcendence by two means. The first was to make the condition of poverty among humankind an instance of that fundamental scarcity, the external poverty of nature, which, for Malthus, was a result of the unalterable imbalance between the growth of population and the growth of subsistence. The poverty amongst humans was only the reflection of the deeper, more fundamental poverty of nature. The second was to make poverty necessary to the production of wealth as the original source of that labour which was the foundation of all the accompaniments of civilisation, such as is found in the discussion of magistrates like Colquhoun, and in the social administration of Edwin Chadwick and the *1834 Poor Law Report* of which he was the chief architect. A *poverty* theory of labour could be said to underlie a *labour* theory of value. Indeed, the constitution of poverty as natural and necessary was one of the most basic premises in the classical political economy of Ricardo, as will now be shown.

In classical political economy there is no postulation of an inherent propensity to exchange and thus no moral basis which frames such questions as the proper reward for labour. Rather, in this new economic discourse, the actions of economic agents are determined by the natural laws of production and distribution. The moral imperatives of justice and equity which underlie the Adamite economy are not pertinent to the formation of this theoretical conception of the economy. If this new discourse retains a place for moral statements, it is no longer a foundational one. Rather, it is the natural laws of population, capital, and subsistence which present each individual and each society with the moral choice to obey their dictates or to transgress them and bring about inevitable personal distress and social disaster. Moral conduct no longer comprises those actions which accord with human nature, but those imposed by an anterior necessity inscribed in nature.

Classical political economy

Smith's *Wealth of Nations* equated the amount of labour ('toil and trouble') expended in acquiring an object with the amount of labour that object could 'command' in the exchanges of calculating subjects. The reward for labour was thus equivalent to the product of labour, at least in the original state of humankind. These propositions, so fundamental to the moral economy of exchange, are denied in the opening pages of David Ricardo's *On the Principles of Political Economy and Taxation* (1951, 1; hereafter *Principles*). Ricardo argues:

> If this indeed were true, if the reward of the labourer were always in proportion to what he produced, the quantity of labour bestowed on a commodity, and the quantity of labour which that commodity would purchase, would be equal, and either might accurately measure the variation of other things: but they are not equal; the first is under many circumstances an invariable standard, indicating correctly the variations of other things; the latter is subject to as many fluctuations as the commodities compared with it . . . . Is not the value of labour equally variable; being not only affected, as all other things are, by the proportion between supply and demand, which uniformly varies with every change in the condition of the community, but also by the varying price of food and other necessaries, on which the wages of labour are expended?

> (Ricardo 1951, 1: 14–15)

Labour has ceased to be the property of human beings which is secretly equalised in the 'higgling' and bargaining of the market. Instead, the concept of labour has been split into two. Ricardo's analysis is not the first to give labour an importance, but it is the first to explode the unity of that notion (Foucault 1970: 253). On the one hand, the amount of labour which goes into the production of a commodity regulates the value of that commodity relative to the value of other commodities. On the other, labour itself has become a commodity, subject to the same regulation by the value of commodities which are essential to its production, and to the same fluctuations of supply and demand. The determination of the price of labour, the wage, is subject to the same mechanisms which determine the price of all other commodities.

Ricardo's theory of wages, or the price of labour as a commodity, describes the outline of a definite *economic* conception of poverty. This conception is provided by the relation between the wages necessary for the subsistence and perpetuation of the labourers, the 'natural price of labour', and the actual or 'market price of labour' (Ricardo 1951, 1: 93). The latter is that which is really paid to the labourer from the natural operation of the proportion of the supply to the demand for labour. When the market price falls below the natural price, the labourers find that 'poverty deprives them of those comforts which custom renders absolute necessaries' (94). Only when such 'privations' have reduced their number, or when the demand for labour has increased, will the market price rise to its natural price, and the labourers 'will have the moderate comforts which the natural rate of wages will afford' (94).

Variations in the price of labour, excluding variations in the value of money, are therefore the result of the supply and demand for labour, and the variations in the price of the commodities on which the wages of the labourers are customarily expended (Ricardo 1951, 1: 97). It is no longer a matter of what the reward for labour *ought* to be, or what level of wages is good for the nation and for the fulfilment of national goals, as it is in the *Wealth of Nations*, but of how wages are determined by a specifically economic reality. In the *Principles* one is no longer dealing with a morally founded, politically defined problem of the various circumstances which enter into the fixing of wages. This, then is the de-moralised economic science, an analysis of the economy as distributional mechanism. The approach to poverty in the *Principles* is completely unsentimental, free from cant, and has left behind the debates on the police of relations of rich and poor. It might implore the poor to marital delay, hard work, and frugality, but it does so in the sombre light of economic logic and not in the manner of the preacherly and berating diatribes which so characterise the social literature of this and succeeding generations. However, it must be emphasised that this does not mean that classical political economy has left behind the supposition of the male breadwinner as head of household. The logic of the economy may be de-moralised, but its imperatives circumscribe a definite form of life for the poor.

This fundamental premise of the new economic rationality of the *Principles* never strays far from the Malthusian maxims and their implications. For instance, the Ricardian system holds that wage levels depend on the ratio of population to capital, the latter defined as the means of employing labour, or, in Malthusian terms, subsistence (1951, 1: 98–100). The accumulation of this capital depends on the productive powers of labour. Where labour is productive and population small, as in new settlements, wages will be high. However, as population increases, and worse land is taken into cultivation, the productive powers of labour decrease and so, therefore, does the rate of growth of capital. Thus there is a tendency for the rate of growth of capital to decrease while the rate of growth of population remains constant (98). In rich countries, then, if the population is pressing against the means of subsistence, and the fertile land is already fully cultivated, the only remedy is a reduction of the number of people, accomplished by the market rate of wages falling below their natural rate (99–100). If Malthus postulated a natural imbalance between the rate of growth of population and that of the means of subsistence, Ricardo was to locate a natural source of scarcity in the diminishing productivity of labour associated with the bringing of less fertile and less well-situated lands into cultivation.

This last theoretical postulate built Malthusian premises into the centrepiece of the Ricardian theory of distribution, its theory of rent. While in the *Wealth of Nations* there was a tendency to reproduce the physiocratic view of rent as emanating from the powers of the soil, for Ricardo the category of rent is crucial to the constitution of the mechanism of distribution. This theory is first stated in his *Essay on the Influence of a Low Price of Corn on the Profits of Stock* (1951, 4: 9–41), published in 1815 and restated in the second chapter of the *Principles*. In it, rent is understood as the means of equalisation of profits between lands of different fertility and situation. The theory is demonstrated by a conjectural narrative which is guided by the Malthusian theme of the constant capacity for the augmentation of the population (1951, 1: 69–72). The narrative commences in conditions in which there is an abundance of fertile land in proportion to the population it must support and in relation to the capital held by that population (69). Under such conditions no rent would be paid on land by virtue of the common principles of supply and demand. With the growth of population, land of second-degree fertility is taken into cultivation and immediately the land of the first quality accrues rent, the amount of which depends on the difference of quality between the two types of land. Gradually, as population progresses ever onwards, lands of third, fourth, and fifth quality are brought into cultivation, each receiving in rent the difference in quality between it and the least fertile land. Rent then can be defined as the 'difference between the produce obtained by the employment of two equal quantities of capital and labour' (71). Thus rent is not a payment on the original powers of nature but on the limits of those powers, the scarcity which is brought into being by the inexorable growth of population.

The Malthusian laws of necessity, inscribed in the natural relation between the rates of growth of population and of subsistence, and educing a particular form of marital conduct among the poor, are constitutive of the distributional mechanism of the Ricardian economy (cf Foucault 1970: 256–257). Thus economic discourse, which presents itself as overcoming the oeconomic or householding conception of the polity, presupposes a necessity that imposes specific forms of domestic life on the propertyless.

In the Ricardian economy the progress of wealth and population is accompanied by a rise in rent and a decline in the rate of profit. So much is this the case that the Ricardian system is haunted by the spectre of a 'stationary state' in which wages become so near to the total return of the capitalist that accumulation ceases, no more labourers can be employed, population remains static, and no more lands are brought into cultivation (Ricardo 1951, 1: 120–122). The scarcity which is inscribed in the laws of nature and which drives the application of labour and capital to the land, and which in turn leads to the pursuit of the conveniences and luxuries afforded by manufacturing production, makes its reappearance as the finality of history in the stagnant balance of capital, labour, subsistence, and population.

For Malthus, poverty is the natural consequence of the relation between population and subsistence and necessary to the maintenance of their actual equilibrium. For Ricardo, poverty is necessary to the adjustments of population to the quantity of available capital which occur because, in the course of time, population will outstrip the growth of capital due to the progressively niggardly character of nature. Human poverty parallels natural scarcity in both the differential theory of rent and the principle of population. Economic discourse is born out of the supposition that the needs of humankind are always in excess of the powers of production, the supposition of illimitable needs and limited resources. The situation of perpetual scarcity, which it presupposes, implies an agent capable of curbing the operation of the constant drive for procreation, the rational, calculating, patriarchal subject.

In Smith's *Wealth of Nations* rent is produced by the very bounty of the land, as a free gift on the produce which is the result of the powers of nature. Agriculture is thus the most productive use of capital stock because in it 'nature labours along with man: and though her labour costs no expense, its produce has its value, as well as that of the most expensive workmen' (1889: 161). Agriculture is here conceived as a direction of 'the fertility of nature' in a way most profitable. The 'labourers and labouring cattle' thus not only produce the value of their own consumption, or of the capital by which they are employed, but return a net produce in the form of a 'free rent to the landlord' (305).

By contrast, in Ricardo's *Principles* rent arises from the fact that under the pressure of the constant tendency of population to increase, the same quantities of labour and capital will yield ever diminishing returns from the land. The more population increases, in Ricardo as in Malthus, the more difficult it becomes for people to procure their subsistence and to produce a profit which permits the production of conveniences and luxuries. Rent refers us therefore to a lack, an intrinsic and progressive absence of abundance on the part of nature. Indeed, if land was all equally fertile and abundant, rent would not exist. Rent is the symptom of the Malthusian crisis of population, of that poverty which is ultimately insurmountable.[2]

Smith had annexed the sphere of exchange from the legislative framework of Political Oeconomy and constituted it as an autonomous realm subject to its own laws. However, these laws are moral ones with specific political implications. The wealth of a nation had been conceived ultimately in terms of that happiness which depends on the degree of liberty and justice among its members, the greatest numbers of whom are the labouring poor. By contrast, classical political economy constructs its objects through laws of production and distribution. The laws which regulate the economy are constituted in such a way as to be indifferent to questions of happiness, liberty, or justice and to be without any necessary political framework. This new object of knowledge, the economy, may have particular implications for forms of ethical conduct, and it may be argued that specific types of government are best suited to its functioning. However, it requires no prior polity for its constitution and it does not arise from the moral proclivities of individuals or collectives. From the standpoint of economic discourse, poverty may be grieved but, unless its relief can be shown to assist in the functioning of the production and distribution systems (as, of course, Keynes would do), this sorrow is in vain. The importance of the emergence of classical political economy for the consideration of poverty was that it portrayed poor relief as the height of undue interference with the working of this new reality of the economy. Given that economic discourse had already inscribed poverty in the very operation of the distributional mechanism, it is unsurprising that the relief of poverty would call forth the wrath of the new economic god.

Ricardo argues that poor relief is founded on the principle that the fund which maintains the poor contains the potential for an indefinite increase 'till it has absorbed all the net revenue of the country, or at least so much of it as the state shall leave us, after satisfying its own never failing demands for the public expenditure' (1951, 1: 106). Like Malthus, he argues that this is because the 'system of poor laws . . . have rendered restraint superfluous, and have invited imprudence, by offering it a portion of the wages of prudence and industry' (107). But whereas Malthus had been inclined to dismiss poor relief as a total waste of expenditure, Ricardo argues that it increases demand for subsistence and therefore entails a diversion of resources away from manufacturing production of conveniences and luxuries, and into the continual satisfaction of mere subsistence 'until all classes should be infected with the plague of universal poverty' (108).

Poor relief subtracts from the net revenue which constitutes the capital by which labour is employed. It thereby reduces the growth of manufacturing production. At the same time it increases the number of the poor and the demand for subsistence. Thus lands of less fertility are brought into cultivation to satisfy this increase in demand, causing the rate of profit to fall and the more speedy onset of the stationary state, a possibility openly entertained by Ricardo (e.g. 1951, 1: 109). The poor laws not only tamper with the natural order of the economy, and the subtle balance between wages, subsistence, and population, but contain within themselves the exhaustion of the dynamism of that economy.

From this position, Ricardo is able to take a gradualist abolitionist stance according to which the poor should be taught 'that they must look not to systematic or casual charity, but to their own exertions for support, that prudence and forethought are neither unnecessary nor unprofitable virtues' (1951, 1: 107). Political economy thus retains a moralising dimension in statements concerning poverty and its relief. However, unlike Smith, the approbation in which it holds the 'independence' of the labourer is not derived from a moral philosophy which asserts liberty and equity as part of the natural condition of humankind. In nineteenth-century political economy, this moralising dimension is restricted to the different conducts of the poor. If Smith argues for the liberty of the labourer on the basis of a moral economy of exchange, in classical political economy the figure of the 'independent labourer' simply condenses the form of life which is appropriate to the irresistible laws which prevail throughout the material universe.

The dual position of the rational, calculating subject as wage-labourer and head of household is no longer secured by his ownership of property and entry into the order of exchanges. Nor is it secured by his position within the patriarchal household. The choice of the form of life of the independent labourer, which entails participation in the labour market on the one hand, and the Malthusian approach to marriage and procreation on the other, is no longer specified by the moral relations between ranks which secure police in civil society, but by natural laws. The poor must simply obey the laws under which they, more than most people, are condemned to exist for their earthly life. The genius of the bioeconomic imperatives discovered by political economy is that they have no justification other than their simple existence.

The notion of labour as a productive activity constitutive of value, first found in classical political economy, has a double reference to poverty. Labour is specific to humankind, and ubiquitous among its greatest numbers, not because it distinguishes human 'species-being', but because the human species is locked into an unrelenting battle to satisfy its multiplying needs in the context of an increasing relative scarcity. It is this battle which calls forth a form of life organised around the wage- and marriage-contracts, and the double identity of the worker as wage-labourer and household head. It is not labour but poverty which is the natural condition of humankind, as demonstrated by the bioeconomic mechanisms of population, subsistence, and capital. Wage-labour and a rational approach to marriage and procreation constitute the double destiny of a species which finds its own unremitting power of generation at odds with the paucity of nature.

But the relations between poverty and labour are not yet exhausted. Ricardo's abstractions on the determination of wages rest on the same presuppositions as the rhetoric of Colquhoun or the theology of scarcity of Malthus. For Ricardo, as for Malthus, poverty is necessary to the adjustments between population and subsistence and so necessary to the operation of the economy, that sphere of the generation and distribution of wealth. But even more compelling is the parallel between Ricardo and Colquhoun: for both, labour not only ensures the survival of the species but also provides the conveniences and luxuries which humankind enjoys as the products of civilisation. If poverty leads to labour, and labour is necessary for both subsistence and wealth, then we can conclude, like Colquhoun, that the ultimate lesson of classical political economy is that just as poverty imposes the norms of the life of the 'independent labourer' at work and at home, so it is necessary to civilisation, to civil society itself.

The crucial distinction, as it pertains to the ethical domain, between the regulation of morals and manners in mercantilist work-police and in the liberal mode of government is the latter's introduction of an emphasis on a sphere of personal responsibility or self-regulation. In mercantilist work-police, the Poor are exhorted to or educated in the ways of an 'industrious course of life' rather than choosing it for themselves. In the liberal mode of government, the poor are given an option, albeit an unsavoury one, of choosing a life of industry (which meant wage-labour), independence (from parochial relief), frugality (in their domestic economy), procreative prudence (or 'moral restraint'), and foresight (by savings), or of facing the insurmountable natural reality by which they, their wives, and their offspring would inevitably perish. There is thus moral precept in the police of the Poor but not self-conscious moral action in the face of poverty, as there would be, at least for the male labourers, after Malthus. This simple shift has enormous consequences for the forms of life which inhere in liberal strategies.

In the liberal mode of government which emerged in the first decades of the nineteenth century, poverty was constituted in a dual relation, to matters of economy, on the one hand, and to those of morality, on the other. It is evident that what distinguishes this mode of government from those which preceded it is not the tendency of its agents to preach certain values. Rather, it is the subjugation of the ethical to the economic, the casting of forms of moral conduct in terms of the laws which regulate production and distribution. Morality becomes a matter for each individual, here understood as each adult male, confronted with an economic necessity inscribed in his relation to nature. In such a manner issues of morality, in so far as they affect the propertyless, retreat into a new domain of personal responsibility and dependency, that which would come to be called the private sphere. At the same time that theorists and revolutionaries were constructing a sphere of liberty and universal rights, a liberal government of poverty was being formed around a particular, patriarchal domain of personal responsibility against the claims of a right to subsistence. The genealogy of the liberal mode of government exists in uneasy tension with the explicit doctrines of classical liberalism.

Chapter nine

Pauperism and the labour market

A definite concept of poverty, which was to be embodied in the new political economy, was forged in the last years of the eighteenth century. But this concept had what might be thought of as an illegitimate half-sibling, pauperism. The latter is the central focus of the final three chapters. Broadly speaking, they complete the investigation into the implications of Polanyi's striking claim concerning the dual implication of political economy and pauperism in the discovery of *society* (1957: 103). In respect of the reform of the poor-law administration, we shall pose the question of whether it can be regarded as a *social* reform and whether, especially in plans of 'less-eligible' pauper management, pauperism was a *social* problem.

This chapter focuses on Karl Polanyi's account of the relationship between forms of relief practice, the problem of pauperism, and the formation of a capitalist labour market. We shall first examine the main aspects of Polanyi's provocative thesis that the reform of poor-law administration in England in 1834 was a crucial condition of the formation of the first national capitalist labour market. This thesis turns on an intepretation of the pre-1834 poor law as a 'Speenhamland' system of relief, and it is with this interpretation we shall begin. Then we shall address whether the *1834 Poor Law Report* (Checkland and Checkland 1974) can be used to sustain the claims made by Polanyi in support of this thesis, as he contends. In the course of this discussion, an alternative account of the definition of the problem and official strategy of this report will be presented.

The tasks contained in these sections are, however, only preliminary to the main investigation contained in the third. There, the core of Polanyi's thesis will be addressed in several ways: first, by producing a concept of what constitutes a capitalist labour market; second, by investigating whether the problem of the *1834 Report* could be read in Polanyi's terms as a problem of the prevention of the generalisation of the labour market; and finally, with the assistance of a key study (Williams 1981) on the institutional form of relief before and after the 1834 reform, by assessing the merits of Polanyi's theoretical positions.

Speenhamland

Karl Polanyi's account of Speenhamland will be familiar to students of
the classic studies in English social and institutional history, those of
Hammond and Hammond (1913: 161–165) and Webb and Webb (1963a:
176–189), written in the early decades of the twentieth century. However,
Polanyi (1957: 280–283) also draws attention to discussions of
Speenhamland in the lectures of Arnold Toynbee (who called it 'Tory
Socialism'), and the economic history of William Cunningham and Paul
Mantoux. We may add that Hammond and Hammond and Webb and
Webb point to the near universality of Speenhamland, while the former
regard it as a replacement of 'ancient rights and possessions' with a
'universal system of pauperism' (1913: 165). Mantoux understood it as
keeping the country quiet during the years of the Napoleonic Wars and,
quite curiously, as removing 'the obstacles which stood in the way of
the great economic change' (1961: 438). While virtually all this classic
literature agrees on the first point, it places Speenhamland, contrary to
Mantoux, as the final obstacle to the capitalist organisation of labour.
Most of these authors would no doubt agree with T.H. Marshall's assessment that Speenhamland is the 'final struggle between the old and the
new, between the planned (or patterned) society and the competitive
economy' (1983: 252). This is the lesson of Speenhamland which, in
any case, Polanyi draws.

Polanyi's account of pauperism itself turns on the diametrically
opposed roles he assigns to the Speenhamland system of relief and the
New Poor Law in relation to the operation of the labour market. Simply,
Speenhamland is supposed to have provided an obstacle to the labour
market, while the poor law after 1834 abolished such obstacles (Polanyi
1957: 79–83, 101, 137–138).

Polanyi had discovered in the works of these early economic
historians, reference to an informal system of widespread relief after
1795, which was named after the place in Berkshire in which it had been
first proposed at a meeting of the justices (1957: 77–78, 280–282). Under
this system, wages were supplemented or paid out of the poor rates by
means of a set of scales published by local magistrates. These scales
set a minimum income for labourers according to the prevailing price
of bread or grain and the size of the labourer's family. The central issue
for Polanyi was that Speenhamland was a form of relief 'in aid of wages'
and therefore incompatible with the emergent wage system (e.g. 280).
It established a 'right to live' regardless of the wage system, and func-
tioned first as a recharged local paternalism to protect the village against
the dislocation caused by rising wages in urban areas, but later spread
to manufacturing districts (77–85, 88–89, 96–102).

Speenhamland, then, represents a conflict between two contrary sets of principles, those of the *market* and those of *paternalism*.

> Under Speenhamland society was rent by two opposing influences, the one emanating from paternalism and protecting labour from the dangers of the market system; the other organizing the elements of production, including land, under a market system, and thus divesting the common people of their former status, compelling them to gain a living by offering their labour for sale, while at the same time depriving their labour of its market value.
>
> (Polanyi 1957: 80)

For Polanyi this system was hence a 'pseudo-humanitarian' one, professing to care for the poor after the fashion of traditional labour protection, while, in tandem with the anti-combination legislation, depressing their wages below subsistence and subsidising the rich in their exploitation of the poor (280–281). Moreover, because its inevitable result was lower than subsistence wages, the Speenhamland system became self-perpetuating and self-expanding.

As Corrigan indicates, this emphasis on the labour market is one of the main emphases in post-war debates on the post-1834 poor law (1977: 42–48). He suggests, however, that its 'moral dimension' has escaped historical attention. For Polanyi, however, these two aspects were irrevocably aligned. He argues that Speenhamland was an 'instrument of popular demoralization' with the 'dehumanization of the masses' leading to a 'grave deterioration of the productive capacity of the masses' and destroying the 'self-respect of the common man' (1957: 98–99). Pauperisation meant that workers preferred relief to wages, and hence such a system of relief contained the potential for indefinite expansion (79–82). The able-bodied and the pauper 'tended to fuse into one indiscriminate mass of dependent poverty' (95–96). It is interesting to note that this theme of moral degeneration, despite its humanist tone, repeats the complaints made by poor-law reformers of the time.

By characterising pre-1834 poor relief as a Speenhamland system, Polanyi wished to make the theoretical point that the configuration of relief practice prior to 1834 sought to protect the local village order by placing paternalist barriers against the 'pull' exerted by the developing industrial centres on an increasingly underemployed agricultural workforce. Polanyi opposes the intent and effects of the Speenhamland system of relief to those of the reform of the poor laws of 1834.

The post-1834 poor law and Speenhamland form, for Polanyi, the opposite poles of the possible effects of relief practice upon the operation of the capitalist labour market. So, while he conceives Speenhamland as an obstacle to the full flowering of the capitalist economy, he regards the New Poor Law as a key starting-point of modern capitalism, putting an end to the 'disastrous attempt to forge a capitalist order without a labour-market' (Polanyi 1957: 80). Similarly, while he places Speenhamland in the paternalistic tradition of labour regulation and protection, he views the reformed poor law as an uncompromising legislative enactment of the principle of *laissez-faire* (1957: 137). Moreover, while Polanyi interprets Speenhamland as having promised a 'right to live', he holds the reform to have attacked and abolished such a right because it was an obstacle to the labour market (Polanyi 1957: 82). Pre-capitalism, paternalism, localism, the right to subsistence, are opposed, point by point, to capitalism, *laissez-faire*, central administration, and market forces. Speenhamland is the fulcrum of transition to a capitalist modernity.

The reforms of 1834 are analysed simply as the negative pole of the earlier 'Speenhamland' form of relief. Polanyi's opposition between 'Speenhamland' and the 'New Poor Law' can be read as fulfilling the particular function of illustrating the proposition that the generalisation of the capitalist labour market can only occur under specific institutional conditions. It relies upon, on the one hand, the granting of a unitary meaning and unitary effects to the configuration of relief practices before 1834, and, on the other, a ready set of oppositions between paternalism and individualism, interventionism and *laissez-faire*, protection and the market, and so on. In opposing the forces of paternalism to those of the market, Polanyi implies that the New Poor Law, like the official self-image of political economy, has somehow broken irrevocably with the patriarchalism of the traditional social order.

The 1834 Report

The ultimate authority for Polanyi, as for similar accounts, remains 'the classic passages of the Poor Law Report' (1957: 281). But the problems of what type of relief practices that *Report* regarded as abuses, what type of objects it regarded as illegitimate, and whether it can be used in evidence of a Speenhamland system, remain unresolved.

The first problem is apparently easy to resolve, for the *1834 Report* supplies us with a direct answer (Checkland and Checkland 1974: 82): 'The great source of abuse is the outdoor relief afforded to the able-bodied on their own account, or on that of their families.' The interpretation of this simple sentence has been almost universally taken by both classic and latter-day poor-law historians to refer to the outdoor relief of all the able-bodied poor (e.g. Digby 1976: 149; Ashforth 1976: 129).[1] However, Williams (1981: 53) has recently argued that the objectionable practice referred to by this sentence was outdoor relief to able-bodied *males* and those considered their dependants. That this has been ignored by commentators may be a function of the framework which views the New Poor Law in terms of a transition between a patriarchal tradition and an individualist modernity of the generalisation of the wage-contract. Whatever the case, this elementary shift of interpretation, with which we concur, has enormous consequences for the analysis of the degree of success or failure of the reformed poor law.

The *1834 Report* distinguishes six types of outdoor relief: relief in kind, relief without labour, the allowance system, the roundsman system, parish employment, and the labour-rate system (Checkland and Checkland 1974: 82, 88). The principal focus of its attack is the allowance system – the category which has been held to refer to the Speenhamland system (e.g. Polanyi 1957: 280). The *1834 Report* defines the term somewhat obscurely as comprehending both relief to those employed at average wages in a district, which it calls the 'payment of wages out of rates', and allowances on account of children for such persons (Checkland and Checkland 1974: 90).

The examples given of the operation and abuses of the allowance system make frequent reference to the practice of supplementing wages by means of scales published and enforced by the magistrates, and sometimes formalised in local statutes. The main body of the *Report* includes copies of such scales from the County of Cambridge, the Town of Cambridge, and from Chelmsford, Essex, all dating from the 1820s (Checkland and Checkland 1974: 94–96). Nevertheless, such passages rely on purely anecdotal evidence and cannot be used in support of claims concerning the prevalence of a Speenhamland system of supplementing wages by bread scales.

The testimony on the allowance system which is quoted in the main body of the *Report* does indicate the nature of the relief practices it found to be objectionable and hence wished to highlight. This testimony demonstrates that it is not the use of scales *per se* which was under attack, but the use of such scales to provide relief to able-bodied men and their families whether or not they are employed (Checkland and Checkland 1974: 96–101).

The *Report* is crucially concerned about relief to able-bodied men, mostly in existing employments, granted as a supplement to wages for the support of themselves and their families. The examples of such relief it gives are often, but not always, formally calculated by the differences between the wage-earnings of the labourer (and sometimes the other members of his family) and the price of a certain quantity of bread which is held to form the necessary subsistence for families of various sizes. The *Report* cites many examples of 'abuses', particularly in the South, which emphasise the lack of sufficient refusal of relief (Checkland and Checkland 1974: 96–97), the lack of distinction between relief and wages on the part of the labourers (98), the extension of relief to those on higher than average wages (99), the formation of an expectation that such relief is given on the addition of new members to the family (100), and the granting of relief to adolescents regardless of parents' income (101–102).

Almost as culpable, however, is the so-called 'roundsman system' (Checkland and Checkland 1974: 102–106). According to the *Report*, this involved the contracting of pauper labour to the farmers at rates fixed by the parish, which then repays the farmer out of the poor rate any payment above a certain sum (102). As examples of abuses, the *Report* complains of the auctioning of paupers, including the aged and infirm (103), and cites one example in which the parish overseers shared out pauper labour among the farmers, including themselves, and paid these labourers wholly from the rates (106). It condemns the roundsman system as a means by which farmers could gain a cheap source of labour subsidies by the poor rates. Moreover, it gives prominence to testimony which argues that this system rewards 'men of bad character' as much as the 'honest labourer' and repeats the assertion made in respect of the allowance system that the pauper labourer comes to regard this relief as his entitlement or right (103–104).

After many pages citing the abuses to which relief to able-bodied males and their dependants is liable, the *1834 Report* notes, apparently approvingly, that 'a class of persons have, in many places, established a right to public support', namely widows (Checkland and Checkland 1974: 114). In a similar vein, it argues that out-relief to the 'impotent' (i.e. the aged and the sick) affords few opportunities for abuses (114–115). Accordingly relief to at least one class of able-bodied pauper, that of widows, is included with the relief to the aged and the sick as not falling among the abuses of the existing poor laws. The *1834 Report* therefore defined relief to the able-bodied male, his wife, and children as the major source of abuse and excluded relief to able-bodied widows from this definition. It fails to address the question of the two remaining classes of able-bodied women, single women without children and single or separated women with children. We may therefore assent to Williams' characterisation of the definition of the problem of the *Report*, while noting the existence of a grey area of able-bodied female pauperism.

The major focus of condemnation of the *1834 Report* is not the generalisation of a Speenhamland system of granting relief according to published scales, but rather all forms of relief, however administered and calculated, to able-bodied males for the support of themselves and their families. The *Report* condemns equally relief to employed male labourers, underemployed or low-paid male labourers, and unemployed male labourers. The historiographical debate over the existence of a Speenhamland system is singularly misplaced from the perspective of the *1834 Report*. Any reconstruction of Polanyi's thesis of the relation between relief practice and the labour market must be made without the shaky supposition that pre-1834 poor practice has a unitary meaning given by the concept of Speenhamland. Similarly, it should be wary of making the assumption that the changing approach to relief embodied in the report is intelligible as a break with patriarchy. Polanyi is correct to understand it as a rejection of paternalism, but he fails to understand that the report advocates a patriarchal 'responsibilisation' of the male labourer and constructs the female poor as his natural economy dependant. Any reconstruction must, therefore, keep in mind the specific definition of the problem of poor relief in the *1834 Report*.

The strategy of the *1834 Report* followed closely this definition of the problem. It made no specific proposals for the transformation of relief practice respecting the aged and infirm, or widows and their children. It almost exclusively concentrated on the evils it understood as connected with the relief of able-bodied male labourers, their wives, and children (e.g. Checkland and Checkland 1974:: 115–123, 167–179). The solution to these evils would be that this class was to be granted relief only under a 'less-eligible' situation than that of the lowest class of 'independent labourer' (335).[2] This principle of less-eligibility would be secured by the granting of relief to such persons only in 'well-regulated workhouses' (375–377). These workhouses would contain various classes of pauper, including children, some old and infirm, able-bodied males, and able-bodied females, each of which would receive 'separate and appropriate' treatment in specialised institutions or within the one institution (430). In such institutions the regime of the able-bodied would render their situation less-eligible by providing them with 'more irksome labour' than the independent labourer, and subjecting them to a 'strict discipline' which would separate men and women, prevent going out or receiving visitors, and proscribe the use of 'fermented liquors' and tobacco (336–340).

The main functions of the workhouse, then, would not be concerned with the reform of individual inmates, with the transformation of their 'souls', but with the repression of able-bodied male pauperism. The internal regime of the workhouse mattered less than its immediate effects in diminishing the number of applicants for relief and the size of the poor rates (Checkland and Checkland 1974: 342–343). By so doing, the abolition of out-relief would have numerous benefits on the labouring populace, improving their industry, increasing frugality, increasing their wages, lessening improvident marriages, and abating their discontent (374). Its effectiveness could only be judged by the degree to which it acted as a *deterrent*. The greatest significance of the workhouse lay in the multiple benefits which would naturally accrue to the behaviour and condition of the labourers. The workhouse was a very blunt instrument indeed.

In order to effect such a policy, the *1834 Report* argued for the necessity of the establishment of a 'permanent and independent authority', a Central Board of Control, which would regulate the overall administration of the poor law (Checkland and Checkland 1974: 398–413). The existing units of relief administration, the parishes, were to be united for the purposes of workhouse management (434). The resultant local authorities would be divested of all discretionary power and charged with the implementation of uniform regulations promulgated by the central board, particularly those concerning the abolition of outdoor relief to able-bodied labourers and their dependants (415–419).

The *1834 Report* hence arrived at a radically new, centralised administrative structure which would ensure that outdoor relief to able-bodied males, on account of themselves or their wives and children, would be abolished and relief to this class only granted under the less-eligible conditions of a 'well-regulated workhouse'. The report arrived at such a strategy without assuming that relief practice had been dominated by a Speenhamland system. The interpretation of the definition of the problem and consequent strategy of the *1834 Report* as a concern with the effects of Speenhamland must be replaced with that of a concern with relief to a specific class of paupers. It is now possible to examine whether such a strategy can be read as an overcoming of the obstacles presented by forms of relief to the formation of a capitalist labour market and, if so, whether it was successful.

The formation of the capitalist labour market

An analysis which posits the near universal existence of a Speenhamland system obscures the diagnosis and strategy of the Commissioners in 1834. But where does this leave Polanyi's theoretical proposition concerning the poor law and the labour market? This proposition is that the reform of the poor law, implemented upon the recommendations of the *1834 Report*, was crucial to the institution of a generalised regime of wage-labour among the propertyless and hence to the formation of a national labour market. To assess its worth, we shall first discuss what constitutes a capitalist labour market. We shall then examine the practices of relief before and after 1834 to ascertain whether the poor-law reform should be understood as overcoming obstacles to the labour market presented by relief practice.

The concept of the labour market

The first feature of the capitalist labour market is that it is, as Polanyi said, 'self-regulating' (1957: 68–76). But what are we to understand by such a term? It is evident that the fundamental condition of such a market is that it functions and reproduces itself without immediate political regulation. To be self-regulating, a labour market does not simply involve the widespread sale of labour-power, but the reproduction of the labour-power of present and future generations of labourers. In a capitalist labour

163

market the sale of labour-power must be the means by which the class of labourers subsist so that their own labour-power, as well as that of a further generation of labourers, is reproduced. In Marxian terms, a capitalist labour market can only exist if the sale of labour-power enables the labourer to procure the means of subsistence which are socially necessary to the reproduction of labour-power. The demonstration of the conditions of existence of this 'self-regulating' labour market would be remiss, however, if it did not recognise the existence of a sphere in which the reproduction of labour-power, and the future labouring population, is socially organised and secured. A labour market is self-regulating in so far as it leaves the future reproduction of the labourers to the putatively natural operation of a private, domestic sphere.

But how are the bearers of this labour-power defined? This is a question which complicates the pure, ideal-typical, concept of the labour market. If labour-power is defined as the capacity to work, then its bearers must be capable of working. This automatically excludes those who, by age or infirmity, are unable to work. The nature of this disability with respect to work is not, however, simply a psycho-physiological matter. It is defined by specific socially constructed categories such as 'old age', and the degree of skill, competence, and dexterity required for participation in forms of work. Further, some characteristics may be regarded as the basis of exclusion from the labour market which are totally unrelated to considerations of the requirements of the work process, such as caste or sex. Therefore, the second feature of a capitalist labour market is that the condition of wage-labour is generalised to a specific population which is defined as able to work through a complex interchange of social practices with physical and psychological attributes.

What is this condition of wage-labour? On the one hand, virtually every sociologist has followed Weber's lead in defining wage-labour as 'formally free labour'. For Weber, one of the necessary features of 'rational capitalism' is the class of free labourers, i.e. a class who sell their labour-power or services 'in the formal sense voluntarily, but actually under the compulsion of the whip of hunger' (1927: 277). That is to say that labourers freely contract to sell their labour-power under conditions of considerable duress.

But why should this be so? What is it about wage-labour that means that only under such adverse conditions will the individual enter into a wage-contract? The simple answer to these questions is not often spelt out by socialist critics of the wage-contract who have concentrated on the inequalities of the conditions under which the contract is entered into. It has been pointed out, however, by Carole Pateman (1988: 146–151), that in the wage-contract the labourer contracts to submit to relations of subordination. Against Marx, she shows that the economic exploitation of the worker, i.e. the appropriation of the surplus value, is 'a consequence of the fact that the sale of labour power entails the worker's subordination' (149). The contract legitimates, then, the domination of employee by employer, the fact that the worker must act in accordance with the commands of the boss. The 'rational' individual who had means of procuring the socially necessary subsistence without contracting to be dominated would, all else being equal, choose such means. This is the theoretical core of the problem of the relation between poor relief, or other forms of welfare provision for that matter, and the labour market. The third feature of the capitalist labour market is, then, that those defined as bearers of labour-power have no reasonable, satisfactory alternative to wage-labour.

As we noted above, for a capitalist labour-market to exist, the sale of labour-power must be the means by which the future labouring population is reproduced. This implies the fourth feature of the capitalist labour market, the constitution of a group that is economically dependent upon wage-labourers' earnings. If we remove the Malthusian assumption that dependants are defined by the laws of necessity which are inherent in nature, it becomes necessary to examine specific practices (legal, administrative, customary, etc.) by which economic responsibility and dependency are defined and apportioned. The obverse side of such practices, it must be remembered, are patriarchal relations of domination and subordination.

It follows that if there *is* an alternative or significant supplement to wage-labour as the means of procuring the means of subsistence for workers and their dependants, then there exists a barrier to the development and operation of a capitalist labour market. A condition of the emergence of a national capitalist labour market is the removal of all such barriers in a nation and the establishment of the institutional conditions by which the sale of labour-power is the sole means of support for those defined as labourers and those constructed as their dependants.

This concept of the capitalist labour market can be applied to poor relief. If poor relief provides such an alternative or supplementary means of subsistence to wage-labour for those socially defined as the bearers of labour-power and their dependants, then such relief prevents the full development and self-reproduction of the capitalist labour market. Under such conditions, however else we may characterise the sale of labour-power, it is *not* self-regulating. Conversely, relief to those who are unable to work, whether through infirmity, law, or custom, cannot be said to be an obstacle to the labour market since these groups are already ruled out of the sphere of paid work. It is only poor relief to those who are psychologically and physically able to fulfil the tasks required by the work process, and are socially constituted as legitimate bearers of labour-power, or relief to 'dependants' of this group, which prevents the emergence of the labour market.

These theoretical issues of poor relief and the labour market may be illustrated by the examples culled from the *1834 Report*. The allowance system it describes permits local employers to maintain a pool of low-paid labourers protected from the competition of higher wages at other places. For these labourers, subsistence is not secured solely by the sale of their labour-power. Nor, it may be added, is their own labour-power or that of the future labouring population reproduced by those wages. Rather, the socially necessary means of subsistence is attained by a combination of wage-labour and relief supplements, and hence the reproduction of both labour-power and the labouring population is not secured by the labour market but by an attenuated labour market in combination with poor relief. Similarly, the roundsman system provides a pool of reserve labour for the farmer at fixed non-market wages. It thus maintains a surplus population without regard to the availability of employment or the existing wage levels throughout the national economy. Together with the continued, if diminished, restrictions on the movement of labourers enacted under the laws of settlement (Rose 1976: 27–28), both the allowance and roundsman systems would limit the formation of a national labour market for able-bodied adult males if their practice was extensive.

Is there, then, any evidence that the pre-1834 poor law did act in such a way and that its reform radically transformed the effects of poor-relief practices upon the labour market?

Relief practice and the labour market

The *1834 Report* objected to various forms of relief which, if they had been widespread, would have prevented the generalisation of the condition of wage-labour and hence the formation of a national labour market. However, the anecdotal use of evidence in that report means that it can only be informative of its own definition of the problem and its strategy for overcoming that problem. The report cannot be used to gauge the extent of various forms of relief before the reform of the poor law. Nor can it be assumed that the strategy enunciated in it was either implemented or effective after 1834. The question of the nature and extent of relief practices in both these periods must be resolved, however, before a conclusive assessment can be made of Polanyi's theoretical postulate of the different functions of relief in respect of the labour market. It is necessary, therefore, to find some means of ascertaining both the extent and nature of relief practices before and after the 1834 poor-law reform. These means, fortunately, have been provided by one recent, ground-breaking work in economic history, Karel Williams' *From Pauperism to Poverty* (1981).[3]

The sole resources used by Williams are the official statistics provided by poor-law authorities before and after 1834. The use of such statistics, and Williams' tabulation and analysis of them, does not imply a naïve acceptance of the 'statistical idea' that they represent an actuality which eludes other forms of evidence. It is not necessary to assume that statistical information forms a privileged discourse which provides 'hard' evidence of the non-discursive referent. The official statistics, and Williams' analysis of them, are employed here simply because they are pertinent to the historico-theoretical question of the relation between forms of relief and the labour market.

Let us, then, begin with the pre-1834 period. Williams points out that the official statistics in this period 'make a very short text with many lacunae' (1981: 36). Indeed, that text consists of only one annual series, that of relief expenditure after 1812, and three major *ad hoc* returns on paupers for 1802–3, 1824, and 1832. There are three salient points to emerge from Williams' tabulation of these returns, as we have mentioned in chapter five. The first is that able-bodied males and their 'dependants' constituted the vast majority (over four-fifths) of the total of persons on relief and made up over a tenth of the total population. Second, there were several varieties of relief, including the widespread granting of money relief and/or the provision of work to the unemployed in almost all urban areas in 1832, the widespread granting of child allowances in both agricultural and industrial counties in 1824 and 1832, and the payment of 'wages out of the rates' in a large minority of districts in 1824 declining to marginality by 1832. Finally, the vast majority of relief under the old poor law took place outdoors.

These findings are contrasted by Williams with the profuse post-1834 statistics. This profusion was attendant upon the establishment of central poor-law authorities (the Poor Law Commission and the later Poor Law Board) charged with the implementation of official strategy and the collection of information to check the degree of efficacy of that implementation. Given the evidence of widespread relief to able-bodied men and their dependants, Williams' analyses of relief to able-bodied men covered by the Poor Law Commission's series from 1839 to 1846 and the Poor Law Board's series from 1849 to 1861 are of special concern. For Williams (1981: 68–69) these statistical series are a privileged resource for answering questions about relief practice and strategy precisely because they are designed to measure the success of that strategy.

His analyses of the post-1834 official statistics show that as early as the 1840s the numbers of able-bodied men receiving outdoor relief had declined to minimal proportions, and that for the rest of the century after 1850 outdoor relief to able-bodied men 'in want of work' (a category embracing both unemployed and underemployed men) fell from minimal to negligible proportions, rarely rising above 1 per cent of the total pauper population. Instead of able-bodied men, their wives, and their children, the poor law now consistently relieved the aged and the chronic sick, who made up over 40 per cent of the pauper population for most of the second half of the century, widows and dependent children on outdoor relief, who constituted about 20 per cent of the total number of paupers after 1849, children as a whole, who numbered over a third of all paupers until the late 1890s, and the insane, who rose from 1 per cent of all paupers in 1842 to around 12 per cent at the end of the century (Williams 1981: Table 4.23, 204–205; Table 4.20, 199; Table 4.18, 197; Table 4.31, 215).

We have already seen that the most dramatic conclusion from these findings concerns the 'line of exclusion' which was drawn against able-bodied men after 1834. It must now be emphasised that such an effect is perfectly in keeping with the official strategy enunciated in the *1834 Report*. Able-bodied men were regularly and extensively relieved in the early part of the century on account of themselves and their families and regardless of their employment status. By the second half of the century this group appears to have been relieved in only negligible numbers. This is a stunning conclusion, overturning received notions of relief practice under the post-1834 poor law which stress the failure of implementation of central policy in the face of local resistance. More significantly, this conclusion is crucial for resolving the problem of the relation of different relief practices before and after 1834 to the formation of a labour market.[4]

These findings can now be used to assess Polanyi's claim that before 1834 the poor law acted as an obstacle to the formation of a national labour market and that the reforms of 1834 were a means of overcoming this obstacle. It has already been argued that child allowances and the payment of wages out of rates are two forms of relief practice which would have prevented the generalisation of the condition of wage-labour among able-bodied adult males. Polanyi's contention that poor-relief practice before 1834 was an obstacle to the development of the labour market is supported by the available statistical resources which show the extensive practice of either or both of these forms of relief at this period. Relief to able-bodied males and their families served to withdraw labour from the operation of the nascent labour market and to protect the local economy by insulating it from the larger forces of the national economy. If Polanyi's supposition of the existence of a Speenhamland system of relief is doubtful, his conclusion that relief was granted in such a way as to prevent the commodification of labour is not.

The pre-1834 existence of money doles or work forms of relief in urban areas may well serve quite a different cause, that of maintaining a pool of labourers on which an already established and expanding labour market could draw. Whether this was the case cannot be resolved within the context of the present discussion. Here we are purely concerned with the establishment of a national labour market and not the operation of such a market in specific localities or sectors of the economy. Nevertheless, even allowing the possibility that poor relief may have fulfilled some different or ambiguous functions in urban or manufacturing areas before 1834, the basic operation of poor relief was such as to provide an alternative or supplementary way of procuring the socially necessary means of subsistence for those adult men who were able to work, and those already in work, and thus formed an internal, politically defined limit to the full extension of the labour market within national boundaries.

If certain relief practices before 1834 formed an obstacle to the emergence of a national labour market, then the triumph of the official strategy enunciated in the *1834 Report* can be read, after Polanyi, as the removal of such obstacles to the generalisation of the condition of wage-labour among able-bodied adult males without means of production. The *1834 Report* had called for the repression of pauperism among able-bodied men and their dependants; it did not recommend abolition of, and offered only scant reference to, the question of relief to the aged, the infirm, and able-bodied widows and their children. These groups continued to be relieved in significant numbers in the second half of the nineteenth century. Among other things, these findings indicate that if the reform of the poor law is interpreted as a condition of the generalisation of the labour market, then the shape of this labour market is determined by a set of assumptions about propertyless males being natural breadwinners and heads of households.

The sex-specific nature of the strategy and practice of poor relief after 1834 is a topic which bears reflection, as does the related question of economic dependency. What happened to able-bodied women? We have seen that able-bodied widows continued to be legitimate objects of poor relief for the official strategy and for the relief practice. The question of able-bodied women without children and those separated from the fathers of their children is more difficult to assess. For the latter group there is the evidence that, while widows and their children made up around 20 per cent of the pauper population for most of the century, all fatherless families totalled only between 18 per cent and 26 per cent of the pauper population at the same time (Williams 1981: Table 4.39, 231). Thus separated and single mothers may have been granted some form of relief, although they and their children constituted less than 5 or 6 per cent of the pauper host. It would seem likely, given that the category of 'widows with dependent children' did not cover other single mothers, that 'disreputable' unmarried or separated mothers and their dependants were largely offered only the 'less-eligible' conditions of the workhouse (Williams 1981: 196).

The case of the single able-bodied woman without children is more difficult to assess. The granting of relief to such a group is not

169

contemplated by the *1834 Report* and does not enter into the categories examined or tabulated by poor-law authorities. The full contours of the operation of the post-1834 poor law cannot be said to be known unless we can discover whether the solicitations of the poor law towards 'reputable' women with children (i.e. widows) extended to single women without children, or whether a 'line of exclusion' was drawn against this group because, like able-bodied men, they must be made to support themselves. Another scenario is that, like 'disreputable' single mothers, they were offered the 'less-eligible' conditions of the workhouse. It is possible, of course, that the numbers of this group were so small that they did not warrant official attention and statistical monitoring. But why? Was this group deterred from requesting relief in the same manner as were able-bodied men, that is, by the deterrent workhouse? Or, given the extensive employment of women in domestic service in the nineteenth century, was this group protected from the vagaries of fluctuations in employment?

Some impressionistic comments can be made on the basis of the majority *Report of the Royal Commission on the Poor Laws* (1909). This report, in its 'Statistical Survey of the Poor Law Problems', addresses the question of the higher rate of female pauperism (232–233). The higher rate and longer duration of time on relief is here put down to 'widowhood' and the fact that the labour-force participation rate of unmarried women is much lower than that of men. The citation of the figures on labour-force participation suggests that unmarried women were regarded as more likely and acceptable objects of relief at this time. The report then appears to confirm such an assumption by citing a general difference in treatment of men and women:

> To whatever cause a woman's appeal to the Poor Law may be due, the relief would generally be required for a lengthened period, whereas except in cases of permanent invalidity and of old age no man would ordinarily be allowed to remain permanently in the workhouse or be given out-relief for protracted periods.
>
> (*Report* 1909: 33)

If relief to men as a whole was less acceptable than relief to women as a whole, it may be that single childless able-bodied women were not subject to the same rigorous exclusion as able-bodied men. This same impression is further fostered by a later statement in the *Report* (1909: 35) that 'there is often greater danger of encouraging idleness in giving out-relief to men than to women'. The general picture sketched in this report is that relief practice was more solicitous to all classes of women than to the corresponding classes of men, with a (slight) majority of male paupers on indoor relief and four times as many women on outdoor as on indoor relief. Still, the only figure for single childless women on out-relief is minuscule, forming approximately 0.3 per cent of the pauper population.[5] This figure is further complicated by the fact that it includes 'ordinarily' able-bodied single women who are temporarily sick. The poor law of the early twentieth century does not appear to have been in the business of assisting able-bodied childless single women. Within the limits of the present study, it is difficult to assess whether this was the result of deliberate policy or whether there were few such women applying for relief.

The consideration of the nature of 'dependency' is far more fruitful. The numbers of children relieved after 1834 formed a large proportion of the pauper population, although, both as a proportion of all paupers and in absolute terms, the numbers of pauper children declined after 1870. Nevertheless, one of the major planks of Malthusian-inspired abolitionism had been that poor relief encourages procreation by removing the natural law that children must be supported by their parents. Further, this objection was incorporated into official policy by the *1834 Poor Law Report* which claimed as one of the specific effects of the less-eligibility principle the 'diminution of improvident marriages' (Checkland and Checkland 1974: 349–351). The practice of the exclusion of able-bodied males, wives, and children from relief after 1834 thus followed the Malthusian assumption that the natural order of things required that the labourer should support himself, his spouse, and their children. Through the proscription of relief to this group, the poor law defines the family unit as a *natural* sphere of private economic responsibility which makes children and wives dependants of the male wage-labourer. The exclusion of this group from relief found the simple justification that it replicated the natural order in which men were so responsible for their families. Through the poor law, the liberal state would assume responsibility for families on the condition they were fatherless or that the male breadwinner was infirm. Within the fatherless category, moreover, it is only widows and their children who are regularly included within out-relief while the disreputable single or separated mother is consigned to the less-eligible disciplinary regime of the workhouse.

The liberal state, through the poor law, sought to define a sphere of private economic responsibility and dependency which only ceased with the infirmity or death of the (male) household head. Unlike the practice of late nineteenth-century philanthropy, educational practices, and social work today, the poor law offered no positive measures for this responsibilisation. Instead, it was founded on a strategy which assumed that a sphere of familial responsibility was natural and that, in the absence of any palatable alternative, such would be the choice of the propertyless labourer. Unlike more recent social security which defines a sphere of state responsibility for all 'single parents', the poor law drew a line between those who could not be supported by a male breadwinner, and

171

those who should be supported by an able-bodied male. It was in this fashion that the reformed poor law instituted Malthusian objectives. What Malthus had held to be a natural law was established in fact, that the able-bodied male was to be held economically responsible for himself and those said to be his dependants.

The delineation of a private sphere of personal responsibility for the propertyless, first explicitly formulated within Malthusian discourse at the end of the eighteenth century, became a central tenet of official strategy in the 1834 reforms and was translated into general relief practice well before the middle of the nineteenth century. Moreover, the effect of the removal of legally sanctioned means of support to members of this category was to remove the obstacle presented by poor relief to the generalisation of the condition of wage-labour as the sole means of subsistence for able-bodied adult males without property. The interpretation of the poor-law reform as an intervention capable of overcoming the barriers to the formation of a national labour market, proposed by Polanyi, can therefore be endorsed. If there is a 'capitalist ethic' the effects of which extended deep into the propertyless masses at the base of the social hierarchy, it was one formulated in terms of the natural laws of population, subsistence, and capital. That ethic was to be implanted in the social body not by positive measures for the transformation of the 'consciousness' of the poor but by the reformation of the key practice of poor relief so as to repress relief to those who would constitute the workers and their dependants.[6]

Chapter ten

Pauper-land

In his tracts on 'pauper management', Jeremy Bentham asserted that 'Wisdom – true wisdom consists – not in the *scantiness* of *measures* – but in the *amplitude* of means' (1843, 8: 397). Here we shall explore the amplitude defined by pauperism as an object of state administration. In this and the remaining chapter, we shall reflect upon the imagery of pauperism, its relations with the concept of poverty, and the nature of the great intellectual and practical edifice to pauper administration constructed by the likes of Bentham, Patrick Colquhoun, and Edwin Chadwick. The formation of a distinctive rationality concerned with the means of administration of pauperism is interesting not simply because it was broad and flexible enough to adapt to the exigencies of particular circumstances and interests, to established practices, and to available resources, although this point must be made in relation to arguments concerning the 'revolution of government' of the 1830s.[1] More surprising is the dissonance between means and ends. Thus the writings, programmes, and approaches to the problem of pauperism are also of intense interest in that they are so evidently *pre*-liberal, or even *illiberal*. Many of the writings on pauperism apparently respect few limits to the sphere of governance, let alone those set by either a private sphere or a self-regulating economy. The liberal mode of government of poverty, as it was constructed around the reform of the poor laws, was forged from programmes and knowledges which contravene almost every one of the sacred tenets of liberal philosophies. A cognate issue is whether or not the problem of pauperism is a *social* problem, if by that we mean the construction of interventions around a dichotomy between private and public spheres. In this respect the nexus between the administration of pauperism and the problem of 'the condition of the labouring population' becomes salient. Finally, it must also be asked, with Foucault (1980a: 159), particularly of Bentham's pauper 'Panopticons', why the governance of pauperism could be understood as both an administrative programme and a Utopia.

The general terrain

Let us begin by examining a passage cited by Webb and Webb (1963b: 18–19) which indicates something of the wealth of associations condensed in the notion of pauperism in the pamphlet and periodical literature on the poor laws in the early nineteenth century.[2]

First, pauperism covers a particular category of juridically-defined agents: 'Pauperism, in the legal sense of the word, is a state of dependence upon parochial relief' (Thomas Walker, quoted by Webb and Webb 1963b: 18). In its second function, however, this legal specificity becomes a codeword for a moral indeterminacy. It becomes all that which is antithetical to the proper behaviours of the poor and partakes of the status of a communicable pathology. The right to relief is 'the admission of a MORAL PESTILENCE', which 'attacks and paralyses whole families', 'infests' both city and country, and 'flourishing' and poor districts, resulting in 'periods of devastating violence' (18). The pauper lives in 'deceit and self-abasement', 'his whole life a lie', and his 'study an imposition' (18–19). The problem of pauperism, 'its very essence', is a kind of fraud, since the pauper lives only by appearing not to be able to support himself and his family, and persisting in his 'irksome applications' under the poor laws.

Perhaps this description is somewhat overstated. Nevertheless, the difference between the imagery of this passage and that of the 'average' tract on pauperism is one of degree rather than kind. Pauperism presents itself to the administrators, the magistrates, the divines, and the medical doctors of this period as a radical challenge to the natural functioning of a political and moral order. In many ways the image and language of pauperism transcends differences between political allegiance, and intellectual, ethical, and religious disposition. Pauperism is associated with moral and physical contagion, with epidemics and mental and physical disease, with political disturbances and crimes, and, above all, with the demoralisation of the labouring classes. Pauperism appears as the violation of the morality imposed by a necessity inscribed in nature. It leads from the corruption of morals not only to indolence and vice but also to actual criminality and political upheaval. Pauperism or indigence – the terms are synonymous – is, according to Patrick Colquhoun, 'one of the greatest calamities which can afflict civil society, since, with certain exceptions, it generates everything that is noxious, criminal and viscious in the body politic' (1814: 107).

Pauperism and poverty

The notion of pauperism displayed the hallmarks of a moral panic among nearly all sectors of articulate opinion. However, it is more significant because it indicates how poverty was thought to be *administrable* for this liberal mode of government. It will be recalled that a corollary of the 'poverty theory of labour' was the proscription of relief and state intervention into poverty. It was the task of administrative reformers to define, by means of this distinction between poverty and pauperism or indigence, the legitimate realm of governmental, both state and non-state, intervention. Thus Edwin Chadwick argued a defence of the Poor Law Amendment Act, of which he was the principal architect, in the following terms:

> The Commissioners might have added that poverty . . . is the natural, the primitive, the general and the unchangeable state of man; that as labour is the source of wealth, so is poverty of labour. Banish poverty, you banish wealth. Indigence, therefore, and not poverty is the evil, the removal of which is the proper object of Poor Laws. Indigence may be provided for . . . but all attempts to extirpate poverty can have no effects but bad ones.
>
> (Chadwick 1837: 18)

This statement encapsulates, succinctly, the principal means by which the liberal government of poverty sought to frame the role of the state in matters of poverty in the first half of the nineteenth century. In the same article, Chadwick defined more precisely this role: 'Poverty was not the object of attack, but rather those circumstances in their environment that turn the poor into the indigent' (1837: 42). The administration of poverty during this period was founded upon the strategy of acting on those circumstances/conditions/behaviours of the poor which constitute the genesis of pauperism.

This distinction between poverty and indigence closely resembles that drawn in the manuscripts of Jeremy Bentham written some forty years earlier. It is unsurprising, given the close association between the two men at the end of Bentham's life, that this should be so (Finer 1952: 28–35). Chadwick served as Bentham's secretary, worked on his *Constitutional Code* (Bentham 1843: 10), and would appear to have been familiar with his writings on the subject. In any case, whatever the significance attributed to this biographical link, the distinction drawn by Chadwick had already been established in the first part of the unpublished manuscript of Bentham's *Essays on the Poor Law of 1796*:

> Poverty is the state of everyone who, in order to obtain *subsistence*, is forced to have recourse to *labour*. Indigence is the state of him who, being destitute of property . . . is at the same time, either unable to labour, or unable, even *for* labour, to procure the supply of which he happens to be in want.
>
> (quoted by Boralevi 1984: 98; Poynter 1969: 119)

175

For Bentham in 1796, as for Chadwick in 1937, only indigence fell within the province of state administration, while poverty remained the 'natural, the primitive, the general and the unchangeable lot of man' (Bentham, quoted by Poynter 1969: 119; Boralevi; 1984, 99). More importantly, the same distinction and conclusion were drawn by the *1834 Report* in its comments concerning the peculiarity of the English poor law. It claimed that:

> In no part of Europe except England has it been thought fit that the provision, whether compulsory or voluntary, should be applied to more than the relief of *indigence*, the state of a person unable to labour, or unable to obtain, in return for labour, the means of subsistence. It has never been deemed expedient that the provision should extend to the relief of poverty; that is the state of one, who in order to obtain a mere subsistence, is forced to have recourse to labour.
>
> (Checkland and Checkland 1974: 334)

The language of Bentham and Chadwick was that which was used to frame the most comprehensive reform of the English system of poor laws since their Tudor inception. If the ends of the New Poor Law were derived from the critique of the relief of poverty first enunciated by Malthus, and made an article of faith by political economy, then the rationality under which the new administration would take shape bears the unmistakable – and often exceedingly illiberal, repressive, and authoritarian – imprint of the programme of pauper management projected by Bentham in the late eighteenth century.

One can, however, discern another, more fundamental, kinship between the new economic logic and this administrative rationality which lay beyond a common participation in poor-law debates. If the former had shown that there was a necessity which would bind poverty to labour, the latter would reveal a different kind of poverty – pauperism – which was both the cause and effect of the breaking of this bond. If it was poverty – that poverty which reflected the poverty already inscribed in the relation between human beings and nature – which called forth the need for labour, and brought forth all the benefits of civilisation, then pauperism – that poverty which so brazenly disobeyed the natural laws which govern human existence – traced the inverse movement towards a relaxation of labour. If labour was the objective expression of the adherence of moral subjects, constituted in the act of the exchange of their only property, that which they held in their own persons, to bioeconomic necessity, then pauperism was a site outside that act of moral constitution, and the violation of that necessity which presaged the demoralisation of the individual and the fall of civilisation into the abyss of inertia. Bentham took the view that:

This aspect of society is the saddest of all. It presents that long catalogue of evils which end in indigence and consequently in death, under its most terrible forms. This is the centre to which inertia alone, that force which acts without relaxation, makes the lot of every mortal gravitate. Not to be drawn into the abyss, it is necessary to mount up by continual effort; and we see by our side the most diligent and the most virtuous sometimes slipping by one false step, and sometimes thrown headlong by inevitable reverses.

(quoted by Poynter 1969: 119; Boralevi 1984: 99)

It was this same association of pauperism with a deadly abyss within the political anatomy which would lead others to demand the immediate eradication of the poor relief which encouraged it and to warn of an impending doom for civilisation if that were not done. For Bentham, however, the correlate of the discovery of this site of social implosion was not moral panic but the elaboration of a new sphere of knowledge and an administrative rationality appropriate to it. In the process of constituting such a field of knowledge Bentham established a set of principles which displaced poor relief by what he called 'pauper management'. It would be impossible to show how pauperism could become an object of rational knowledge and be used to form the field of intervention for the state under the liberal mode of government if we did not understand Bentham's knowledge and practice of pauper management.

This does not mean, however, that we should regard Bentham as liberal in his approach to poverty, or take his pauper Panopticons, with their self-avowed utopian aspirations, as forerunners of the mid-nineteenth-century workhouse. Bentham furnished the principle of less-eligibility of 1834 and the means to put it into practice, the workhouse. However, it was the *deterrent* rather than the positive dimension of what Foucault would no doubt call Bentham's 'semio-technical' programme which became manifest in the reform of the administration of relief.

Bentham: pauperism and government

The table of pauperism

On September 1797, Bentham addressed a letter to the editor of the *Annals of Agriculture*, Arthur Young, entitled 'Situation and Relief of the Poor' (Bentham 1843, 8: 361–362). In it a project was outlined for the collection of information to form the raw material for two volumes, 'Pauper Systems Compared' and 'Pauper Management Improved'. The project required a mode of knowledge which was both statistical and taxonomic. Its statistical aspect was embodied in a blank 'Pauper

Population Table', 'being a Table framed for the purposes of collecting
an account of the Pauper Population in as many parishes, etc., as I may
be able to obtain it from' (361). Bentham sent the Pauper Population
Table to Young in the hope that parishes would return lists of all paupers
and their particulars. According to his editor, Bowring, it is probable
that he obtained few returns (356).

Nevertheless, the form of knowledge which is appropriate to
pauperism cannot be a simple matter of the documentation of the
particulars of each individual. Each individual must be treated as a *case*
(cf Foucault 1977a: 189–192). But in order to effect such a treatment,
it is further necessary to bring an exhaustive system of classification to
bear on this documentation. The capacity for making such a classification is given by the other table sent to Young, the Table of Cases Calling
for Relief, which Bentham called a 'general Map of *Pauper-Land*, with
all the *Roads* to it' (1843, 8: 361).

The Table of Pauperism, as we shall call the form of knowledge
instanced by this second table, may be thought to be merely an extension
of the classificatory system of the Discourse of the Poor in the seventeenth and eighteenth centuries. Yet, unlike that earlier discursive form,
this system of classification does not attempt to divide the 'numbers of
the Poor'. Its object is quite different. It is not a table of the complete
population of 'the Poor' but only that segment of the population made
up of 'cases calling for relief', and is thus premised on the distinction
made by Bentham in the previous year between poverty and indigence.
It was shown that 'the Poor' were constituted in earlier governmental
discourse as among the things to be administered by the state. Here
poverty has been removed from the proper objects of adminstration and
as an object of classification. Poverty is unclassifiable. It is the unalterable
and general state of humankind and therefore indivisible by any system
of classification. Moreover, because poverty is the source of that labour
which is the motor of civilisation, the condition of poverty, although
eternal, opens on to the possibility of history and progress. Only
pauperism is left fixed and immobile, outside the moralising dimension
of labour. It is the result of an antithetical process, leading not to
production, history, and civilisation, but to inertia. Because of this
subversion of the historical dynamic it is appropriate that pauperism alone
can be located within the fixed grid of the table. The map of 'Pauper-
Land' shows the topography of a region which falls outside history and
threatens its dynamism.

The rationale for the two tables reveals the form of knowledge which
is appropriate to the whole region of indigence. The Pauper Population
Table is contrived for the purpose of collecting information of the
'permanent stock' of paupers on indoor and outdoor relief (Bentham
1843, 8: 365). Such a table, however, cannot show all those who may

call for relief, for it misses the 'degraded classes', all those 'whose condition shuns the light', from thieves to beggars and prostitutes. The Table of Cases Calling for Relief is of a far more general type, casting within a representational form of knowledge the totality of possible cases that are found in Pauper-Land. It comprises

> Every individual that can ever enter into the composition of the general mass:- *the coming-and-going stock*, as well as the *permanent*:- the *able-bodied*, as well as the *infirm*:- those who, under the existing order of things, come in but for *casual relief*; as well as those who, under the system of *community maintenance*, are *constantly* in the *House*; and those who, under the system of *home-maintenance*, are *constantly* upon the list of *pensioners*.
>
> (Bentham 1843, 8: 365)

The Table of Pauperism is a form of knowledge which seeks to bring an exhaustive order to that region of the body politic which is shrouded in obscurity and opacity, the abyss of indigence (cf Bahmueller 1981: 5–6). Among the 'Observations' appended to the Table, Bentham states 'that every provision which regards the indigent, in the lump, either as virtuous or as viscious – either as objects of pure compassion, or as objects of pure coercion or pure neglect – must be fatally erroneous'. The mode of combating the moral and administrative contingency represented by pauperism requires, for Bentham, the analytical clarity of the Table. Thus this form of knowledge is subservient to three practical subjects of consideration, according to the note at the top of the Table:

1 The nature and degree of prevalence of *each efficient cause of Indigence* (the degree being measured by the number, absolute and comparative, of the Individuals reduced to Indigence by each efficient cause);

2 The *cause, degree*, and *duration*, of the inability in respect to *Work*;

3 The *mode* and *degree* of *Relief* or *Prevention*, practised or practicable, adequate or inadequate, eligible or ineligible.

(Bentham 1843, 8: Table of Cases etc)

Against the chaos of pauperism, then, the Table of Pauperism classifies by means of a determination of efficient causes, locates each class in respect of labour-capacity, and thereby deduces the mode of relief or prevention necessary.

Causes may be 'personal or internal' or 'external'. The former may be of 'perpetual', 'long-continuing', and 'casual' duration; the latter are all of 'uncertain duration'. The internal causes are infirmity of mind, infirmity of body, 'non-age', inability with regard to work, and unwillingness with regard to work. The external causes are loss of work, inability to obtain work, and loss of property. Under these eight causes are arranged twenty-two cases calling for relief which are, in turn, further subdivided into a total of 137 subcases. Each of these cases and sub-cases, including those indigent through perpetual infirmity of mind or body, are referred to as 'Hands'. The reason for this is given in obser-vation (a) of the Table: 'The word *Hands* is chosen, as bearing reference to *Employment*, serving thereby to point the attention to the consideration of *Employment*, to which persons thus characterised, may respectively be competent or incompetent'. The Table of Pauperism, as a map of Pauper-Land, is organised in reference to that sphere which is its other, the sphere of labour and the order it brings. Labour provides the indispensable point of reference for each classification. It is the origin and the end of the form of knowledge which is the Table of Pauperism. At the origin of pauperism, and the knowledge of it, is the incapacity of individuals to obtain their subsistence by labour. The end of the knowledge displayed in the Table is the proper mode of management of each class of pauper, including the appropriate labour for each.

To understand the 'pervasive repressiveness', the soul-destroying regimentation, the scant regard for civil liberties, and the near absence of emotional sensitivity of Bentham's pauper Utopia (Bahmueller 1981: 2), it is necessary to recognise that we have entered a new region beyond the imperative of self-supporting labour. We have crossed over to the unthinkable for the Adamite economy of exchange, into the moral abyss and administrative confusion of Pauper-Land, a region devoid of the one rational action which establishes the civil individuality, and even the humanity, of the propertyless class, and guarantees order to the activities of the mass of humankind, the exchange of labour.

Bentham's pauper establishments

The Table of Pauperism is a form of knowledge which comprehends indigence as specific cases which are the products of different causes and which could be governed only by means appropriate to each. There is thus an equivalence between knowledge and administrative response for each individual case. More significantly, however, there is a fundamental equivalence between the Table of Pauperism as a whole and the practice of pauper management.

> To state the particular use, the contemplation of which gave birth to each distinction, would be to state the plan of provision in contempla-tion for each class:- to state the particular plan of provision in contemplation for each class, would be to give the entire work of which this paper is but an offset. This much, however, may be observed, that of all the classes there distinguished, there is not one, the

circumstances of which have not in the framing of the plan of provision been specially taken into account.

(Bentham 1843, 8: 365)

Bentham's 'industry houses' were not simply pragmatically designed administrative enclosures. They were to be the practical equivalent of the knowledge of pauperism, the manifestation of such knowledge in concrete form. If the Table was to bring to light the manifold and hidden forms of pauperism, the houses would form a series of chains across the kingdom, a 'net-work' which would forever remove administrative particularity, dispersion, and disconnection (Bahmueller 1981: 5). Within them, paupers were to be located and grouped according to their work-capacity in the same manner as they were laid across the Table. Their sequestration would mirror its closed space. They would be subject to strict modes of *separation* and *aggregation* in the same way that each pauper was treated as a separate case with characteristics which determine its relations with other cases. And finally, just as the totality of cases were spread out across the Table before the rational subject of knowledge of pauperism, so too, in the house, paupers were to be subject to the 'censorial' eye of their governors, or at least to its omnipresent possibility, under the principle of central inspection.

This brings us to the design of Bentham's workhouses. They were to be designed, like his prisons, as Panopticons, the architectural features of which are familiar to the readers of Foucault (1977a: 195–228). The latter was concerned to stress the way in which the Panopticon 'individualised' its inmates (200–202). He argued that the design constitutes them as 'objects of knowledge' rather than as subjects of communication. This happens because of the system of visibility set up by the Panopticon. In it, the inmates are conscious of their constant visibility from the central inspection tower which they can always see but, by slats or blinds, into which they cannot see. Moreover, communication between inmates is denied due to the lateral invisibility between the cells at the periphery of the building. According to Foucault, each inmate is placed in a position of 'sequestered and observed solitude' and forms, from the perspective of their guards, a 'multiplicity that can be numbered and supervised' (201). It is important to note that, although each inmate is aware of the mechanism of surveillance, he or she can never know when it is in use. Therefore, Foucault concluded, the Panopticon encapsulates the principle that power should be both visible and unverifiable, at least from the perspective of those upon whom it is exercised.

While we can accept that Bentham's houses of industry used such tactics of visibility to normalise paupers, it would be highly reductive of their polymorphous character to reduce them to ideal schemas of disciplinary power. Bentham's pauper establishments are not simply machines to produce 'docile and obedient' bodies but multi-functional nodes within a total network for the quarantining and prevention of pauperism.[3]

Before exploring some of these functions, let us consider another, relatively underdeveloped image of the Panopticon given by Foucault. In a short paragraph (1977a: 205), Foucault presented a striking comparison with Le Vaux's royal menagerie at Versailles. There the king's central salon looked out, through large windows, on to cages containing different species of animals arranged at the periphery of an octagonal building. This menagerie should not be viewed as curiosity but as the embodiment of the naturalist's knowledge, just as Bentham understood his pauper Panopticon as the embodiment of the Table of Cases Calling for Relief. The knowledge-function of the menagerie and the pauper establishment are intriguingly similar: both involve the drawing up of differences, the observation and assessment of characters, behaviours, and symptoms, and both allow the making of classifications. Paupers, like the species of the naturalist, are distributed according to fixed types defined by a given set of invariable attributes. It is these attributes of the different classes of pauper, rather than their potential for normalisation, which formed the basis of their distribution in the Panopticon. Consider, for example, Bentham's principle of vicinity.

Principle of Vicinity: Next to every class, from which any inconvenience is to be apprehended, station a class unsusceptible of that inconvenience. 1. Next to the raving *lunatics*, or persons of *profligate conversation*, place the *deaf and dumb*, if included in the same establishment, and separated as to sight. 2. Next to *prostitutes*, and other *loose women*, place the aged women. 3. Within the view of the abodes of the *blind*, place melancholy and *silent* lunatics, or the shockingly *deformed*.

(Bentham 1843, 8: 372)

The comparison of the pauper establishment with the menagerie can only be taken so far. It should not be thought to imply that paupers were regarded as wild animals. Bentham, in fact, was inclined to regard them as similar to *domesticated* animals, 'that part of the national live stock which has no feathers to it and walks with two legs' (1843, 8: 366–367). This is indeed an appropriate comparison for post-Adamite pauper management. Paupers, it is true, due to their descent from poverty, and their incapacity to provide for themselves through labour, have ceased to be rational subjects of labour and exchange, and thereby have forfeited their 'species-being' as humans. Yet one could not say that paupers have become animals in the wild, for the latter are able to provide their own subsistence. Paupers, for this type of administration, were neither beast nor quite fully human, but belonged to a semi-socialised, hyper-natural interworld. Pauper management might be thought of as dealing with a region which cannot be assimilated into the dichotomy in nature between the rational, labouring, human subject and the animal 'kingdom'. It has thus more than a passing resemblance to animal husbandry, tending and directing the indigent to prevent them becoming burdensome and turning them to the benefit of humanity. Pauper management is thus about directing sexual desire and procreation, preventing contagion and disease, averting dangers, and placing them in arrangements which fostered those qualities which are beneficial to civilisation.

Bentham's pauper establishments, however, cannot be reduced to a single figure, whether to disciplinary mechanisms of normalisation, or to the sites where the social engineer-cum-naturalist arranges different species of pauper. Foucault asserted (1977a: 205) that the Panopticon was polyvalent in its application; it must be added that it was multi-functional, at least in respect of paupers.

This can be illustrated by considering the purposes for which this architectural form was to be used in Bentham's plan of pauper management. These purposes first of all come under the heading of 'separation'. Although Bentham proposed four 'means of separation' (separate huts, forms of building, ways of laying out land, and separate hours), it was to be the form of the common building with its uncommunicating divisions which secured the major separation functions (Bentham 1843, 8: 372). Separation was justified for a variety of functions, including the 'preservation of *health* from infection', the preservation of morals, decency, and unsatisfiable desires, security against all types of annoyances, occasional concealment of the paupers against 'the *censorial eye* of the governing class', security of the governing class against the 'evil-disposed' among the governed, and educational, moral, and experimental distinction between 'the *indigenous, quasi-indigenous, extraneous* and *coming-and-going stock* of the *non-adult class* (Bentham 1843, 8: 372).

The purposes for which aggregation, on the other hand, was useful were 'matrimonial society', 'family society', 'nursing attendance', 'medical attendance', 'moral superintendence', 'instruction and direction of labour', and 'intercommunity of work and labour' (Bentham 1843, 8: 372).

These purposes of separation and aggregation reveal the pauper establishments as multi-functional, combining elements of the quarantine station, prison, school, hospital, nursing home, manufactory, and research institute. Bentham's pauper Panopticon is not simply a diagram of power but a programme for an enclosed, alternative economy and polity for those who descended into an amoral abyss. Indeed, in his letter to the *Annals* he regarded his plans for pauper management as Utopia (1843, 8: 362). Given that it *is* odd to describe a poorhouse as a Utopia

(Himmelfarb 1970: 114), we should ask of its various functions in what ways could that be so.

First, the pauper Panopticon partook of the very imagery of the epidemic by which pauperism was conceived in the pamphlet and periodical literature of the time (e.g. Chalmers 1832: 399–400).[4] As that imagery drew upon the figures of the leper and the plague victim, so Bentham's pauper establishment was designed in such a way as to superimpose the rituals of exclusion which had been characteristic of the treatment of lepers upon the 'tactical partitioning' characteristic of the quarantine regulations during plagues and epidemics (Foucault 1977a: 198). Under Bentham's plan no relief would be offered except upon entering the pauper establishment, and the partitioning of paupers was justified in terms of the prevention of both physical infection and moral corruption (1843, 8: 369). Pauper management is utopian as a plan which prevents the most fundamental dangers to the existence of civil society, and thus averts the real possibility of a dystopia.

Second, the pauper Panopticon takes the most ambitious functions of the classical workhouse and projects them on to a utopian scale. It reiterated – and enlarged – the eighteenth-century dream of setting the Poor to work. The incapacity to work would become only a relative matter: 'Real inability is relative only i.e. with reference to this or that species of employment or this or that situation' (Bentham 1843, 8: 382). Because the division of labour would be pushed to the utmost, the 'all-employing principle' would hold. Not only would children be apprenticed from the earliest possible age, but the blind would be employed in knitting or spinning, the bed-ridden with inspection, and duties could even be found for the insane. Thus the classical distinction between the impotent and the useful would no longer hold. Bentham's pauper establishment expands upon the classical workhouse ideal of being a self-subsisting institution, in which paupers would provide for their own needs under the principle of 'self-supply' (1843, 8: 382–383). The pauper establishments were to be utopian in so far as they rid society of the poor rates and a burdensome population.

Bentham's objectives in the sphere of employment never strayed far from the ideals established by those who first advocated setting the Poor to work in the seventeenth century. However, his methods for achieving their goals are more finely calibrated and more economical, and ultimately sought a greater degree of efficacy. They belong to a theory and practice of punishment found in eighteenth-century writings on government and law, which Foucault called 'semio-technique' (1977a: 93–103). Semio-technique uses the penalty as a sign. The penalty signifies the infraction in such a way as to direct each individual who is treated as a rational subject. It does this by associating the infraction with pain, and the desired behaviour with happiness, or with the avoidance of pain. The primary goal of a semio-technical system would be prevention or *deterrence*.

Pauper management aimed at affecting the behaviour of all paupers, potential or actual, in order to prevent pauperism and deter unwarranted applications for relief. Therefore it designed each measure as a sign to instruct the poor in the calculation of their own interests. If the poor were tempted to accept relief in preference to the hardships of labour, then a system of relief which was linked to labour under the irksome conditions of the Panopticons would remove the temptation to choose pauperism and impress upon the labouring poor the necessity of working for a living. Inside these establishments, the necessary link between the labour expended and the resultant earnings would be strengthened by the 'self-liberation' and 'earn-first' principles (Bentham 1843, 8: 383). Under the former, the rule would be established that paupers must work off the value of their relief before they could leave the house, and, under the latter, all able-bodied paupers would be compelled to work before eating. Such rules would act as signs to the pauper of the fundamental dependence of their subsistence upon their own labour, and not upon others'. As a system of signs instructing the pauper on the fundamental truths of human existence, the Benthamite system is utopian because it discovered a secure means of relief which not only respects but reiterates the laws of nature.

The pauper Panopticons were to function according to a set of rules which regulated all activities each day of the week. These rules are a veritable panoply of signs which seek to instruct the paupers. It is perhaps unsurprising that the establishment embrace a multiplicity of educative functions and give particular attention to the young. Child labour, from the age of four to twenty-one, under the 'apprenticeship principle', would be incorporated within a system of instruction. Bentham claimed that among the advantages of such a system would be the intellectual, moral, and religious instruction of children, the breeding of a systematic frugality among them (by means of 'Frugality Banks'), the prevention of vice and criminality, the certainty of employment during training and after, and the chance of promotion to rank and affluence (435–439). Further, internment of children in the House would be far healthier than an outdoor pauper upbringing due to the reduction of infant mortality, the constant medical and nursing attendance provided, and the ventilation and sanitary living conditions (Poynter 1969: 136). Bentham's educational programme, 'Chrestomathia', developed from his plans for pauper apprentices. Indeed, the standard of education he envisaged for them was to be such that he hoped that the upper classes would send their offspring to the House rather than to private schools (Bentham 1843, 8: 424–428; Poynter 1969: 137). At the point in which the educational and medical arrangements for pauper children come to embody the end of contingency and opacity, Bentham's pauper management arrived at a utopian condition for the upbringing of children.

The task of pauper management sketched by Bentham, and embodied in his pauper Panopticons, is a project which is irreducible to a simple classification of modern and pre-modern forms of discourse and institutional practice. It stands as the summation and culmination of earlier programmes of exclusion, sequestration, and make-work, and as the harbinger of the medical and educative functions of later state administration. Furthermore, it encompasses functions which belong neither to the wise administration of the Poor, as it was conceived in the seventeenth century, nor to the nineteenth-century liberal mode of government of poverty. In a manner which would have been unthinkable for a Matthew Hale a century earlier, or for the partisans of liberalism and socialism in the nineteenth and twentieth centuries, the pauper Panopticons were to be places for the augmentation and dissemination of 'Useful Knowledge', places of social experimentation (Bentham 1843, 8: 424–428). In this final sense, they are thus utopian because they are constantly self-improving establishments.

Bentham envisaged that his pauper establishments would become massive laboratories in which research could be undertaken in a wide number of fields. These included medicine, both therapeutic and dietetic, mechanics, chemistry, domestic economy, technical economy, husbandry, meteorology, bookkeeping, and logic (Bentham 1843, 8: 425). It also included a study of the effects of sexual relations upon the health and development of apprentices at various age intervals in order to discover at which age the 'comforts of matrimony' were most compatible with physical and intellectual maturation (Bahmueller 1981: 171–174). Bentham concluded:

> *Fiat lux* were the words of the Almighty: *Fiat experimentum*, were the words of the highest genius he ever made. O chemists: much have your crucibles shows us of dead matter; but our industry house is a crucible for men.

> (Bentham 1843, 8: 437)

Bentham's scheme belongs to a unique, relatively coherent, programme of management which brought available techniques and institutions into contact with the dystopia of contingency, contagion, and chaos of pauperism. Because pauperism represented all that was alien, opaque, and obscure in the ideal kingdom, a systematic mode of combating it would have to discover and represent an ideal of total transparency, illumination, and clarity. Bentham's Utopia is one of complete transparency, visibility, and inspectability. What is most significant about Bentham's scheme is that in the course of describing such a Utopia it was able to evince a particular form of administrative rationality which was flexible enough to adapt to more concrete situations, while rigorous enough to establish protocols for the reorganisation of the administration of assistance to the poor.

The principles of pauper management

We shall now seek to understand why Bentham differed from so many of his contemporaries who demanded the abolition of poor relief. We shall look at Bentham's general defence of public relief and his arguments on the particular principles which this relief must respect.

Bentham's ken is rather wider than that of the political economists. In his *Theory of Legislation* (1950) he placed four 'subordinate ends' of legislation under the ultimate end of utility or the general principle of the 'greatest happiness of the greatest number'. These ends were: to provide subsistence, to produce abundance, to favour equality, and to maintain security (1950: 96–97). Security, which included security of person, honour, property, and condition, assumed paramount importance (96). Bentham in fact lifted the subordinate end of security to the top of the hierarchy of the ends of government, so that conflict with other ends are invariably resolved in its favour (Boralevi 1984: 97–98).

The conflict between equality and security must always be resolved in favour of the latter (Bentham 1950: 120). Security is the 'foundation of life', on which 'subsistence, abundance, happiness, everything depends'. Perfect equality, however, is a 'chimera' and all that can be done is to diminish inequality. Further, security leads over time to greater equality. Bentham argued that security is a condition of the progress of agriculture, manufactures, and commerce, which inevitably produces a more equal distribution of property (122–123). The poor, he concluded, benefit from security as well as the rich, while 'equality, if taken as the basis of the social arrangement, will destroy both itself and security at the same time' (123).

The relation between security and subsistence is more complex. On the one hand, Bentham was inclined to argue that subsistence was not a matter of direct interference by government and could only be promoted indirectly by offering security to the fruits of labour, property (1950: 100). On the other hand, he invoked the end of security to justify the relief of indigence: 'The only sure means of protection against the effects of indigence consists in furnishing necessaries to those who are in need of them' (385). Among these effects are all the offences persons who are starving might be driven to in order to supply their wants. Governments must therefore provide subsistence to those who cannot provide for themselves, not because it is desirable to have greater equality, but because security must be maintained against the potential dangers of the indigent.

It was in this manner that Bentham could provide a rationale for poor relief which both respected and transcended the limitations of purely economic considerations. Bentham's theory of government, born out of eighteenth-century jurisprudential discourse, enabled him to place narrowly economic functions of subsistence and abundance within a context provided by the consideration of security.

Why could not the functions of poor relief be discharged by Christian charity, after the manner that would be suggested by the Reverend Chalmers (1912: 213–220)? Chalmers was to argue, somewhat later, that abolition of compulsory poor relief would unblock the 'fountains' of Christian charity, including the habits and economies of the people, the sympathy of the rich, the kindness of relatives, and the feelings of mutuality among the poorer classes. For Bentham, all these sources were capricious. Private charity, inspired by these feelings and emotions, consigned too important a task to obscurity and contingency. The problem with the principle of sympathy was that it afforded no 'objective criterion' of moral and political judgement (unlike the principle of utility), that it depended on the vagaries of sensibility and ought therefore to be called the principle of 'caprice' (Bentham 1950: 21n.; Boralevi 1984: 101; Poynter 1969: 124). Charity could err on the side of 'severity' or 'lenity' and it could be partial in its application (Boralevi 1984: 101–103). Charity was too open to the partiality, peculation, and corruption of unreformed forms of government. In this respect, the fountains of Christian charity were no better, if not worse, than the parochial administration of relief. Sympathy and benevolence, whether of the rich or of the parish, were not firm grounds for the administration of relief. This is not to deny the contribution of such moral sentiments. Indeed, Bentham (1843, 8: 428–430) left a place for charity in his plan of pauper management. Charity was not to be discouraged but regulated by law and strictly placed within a publicly enforced system of assistance and provision.

This was the basis of Bentham's advocacy of a centralised authority for paupers, of which he presented two versions. The first was a 'National Charity Company' (Bentham 1843, 8: 369–372); the second an 'Indigence Relief Ministry' (1843, 9: 441). The shift from a contract system to a state ministry, however, should not be taken to indicate a fundamental change in Bentham's views on the role of the state. Rather, as Boralevi (1984: 103) and Poynter (1969: 131) have shown, it is more likely that the shift reflects nothing more than Bentham's assessment of the different capacity of state administration in the 1820s, when he was drafting the *Constitutional Code* which included such a ministry, from that of the 1790s, when he proposed his system of pauper management.

The proposal for a National Charity Company was sketched in the late eighteenth century in *Pauper Management Improved* (Bentham 1843, 8: 369–372; Bahmueller 1981). The managing authority was to be a joint-stock company, run along the lines of the East India Company, the central board of which would have the power to raise capital, purchase land and construct buildings, and even to apprehend beggars and vagrants (Poynter 1969: 130-133). The Company was to be responsible for all aspects of the relief of the poor, including not only the 250 large houses of industry evenly dispersed across the nation, but also a multiplicity of 'collateral aids' for independent labourers and their families (Bentham 1843, 8: 373-379).

The Company was thus to be run on a contract basis as a profit-making venture. Its efficient management was to be ensured by means of self-interest, under the 'Duty and Interest Junction Principle' (Bentham 1843, 8: 380). Perhaps discovered in the writings of Burke in the 1780s, this principle was founded on the idea that 'a man may be said to have an interest in an object if it is a source of pleasure or pain, or security against pain' (quoted in Bahmueller 1981: 181). For employees and governors in the houses, this took a pecuniary form, not of fixed salaries, but of rewards and penalties. Hence, under the 'Life Assurance or Life Warranty Principle', the salaries of governors would vary according to the infant mortality rate, and the matron-midwife would pay head money for each woman who died in childbirth (Bentham 1843, 8: 381).

It is most likely that Bentham's use of a contract system of management in the 1970s was dictated by his view of the current condition of state administration, which he saw as liable to procrastination, lapses of parliamentary confidence, jobbery, and fund-raising difficulties (Poynter 1969: 131). That Bentham had later shifted in his view of the capabilities of state administration is evidenced by the inclusion of an Indigence Relief Minister among the thirteen specialist ministries in his Constitutional Code (Bentham 1843, 9: 441). Because the Code does not go into the details of the functioning of the particular ministries, it is difficult to assess the extent of their powers. Clearly, they were not to be minimal, since the Minister was 'to give execution and effect to all institutions, ordinances and arrangements, emanating from the Legislature, in relation to the relief of the Indigent'.

Bentham's administrative Utopia follows directly and without contradiction from the same principles as the moral economy of exchange. We have to go no further than the very principles enunciated by Smith to understand how Bentham could arrive at his exceedingly illiberal, authoritarian, and even repressive administrative regime, which would amount to an alternative, fully regulated economy within a wider state operating under the principles of economic liberalism. Bentham, unlike Smith, recognised one set of circumstances in which it is possible for the propertyless rationally to choose *not* to exchange their labour. This exceptional set of circumstances was summed up by Bentham in this statement:

If the condition of persons *maintained* without property *by the labour of others* were rendered more eligible than that of persons maintained by their *own labour* then, in proportion as the existence of this state of things were ascertained, individuals destitute of property would be continually withdrawing themselves from the class of persons maintained by their own labour, to the class of persons maintained by the labour of others: and the sort of idleness, which at present is more or less *confined* to persons of *independent* fortune, would thus extend itself sooner or later to every individual . . . till at last there would be *nobody* left to labour at all for anybody.

(quoted in Poynter 1969: 125–126)

The Adamite regard for the labourer as rational subject of exchange becomes, when poor relief is taken into account, a problem of the relative eligibility of conditions of labourer and pauper. It is this problem which was to guide the conditions under which relief could be granted. If relief was to appear more comfortable, desirable, or suitable than the situation of the ordinary labourer, then the poor, as rational subjects, would choose relief over labour. If one assumes labour is necessary to the creation of subsistence, wealth, and civilisation, it follows that relief should only be offered under conditions which preserve the rational preference for labour. This can be done, argued Bentham, only by granting relief to the poor person in such a way that 'public provision should appear less eligible to him than the provision resulting from his own labour' (quoted in Poynter 1969: 126).

Under this principle, Bentham's plan was not content merely to denounce the status of the pauper as morally inferior to that of the independent labourer. It would make that inferiority a feature of the actual conditions under which relief was granted. These conditions, in turn, would signify that inferiority. Moreover, they would signify that by preferring relief to labour, the pauper forfeits his treatment as a rational individual and hence his civil individuality and status of worker. The semio-technical element of the conditions of relief reveals how it is possible for those conditions to be at once designed as ideal provinces within the kingdom and to be less-eligible. In other words, it reveals how Utopia can be a deterrent!

An ensemble of signs signify the status an individual acquires when 'choosing' relief, the status of pauper. Bentham proposed a revival of the old practice of 'badging' of paupers by making uniforms compulsory. But was this not an infringement of the dignity of the pauper? Bentham thought not. The uniform was a sign of his or her station, it merely 'marks the class in which it finds' the pauper, and cannot thereby be said to degrade him or her (quoted by Bahmueller 1981: 162–163). Uniforms signify order, tidiness, recognition, and distinction. Because of the latter they could be used as forms of punishment and reward. A less-eligible condition does not have to be one which is materially worse than that of the lowest labourer, who might well be in a state of great impoverishment and lacking the material means of life in times of scarcity. It is one which is *signified* as less-eligible, and what better way to signify that than by a condition which deprives the pauper of common dignity and personal liberty? If this deprivation of freedoms is condemned as tyrannical or unjust, Bentham could reply that this was more than offset by the freedom from want (1843, 8: 436). Reliance on public assistance implied a civil as well as an economic incapacity and legitimated – nay, necessitated – forms of public regimentation: 'Soldiers wear uniforms, why not paupers? Those who save the country, why not those who are saved by it?' (quoted by Poynter 1969: 126).

Similarly, the pauper establishments did not simply use the architectural plans of a model prison. They were very much like prisons themselves. Bentham envisaged a rounding-up of the pauper population on their opening. He wanted their governors to have continued powers of apprehension, and control over all aspects of paupers' daily lives when once inside, including when they would be able to leave. With their 'punishment book' to record petty infractions, their two perimeter fences, between which would grow timber plantations, and their movable 'watchhouses', the houses of industry become more like fortified prisons than almshouses. All this, however, was not a form of punishment. Bentham claimed that 'in the provision there made there is nothing that can with propriety be termed a punishment' (quoted in Bahmueller 1981: 150). These were all merely appropriate to the civil incapacity of being unable to procure one's own subsistence through labour.

As Boralevi has shown (1984: 105–106), although absolute sexual liberty was one of Bentham's principles, it did not extend to paupers. If paupers could not be the best judge of their own self-interest in the exchange of labour, and were hence disposed to vice and crime, then they could not best judge their own sexual behaviour. The unchaste female hands, prostitutes, unwed mothers, brothel-keepers, and procuresses, would be kept in a detached building (Bentham 1843, 8: 373). The maintenance of 'female virtue' under the governess and her subordinates would be more assured than in the best families. Wives could find asylum in the house against tyrannical husbands, and husbands could be assured of their wives' fidelity while in the house. The opportunity for 'conversation with the other sex' would come only 'in a safe manner and at safe times' (Bahmueller 1981: 169–170). That Bentham took every opportunity to assure his readers of his intention to 'preserve chastity' in his pauper arrangements is due no doubt to fear of failure if his plan were thought to allow for the sexual promiscuity allegedly found in eighteenth-century poorhouses. However, such a claim is perfectly

191

consistent with the principles and would-be practice of Benthamite pauper management. Under the principle of the less-eligible conditions of relief, Bentham held that the mere incapacity of the poor to subsist through labour was sufficient to warrant a denial of common liberties and moral self-determination. That this is so fundamental to his scheme is borne out by the fact that many of the cases in Bentham's classification had causes which could in no way imply a diminution of moral capacity (e.g. casual-stagnation hands, periodical-stagnation hands, those with infirmities, etc.).

This principle, promoted by Bentham in his plans for pauper management in the 1790s, was to become the guiding light of the reformed poor law. The *1834 Poor Law Report* expressed it in these terms:

> The first and most essential of all conditions, a principle which we find universally admitted, even by those who practice is at variance with it, is that his [i.e. the pauper's] situation on the whole shall not be made really or apparently so eligible as the situation of the independent labourer of the lowest class.
>
> (Checkland and Checkland 1974: 335)

There were many differences between Bentham's plan and the reformed poor-law administration after 1834. Nevertheless, it is incontrovertible that the crucial distinction between poverty and indigence, and the granting of relief in such a way as to make this a distinction of actual condition under the principle of less-eligibility, are both first found in the tracts of Bentham. It may well be the case that 'semio-technique' is superseded by a new 'politics of the body' in the field of punishment (Foucault 1977a). Shorn of its utopian ideals and ambitions and its polyvalent functionality, this semio-technique will survive in a region adjacent to but quite distinct from punishment, that of the administration of relief. Bentham's pauper Panopticons may be safely left to the peripheral 'chamber of horrors' of the history of poverty and its relief. The principles which animated them, and the means by which they were supposed to operate, did not. The mid-nineteenth-century workhouse is a crude instrument compared to the gaudy grandeur and finely-tuned regulation of Bentham's plans. Its necessity and justification, however, would still remain as a sign to all who should look upon it of the degraded status and civil dependence of pauperdom.

Chapter eleven

The mechanisms of prevention

One of the functions of Bentham's Table of Cases Calling for Relief was to ascertain the mode of *prevention* of pauperism. Indeed, one could say that both his scheme of pauper management and the actual reforms of 1834 sought to establish an apparatus to prevent the pauperisation of the labouring population. This notion of prevention assumed, at this period, an increasing number of guises in the discussion of poverty, and was prominent in arguments for a police force as we know it. Before investigating arguments for the latter, it is instructive to examine the principle of prevention at work in a body of writing which, at first glance, might be thought to evince a somewhat different perspective from that of Benthamite administration, that of Robert Owen.

Owen enters into the debate on pauperism and the poor laws briefly in the second decade of the nineteenth century with his proposals of village settlements, the famous Parallelograms of Paupers in which 1,200 persons would be employed and educated in self-supplying communities for their own mutual benefit. Owen was a manufacturer who saw the development of manufacturing as the cause of distress, an agitator for factory legislation who advocated spade cultivation, a critic of political economy and competition who was contemptuous of religion – a kind of admixture of the philanthropic and agrarian elements of a secular Toryism, utopianism, and inchoate socialism.

The fact that Bentham had been induced to invest in Owen's mills at New Lanark in 1813 (Halévy 1928: 285) perhaps symbolises the tenor of a period in which the social outcome of demographic, political, and economic changes had not yet been resolved into clear lines of intellectual demarcation and partisanship. It is worth noting, in passing, that unlike many of his other investments, this was one which yielded a profit for Bentham!

Our interest here, however, is in Owen's statement of the preventive imperative of his early nineteenth-century plans. In the *Report to the Committee of the Association for the Relief of the Manufacturing and Labouring Poor* included in his *A New View of Society* (1818), Owen, although a staunch anti-abolitionist, condemns the poor laws in the Malthusian language of the day, and argues instead for a preventive plan for the poor, particularly in regard to the habits passed between the generations. He argued that until laws are framed on the principle of prevention 'it will be vain to look for any measures beyond partial temporary expedients, which leave society unimproved, or involve it in a much worse state' (Owen 1818: 19–20). Yet, despite the trajectory his thought would take, and his already articulated conception of human nature, this change is not thought of as a problem of emancipation but, as in Benthamite administration, as one of management. It would be 'a material improvement in the management of the poor to place them under such circumstances as would obviously unite their real interest and duty, and remove them from unnecessary temptation' (10).

Management was thus conceived as a practice of acting upon the 'character' of the poor by placing them in those circumstances 'which, being congenial to the natural constitution of man, and the well-being of society, cannot fail to produce the amelioration in their condition, which all classes have so great an interest in promoting' (Owen 1818: 13). But whatever the communalism drawn from it, these congenial circumstances are conceived in exactly the same manner as in Bentham's own 'parallelogram' of paupers, his Panopticons, as circumstances which are designed to instruct in the intimate linkage between interest and duty, between subsistence and labour.

The field of knowledge of the poor came to be occupied by an interplay between character and circumstances or conditions. However, this field remained *pre*-sociological and *pre*-social in so far as it maintained a static reference to the natural constitution of humankind, and a theory of motivation and action anchored in the rational, calculating subject we first found in Adamite moral economy. Under such a theory, if the poor are placed in circumstances suited to their nature, their vicious characters will improve. If, on the contrary, they are allowed to lead the unnatural existence of the pauper in which their duty to labour is not supported by a private interest in their own subsistence, then their characters will degenerate. Generally, then, the discussion of the poor in the early nineteenth century was conducted around the means by which the prevention of this degeneration could be implemented. In this context, then, to prevent meant to act on the circumstances and conditions which pauperised the poor. This concept of a preventive form of management of the poor was addressed in a variety of ways at this time. One proposed solution was contained in the argument for a preventive police.

Colquhoun's preventive police

We are now in a position to take up our earlier concern with police.

The shift in the discourse of police is crucially linked to the liberal transformation in modes of government.

The transformation of the meanings and functions of police can be illustrated in the writings of Patrick Colquhoun, particularly his *A Treatise on Indigence* (1806) and *A Treatise on the Police of the Metropolis* (6th edn, 1805). It should also be noted, however, that Edwin Chadwick's career was launched with his influential unsigned article on 'Preventive Police' in the *London Review* in 1829 (Radzinowicz 1956: 448–474). This article brought Chadwick into contact with Bentham, who a few weeks later would engage him as a secretary and entrust him with the task of writing two sections of his *Constitutional Code*. Bentham, a close associate and admirer of Colquhoun, had himself written extensively on police matters since the last quarter of the eighteenth century. Despite their differences, what is significant in the new approach to matters of police exemplified by Colquhoun and Bentham, and later by Chadwick, is the presence of a panoply of measures specifically designed for a systematic, effective, and economical strategy for the prevention of crime. These measures include the establishment of a perpetually vigilant body concerned with the detection of crime governed by a central board; an agency to collect such intelligence to ascertain the types and causes of crime; a ministry of police; the cultivation and employment of spies and informers; and the systematisation of rewards. The question of the reform of police and the reform of poor relief are linked not only by the common strategy of prevention, but also by the articulation of this strategy upon the terrain of pauperism.

Colquhoun's new science of police and his reforms can be conceived first as the assertion of the juridical rights of individuals against the arbitrary despotism of existing regimes of punishment and police regulation; second, as the concern to develop police as a permanent administrative apparatus of prevention; and third, as the identification of pauperism as the region within the population which is most closely associated with the commission of crime.

On the first point, Becarria had already criticised the French system of police as the narrow-minded pursuit and reduction of the 'turbulent activity of men to geometrical harmony without any irregularity or confusion' (quoted by Radzinowicz 1956: 427). Colquhoun used this critique to advance his own arguments: 'It will not be altogether possible, amid the various attractions of pleasure and pain, to reduce the tumultuous activity of mankind to absolute regularity: we can only hope for a considerable reduction of the evils that exist' (1805: 73). Colquhoun employed the *Ideologues'* semio-technical critique of existing modes of punishment to arrive at his understanding of police. If there are too many regulations, if they do not discriminate between slight and serious offences, if punishment is out of proportion to the crime, if capital punishment is used for all manner of offences, then 'State Policy' will have 'the appearance of a cruelty not less severe than any which is exercised under the most despotic Governments' (Colquhoun 1805: 32–39). Police must be reformed because existing measures lead to an infringement of the liberties and rights of individuals and to tyranny. The new science of police specifies the global project of general happiness characteristic of the *Polizeiwissenschaft* in relation to a new juridical individuality, the rational, calculating subject. Police had become the 'art of conducting men to the *maximum* of happiness and the *minimum* of misery' (72).

The second way of conceiving the novelty of this new police is by considering how it safeguards the rights of the individual by setting up an apparatus, completely separate from judicial power, for the prevention and detection of crime. In this regard Colquhoun went somewhat further than Bentham. Where the latter had preserved the eighteenth-century classification of police so that 'the prevention of offences' was but one among eight departments (Bentham 1843, 3: 169), Colquhoun offered a newer, more restricted definition:

> Police in this country may be considered as a *new science*: the properties of which consist not in the Judicial Powers which lead to *Punishment*, and which belong to the Magistrates alone; but in the PREVENTION and DETECTION OF CRIMES, and in those other Functions which relate to INTERNAL REGULATIONS for the well-ordering and comfort of Civil Society.
>
> (Colquhoun 1805, preface, original emphasis)

This new police used the notion of prevention to argue for a permanent apparatus charged with the 'intricate and laborious investigation' into the causes of crime, and the dangers to private and public property and security, and with the implementation of measures to avert such dangers and crimes. While police had earlier been the condition of order of a well-governed community, and the regulations which establish this condition, it now became the techniques for the preservation of order ('keeping the peace') by the prevention and detection of dangers to that order (crimes). It is paradoxical, perhaps, that during the same epoch in which 'oeconomy' as a set of techniques of government was displaced by a quasi-autonomous reality to which political action must submit, police ceased to be a positive condition of the polity and became a technique of security.

For Colquhoun the delimitation of the field of action of police was conceived in terms of the problem of indigence. This is the third point. The condition of pauperism was closely allied with the causes of crime. Indeed so much was this the case that Colquhoun produced his 'Table of the Indigent and Criminal Classes of Great Britain' (1806: 38–43).

He argued that indigence produced a disposition to 'moral and criminal offences' and therefore 'it will be found impracticable to ameliorate the condition of the poor without taking effectual measures at the same time for the prevention of criminal offences' (49).

Thus the key rationale for the establishment of a police force concerned the familiar fear of the effect of the descent of poverty into pauperism. The 'useful Poor' by their industry are the 'actual pillars of the State' (Colquhoun 1805: 365). Therefore, they 'merit the utmost attention of all governments, with a direct and immediate view of preventing their poverty descending unnecessarily into *indigence*' (366). Indigence or pauperism is thus the result of a progressive breaking down of the barriers which uphold 'honest industry' and the 'influence of moral principle' in what Colquhoun saw as a new world era (562–564). It is at the level of this progressive descent that Colquhoun ultimately defined the fundamental target of his police.

> It is not pecuniary aid that will heal this 'gangrene': this 'Corruption of Morals'. There must be the application of a correct system of Police calculated to reach the root and origin of the evil . . . . In all branches of Political Economy, there is none which requires so much skill and knowledge of men and manners, as that which relates to this particular object.
>
> (Colquhoun 1805: 358–359)

So while economic discourse was forming a conception of poverty as governed by natural laws and necessary to the functioning of the economy and the production of wealth, Colquhoun's new science of police sought to preserve this poverty by preventing its collapse into indigence, from whence would come the temptation to crime and vice. His police would do this, however, not by the less-eligible sequestration and disciplining of pauperism, but by the establishment of an intelligence and supervisory mechanism to prevent those modes of conduct which transformed the poor into a danger to the security of the state, property, and life. If Benthamite administration sought a partition which signified the difference between pauperism and poverty, police would seal off poverty from the temptation to crime. In the new science of police, pauperism, indigence, mendicity, vice, and crime begin to form a coherent chain of signifiers which specify the contours of a definite mode of life of poverty.

Although closely associated with the criminal, the indigent remains a relatively distinct category for Colquhoun. On his Table (1806: 38–43) there are the 'casual poor' who are occasionally thrown on relief in times of lack of employment as well as those who, by their age or infirmity, are unable to labour. The point at which the indigent and criminal are linked on Colquhoun's Table was represented by the estimated 1,320,716 members of the population of Great Britain who 'live chiefly or wholly upon the labours of others' (43). Thus, there is an omnipresent possibility of the movement between indigence and criminality. There are those persons who lack work and gradually grow accustomed to idleness, whose energies become dissipated and who then 'connect themselves with those who live by petty or more atrocious means, and contribute in no small degree to the increase of the general phalanx of delinquents' (354). Once this occurs, the children of this group become ignorant of any other means of subsistence, and 'resort to devices which early corrupt their morals, and mar their future success and utility in life' (355).

It might be argued that, despite their significance in the history of police reform, these writings are of minor importance compared to the great intellectual achievements of their age. It can be replied that in their frankness and their concern with practical objects they reveal as much about social transformation as their more notable contemporaries. The writings of Colquhoun illustrate the terms in which the implantation of an administrative infrastructure to provide security for the operation of capitalist social relations could be conceived. Moreover, they exemplify the polymorphous nature of an administrative rationality concerned with the problem of pauperism. The aims of this rationality, whether in the fields of poor law reform, police reform, or a host of other projects of state administration, remained the preservation of poverty and the dispauperisation of the labouring masses. It is the means employed which differed in each case.

In the pages of the economists, a liberal governance of poverty was constructed around a liberal economy symbolised by the independent labourer. To the jurists, magistrates, and administrators, this economy would only be secured by the walls of the workhouse which signified to the labourers outside their difference in status to that of the pauper. Yet such a difference could only be sustained through a concert of measures which checked the constant temptation to vice and crime. Out of such crude mechanisms, a form of life consistent with the contractual exchange of labour-power, and the patriarchal responsibility of the worker, was in the process of being fashioned. The economy was self-regulating, and the poor would become wage-labourers, to be sure, but only in the space defined between crime and pauperism. Between the social implantation of a mechanism for the prevention and detection of crime, a police, and the institutional face of the distinction between labour and relief, the workhouse, the propertyless were granted the juridical individuality of the worker with the implicit patriarchal status of breadwinner.

In both cases, the preventive nature of the remedy to pauperism and its effects required the establishment of a permanent, centralised apparatus of state administration. By a strange twist, then, the liberal proscription of the relief of poverty on the grounds that it was governed by natural laws, does not lead to a minimal state, as might be expected, but to a fundamental reorganisation and extension of the powers and prerogatives of state administration.

In the previous chapter we sought to understand how the constitution of an administrable domain was made possible though the notion of pauperism. For the most part, this theme has been addressed in terms of the problem of establishing the efficacy of this administrative discourse in guiding the reform of the poor law. As Colquhoun's new science of police illustrates, however, the same field of intervention could be employed to argue for the necessity of administrative structures not directly connected with matters of relief. Here, the problem of pauperism begins to become attached to a chain of effects which marks the spiral of the labouring poor into degradation. As yet, the conditions of labour itself have not been understood as a possible source of such a movement. In the recognisably *social* investigations of the 1830s and 1840s, labour is no longer simply an end of the governance of poverty. The form that labour takes is viewed as having deleterious, demoralising, and pauperising effects. The social question comes to be formed against a concern with the conditions of the labouring population.

The condition of the labouring population

The problem of pauperism occupied a key place in a particular form of social investigation which became prominent in Britain from the fourth decade of the nineteenth century. This form of investigation might be called 'the condition of the labouring population' after that which it constructed as its object. A contemporary form of social investigation in France called *l'économie sociale* shared its characteristic concerns with pauperism and with the effects of the urban–industrial organisation of labour (Procacci 1978).[1]

For the liberal mode of government in the first half of the nineteenth century, poverty was rendered administrable through this notion of pauperism which is constructed in relation to a specific theoretical discourse on the economy, a particular understanding of the moral position of the labourer and *his* family, and a specific conception of state administration. Pauperism came to be emblematic of the rationality which was immanent to this governance not because it is the expression of an essential economic logic but because it marks the more or less coherent assemblage of specific social practices, theories, programmes, and interventions.

There are important differences between the notion of pauperism in *l'économie sociale* and in pre-1834 English discussion. For example, where the former defined pauperism as an urban phenomenon and identified it with characteristics of mobility and independence from social control (Procacci 1978: 64–65), the poor-law debate regarded pauperism as an agrarian problem associated with the stagnation in the mobility of labour caused by poor-relief practices and the law of settlements. Where the French analyses spoke of the breakdown of relations of subordination, the debate around the poor law contrasted the dependence of the pauper with the independence of the wage-labourer. Doubtless these shifts in the notion of pauperism are due to the different contexts of the respective debates. '*L'économie sociale*' is a phenomenon of the 1840s focusing on the ill effects of urbanism and industrialism while the poor-law debates were initiated at the turn of the century and dealt with problems of rural distress, famine, and the institutional barriers to the taking up of wage-labour by the poor. The differences, however, which are mirrored in the English literature after the 1830s, indicate something of the pivotal role played by the reform of the poor law in the emergence of the 'social question', and, indeed, of the whole field of social problems.[2]

Eugène Buret in his award-winning essay of 1840 proposed a new form of study, one which would supplement the analysis of wealth with that of distress and hence provide a veritable critique of political economy. He asked:

> Is not the study of distress an integral and necessary part of political or social economy, or the physiology of society, as it may better be called? We do not consider the statement that the picture of the wealth of nations must be confronted with the picture of the distress of nations is merely a play on words. The latter part of the science does more than supplement the former; it provides a test, a critique and a means of verifying it.

(Buret, quoted by Chevalier 1973: 143–144)

Buret's question should be considered if we are to understand *how* poverty was to become a – if not *the* – characteristic concern for the 'moral sciences', and hence play a central role in the development of statistical social science. While the 1840s gave birth to Marx's much more famous critique of political economy, they also gave rise on both sides of the Channel to a far more immediately successful critique which would lead to the forebears of empirical sociology. In France, this critique urged that, adjacent to its great wealth, the new urban and industrial scene reduced whole populations to a slow starvation accompanied by both physical and moral distress; that alongside the greatest achievements of civilisation is a state of barbarism, vice, and destitution, which threatens that very civilisation by producing a class dangerous to the social order (Chevalier 1973: 139–144).

Contrary to the prognostications of political economy, the 'so-called social science', as Buret put it, poverty and vice are not exceptional but permanent effects of the state of industry, of trade and commercial crises, of fluctuations in the demand for labour, and the concentration and multiplication of 'nomads' (Chevalier 1973: 139). These were Frégier's 'dangerous classes' who, due to their ignorance and insecurity of subsistence, are the fertile ground for crime: 'The poor and vicious classes have always been and always will be the most productive breeding ground of evildoers of all sorts; it is they whom we shall designate as the dangerous classes' (Frégier, quoted in Chevalier 1973: 141). The dangerous classes are both a problem for governments, and also, as Buret said, a threat to the certainties of economic science: 'This ever-growing accumulation of social distresses has caused governments serious alarm and has sadly disconcerted the optimism of the science of wealth' (140).

Chevalier argues (1973: 134–136) that this French social economy was remarkable for its English-style analyses and themes, bringing together the Malthusian principle of population and the researches into pauperism undertaken by the Scottish minister, Dr Chalmers, as well as the insights of the reform of the English poor law. For example, Buret, whose essay was entitled *De la misère des classes laborieuses en Angleterre et en France*, stated: 'In our project England was a central point of our research, for it is there that recent surveys and applications of new laws to pauperism have enabled an intelligent curiosity to grasp the social mystery we are trying to solve' (quoted by Chevalier 1973: 134).

In England what might misleadingly be styled a *critique* of political economy led to the elaboration of the 'statistical idea'. The imperative for the Statistical Movement, and for the establishment of the various Statistical Societies from the 1830s, was not a rejection of political economy but an increasing concern of those economists who sought to influence policy but 'found that they spoke with many voices' (Abrams 1968: 12). Such a plurality, at least in the first instance, found its roots in the split between, on the one hand, the alliance of Whig-liberalism with Ricardian optimism and Benthamite administrative reform, and, on the other, Malthusian pessimism, defence of the landlords, abolitionism, and legislative quietism (Finer 1952: 20–25). The London Statistical Society's concern was to be with 'facts calculated to illustrate the condition and prospects of society', as its first constitution read. However, the problem that preoccupied it from the start was the integration of the statistics of poverty with the operation of the economy, the problem of the existence of poverty in a self-regulating economy, and its model of progress (Abrams 1968: 13–23).

The investigations of this period locate another role for labour and its conditions, apart from that of the necessary consequence of the poverty inscribed in the laws of the economic order. For classical political economy, and indeed for Bentham's pauper management, labour was unproblematic. For them, poverty was the condition of having no surplus labour in store, and the sale of labour was the natural means by which the greatest segment of the population would subsist. By labour the poor were both integrated into civil society and made the producers of wealth and all the advantages of civilisation. The beginning and end of any system of relief should be to dispauperise the population, and return them to independent (i.e. wage-) labour. The only problem for such discourses was how to ensure that the propertyless poor would exercise their rational preference for labour.

The later social investigations start from exactly the opposite problem, the fact that labour now becomes an element in the disintegration of the social order and the demoralisation of the masses. A concern with the conditions of labour emerges against the background of a new urban question, in a new style of analysis which is crucially undertaken by medical doctors, administrators, state servants, and social reformers. Despite the differences in content and the different sites from which they were enunciated, the common theme of these reports and investigations is that the form that labour takes under urban and industrial conditions is inadequate to the installation of a comprehensive integration of the poor. Such an inadequacy is typically expressed as a tripartite problem, composed of physical, moral, and social dimensions.

In this literature, the question of pauperism still occupies an important position in the hierarchy of effects of the conditions of the labouring classes. Howevever, it presupposes that the war on 'indiscriminate' poor relief has been won, as it had from the standpoint of the reformers, at least by the 1840s. Pauperism is one among many effects of the conditions of the labouring classes, even if it still retains a certain privilege. This can be evidenced by the way the theme of degeneration organises the discussion of such attributes as disease and epidemic, delinquency, vice, crime, and ignorance.

Gaskell (1833: 1–13), for example, argued that the decline in the 'moral, physical and social conditions' of the manufacturing labourer was due to neither poverty, factory labour as such, nor lack of education. Rather, he urged, the replacement of domestic manufactures by steam-driven machinery occasions the 'separation of families' and the 'breaking-up of households', so that the domestic ties which bind humans to those 'instincts and social affections' which make them 'respectable and praiseworthy' members of society are torn asunder (7–8). The problem of social affection again manifests itself in the theme of the 'division of interest' between masters and men, evidenced by the truck and cottage systems of the former and the combinations of the latter (4).

Such a diagnosis leads Gaskell's analysis into an unusual critique of the industrial organisation of labour which is constantly open to the possibility of becoming an apology for it. On the one hand, he suggests that the operative is reduced to a 'mere watcher or feeder of his mighty antagonist' (Gaskell 1833: 9–10). Moreover, he argues that the atmospheric conditions and repetitive tasks found in the factories have grave effects upon the complete cycle of human maturation (173–212). On the other, he concludes that children are fit for factory labour for eight to ten hours from the age of nine or ten (200). The reason for this apparent subversion of the analysis is close at hand: 'The employment of children in manufactories ought not to be looked upon as an evil, till the present moral and domestic habits of the population are completely reorganised' (209). Thus, the real evils of infant labour arise from the degeneration of domestic relations among the labouring population. This ensures that children are already in poor health – and predisposed to moral degradation – prior to entering the factory, which merely compounds a pre-existing problem.

This concern with the breaking up of domestic ties as the basis of working-class ills may explain Gaskell's preoccupation with morals, particularly the sexual behaviour of the young. The second chapter deals with the 'influence of temperature upon physical development and morals' (Gaskell 1833: 68–86). The temperature of the new steam manufactures, together with the absence of propriety of manners, and lack of proper supervision on the part of mill-owners and overlookers to replace domestic ties, is said to lead to the early onset of puberty and early engagement in sexual intercourse. The result in that 'the crowding together numbers of the young of both sexes in factories is a prolific source of moral delinquency' (68). Indeed, Gaskell is concerned with the distortion of the sexual and reproductive functions at every stage of human life. In successive chapters (144–147, 162–165), for example, there are accounts of the 'destruction of maternal love' in the women in factories and the decline both of female physiology and feminine attractiveness (the 'Lancashire witches'). The ill effects of the industrial system are consistently understood through the social condition of the population, one which leads to reciprocal interaction of moral with physical deterioration. Indeed, the *social*, in so far as it is here nothing more than the mode of life of the manufacturing people, is the bridge between the moral and the physical.

If one follows the theme of this double, moral and physical, degeneration of the labouring population under the new 'social system' of labour and the conditions it presupposes, one is returned to the problem of pauperism. James Phillips Kay (later Kay-Shuttleworth), who became an Assistant Poor Law Commissioner in 1835, but is now perhaps best remembered for his work in the field of public educational reform (Corrigan 1977: 197–237), argued that an examination of his statistical findings concerning Manchester showed the 'concomitance of pauperism with moral and physical degradation', and that pauperism spreads most rapidly in ignorant and demoralised populations, in particular the immigrant Irish (Kay 1832: 29–32). Pauperism is here not simply the effect of dependence on relief but the culmination of the degenerative effects of the conditions of life of the labouring population.

Kay's study, which its author was later to see as linked to the forming of the Manchester Statistical Society (Corrigan 1977: 201), is only incidentally concerned with the effects of the industrial system *per se*. It does mention, nevertheless, the theme of the debilitating effects of industrial production, in which 'dull routine and ceaseless drudgery', like the 'torment of Sisyphus', leads to a slumbering intellect and the 'habits of an animal' (Kay 1832: 8). Kay's problem, however, was ultimately an urban one. According to his account the Manchester working classes live in densely packed houses, have inadequate diet (largely due to the Irish introduction of the potato), display a 'barbarous disregard for forethought and economy', and spend their gains in debauchery in the tavern (6–8). Their abodes are crowded upon 'narrow, unpaved, and almost pestilential streets; in an atmosphere loaded with the smoke and exhalation of a large manufacturing city' (10). Further, the working-class districts are unsewered, and the houses are without proper ventilation or cleanliness, and lack privies (13).

The net effect of the combination of these heterogeneous factors is conceived in terms of 'dissipation', 'depression', or 'degradation', terms which again encompass both the physical and moral state of the labouring population. Kay was clear that the form of labour, the type of diet, and the conditions of habitation not only depress the physical strength and mental capacity of the labourers, but also destroy their ' moral dignity,' so that they sink into 'sensual sloth' or revel in 'degrading licentiousness' (Kay 1832: 11). This moral degeneration, furthermore, reinforces and extends the ill effects of physical agencies upon the population, leading to a predisposition to contagious disease (13).

Kay's understanding of the urban conditions of the manufacturing population, and indeed his whole professional life as a state servant for the next two decades, stands at the intersection of the 'statistical' idea with the 'educational idea' and the 'sanitary idea'. Thus he realised from the start that the conditions he sought to describe were intimately associated with the cholera and typhus epidemics.

> The state of the streets powerfully affects the health of their inhabitants. Sporadic cases of typhus chiefly appear in those streets which are narrow, ill-ventilated, unpaved, or which contain heaps of refuse, or stagnant pools. The confined air and noxious exhalations, which abound in such places depress the health of the people, and on this account contagious diseases are most rapidly propagated there.
>
> (Kay 1832: 14–15)

In such a way, the link between the insanitary conditions of the labouring class and epidemic disease could be used to argue for public health measures and regulation. Such arguments would be reiterated by the major exponents of public health over the next decades, especially the *1842 Report on the Sanitary Conditions of the Labouring Population* (Chadwick 1965). That report argued that the various forms of epidemic and endemic disease were caused by 'atmospheric impurities produced by decomposing animal and vegetable substances, by damp and filth, and close and overcrowded dwellings' (422).

The aetiology of epidemics was thus linked to the pauperising conditions of the labouring classes. As Flinn's introduction shows (1965: 62), this theory of epidemic disease was based on Ferriar's 1810 argument that contagion was propagated by an impression on the olfactory nerves. Later, others, such as Southwood Smith, argued that the putrefaction or decay of animal or vegetable matter gave off a compound called 'miasma' which was supposed to enter the human constitution by smell. It was thus possible to argue, as did the *1842 Report* (Chadwick 1965: 422–425), that this miasmic contagion was most likely under conditions in which atmospheric impurities were created by the dampness and lack of ventilation of dwellings, the effluvia and refuse which accmulated in the streets and houses, the open sewers, and the lack of proper drainage, as well as the lack of cleanliness, poor domestic economy, and filthy habits of the poor.

It is significant that this theory of contagion was held in opposition to the localised and monocausal theories which were increasingly dominant in other fields of medicine and among other groups of doctors. Indeed, Chadwick chided 'the medical controversy over the causes of fever . . . [as] prejudicial in diverting attention from *the practical means of prevention*' (quoted by Finer 1952: 218, original emphasis). In the field of public health, the most successful reformers adopted a model which admitted the influence of a body of factors in the environment (Pelling 1978). Indeed, they led to conclusions, at least in Chadwick's estimation, that civil engineers rather than physicians were to be the most important agents of change in the health of towns. In any case, one of the most striking aspects of the sanitarian theory of contagion was how it fitted nicely the broader concern with the conditions and mode of life of the labouring population and created a rationale for a very broad consideration of aspects of these conditions.

An example of this is how the public-health reformers resurrected the old theme of domestic economy which can be found in eighteenth-century writings from Defoe to Eden. Here the aetiology of epidemics and the consequent principles of sanitation become a way through which modes of life of the poor could be compared and evaluated. Chadwick, like Kay and Gaskell, is centrally concerned with the effects of the neglect of domestic economy. The *1842 Report* contrasts the 'honest, frugal housewife' who 'is ever discharging some household duty in a spirit of placid contentment' with the one 'totally ignorant of all habits of domestic economy' who drives her husband to the alehouse to seek that comfort which he is missing by his own fireside (Chadwick 1965: 205–208). In a similar vein, the comparison between the attitude to children on behalf of two different groups made by Mr Wood of Dundee and quoted by this report can be considered:

> There are many families among the working classes who are in receipt of from 15s. to 22s. per week, who are insufficiently clothed, and whose houses as well as their person appear filthy, disorderly, and uncomfortable. There are other families among them, containing the same number of persons, whose incomes average from 10s. to 14s. a week, who are neat, cleanly, and sufficiently clothed, regularly and suitably fed, and whose houses appear orderly and comfortable. The former class care little for the physical comfort, and far less for the intellectual, moral and religious education of their children. . . . The latter class on the contrary are most anxious to give their children a good education . . . . The former class again grasp at every benefit which the charitable institutions of the place have provided for the poor . . . . Whereas the latter . . . very often present their medical attendant with a small fee.
>
> (Chadwick 1965: 209)

It is unsurprising that this comparison should be made to draw the conclusion that it is among the former, grasping class that 'contagious, febrile diseases are most commonly found' (Chadwick 1965: 209). The form in which the aetiology of epidemics was conceived allowed a specific conception of the relation between poverty and disease. The conception was not held to demonstrate the necessity for the overcoming of poverty, but for corrective interventions upon certain of the habits and conditions found among the poor. When public-health reformers examined the conditions of the working class they did not simply find 'intolerable' conditions, but a complete pattern of behaviour and life style, composed of an array of habits and conditions made pertinent by a particular theory of contagion. It is striking that this theory of the aetiology of epidemics isolated precisely those conditions and behaviours which were constitutive of pauperisation.

Pauperism is no longer simply the source of a moral contagion but both the cause and effect of disease. On the one hand, disease, particularly the typhus and, to a lesser extent, cholera epidemics, was now conceived to have its origins among the most pauperised sectors of the labouring population. On the other, disease was recognised as a factor which led to pauperism through the premature death of some breadwinners and the diminished productive capacity of others, through the creation of widows and orphans, and by throwing families on to poor relief and leading them to a life of vice and crime (Chadwick 1965: 254–257).

The theory of contagion was complemented by parallel and over-lapping developments in the field of vital statistics. As Flinn has noted (1965: 14–16), a rise in mortality rates was first noticed by the Census Commission in Britain in 1831. When the reports of Drs Kay, Arnott, and Southwood Smith were presented to the Poor Law Commission in 1838 they emphatically fixed the blame for the increased incidence of disease and mortality upon squalid urban conditions. The *1842 Report* would dramatise the effect of typhus on the mortality rate in the following terms: 'The annual slaughter in England and Wales from preventable causes of typhus which attacks persons in the vigour of life, appears to be double the amount of what was suffered by the Allied Armies in the battle of Waterloo' (Chadwick 1965: 78).

Political intervention and debate increasingly took place over such 'vital statistics'. This form of knowledge was pioneered by William Farr who, from the Registrar General's Department, classified causes of death in a 'statistical nosology' (Flinn 1965: 26–28). From such a study, Farr concluded that if the legislature had 'not the power to call the Dead up from their graves, it can now close thousands of graves now opening' by measures for cleaner air, proper waste disposal, and so on (quoted by Flinn 1965: 29).

Thus the administrators and statisticians envisaged a government of the conditions of life of the population made possible by a form of knowledge which allowed its diagnosis, vital statistics, and by the social investigation into the labouring population which focused on the cor-relates of poverty. But the imagery of war and mass death which was drawn from these knowledges could be used for a more fundamental indictment of the regime of the government through the economy, that which is delivered by Engels when, upon examining such 'blue book' material, stated: 'Hence it comes, too, that the social war, the war of each against all, is here openly declared' (1973: 60). One of the major themes of Engels' famous text was the charge against the bourgeoisie of 'social murder' which he sustained by maintaining that this class, through such forms of knowledge, knows that it is inflicting premature death upon its victims among the working class (393–394). The paradox of Engels' text is that the statistical and investigatory knowledges which would be employed to organise and expand the sphere of social interven-tion of the liberal state by factory, public-health, and education legislation, are here used to indict the regime of the bourgeoisie as one of '*laissez-faire, laissez-aller*' (276).

This social-investigatory literature both subverts and reinstates the privileged position held by pauperism in the discussions of the poor laws. At first approach, pauperism is here only one of a multiplicity of effects of specific conditions and habits, together with crime, disease, vice, and moral degradation. Nevertheless, the literature retains the use of the term pauperism to encapsulate the whole constellation of deleterious effects (e.g. Kay 1832: 28–43). Moreover, the focus of this literature remained remarkably consistent with Chadwick's (and Bentham's) earlier formula of the legitimate realm of state intervention into poverty as 'those conditions which turn the labouring poor into the indigent'.

One can say that the notion of pauperism was employed in a symmetrical fashion in the strategies for the reform of the poor laws and in arguments for the improvements in the sanitary conditions of houses, streets, and workplaces. In the former, the problem was the reorganisation of relief so that the labouring class would not be unduly tempted away from selling their labour for subsistence. In the latter, intervention would involve the removal of those conditions which led the labouring population into pauperism. In the one the problem was to make the condition of the pauper signify its less-eligibility; in the other, to make the condition of the labourer really more eligible. The notion of pauperism could be used, then, not simply to institute relief practices which constituted the poor as wage-labourers or their dependants, but as a grid by which certain modes and conditions of life among the propertyless could be established and fostered. Such a formulation of the sanitary problem respects no division between necessary, purely technical, public-health measures to lower rates of mortality and incidences of disease, and interventions to promote specific modes of moral conduct among the poor. In Chadwick's case, we can concur with the view that his Benthamite discipleship has perhaps been overstressed to the detriment of his particular moral and political understanding (Corrigan 1977: 264).

The 'condition of the labouring population' literature is not subversive of the aims of classical political economy and the Table of Pauperism despite the fact that it makes problematic the new urban–industrial organisation of labour in a way which neither of the earlier discourses could. Its focus on the conditions of labour offered a critique of political economy in so far as labour could no longer be regarded as an unmitigated solution to the distresses of the poor and could itself be the source of those distresses. However, this critique was not one which sought to argue for the overcoming of wage-labour or for the transcendence of poverty, but for a mode of state administration which could support, reinforce, and maintain both wage-labour and a life style organised around a domestic sphere of familial responsibility and dependency. Chadwick's shift, discussed by Finer (1952: 210–223), may be emblematic of this. He moved from conceiving sanitary reform as focusing upon the single dwelling-house, to its place in the 'venous and arterial system' of the water supply, drainage, and sewerage of towns. This nicely captures the sense in which liberal administration had to come to grips with more than the isolated private sphere of responsibility it sought to establish by the reform of the poor laws. The destiny of liberal governance would be found in the social, moral, and physical structure which shaped such a sphere. This liberal mode of government would find itself taking charge of forming and sustaining the domestic and work relations that nascent economic discourse assumed to be natural.

There is a shift of emphasis between the respective problems of pauper management and the literature on the condition of the labouring population. But such a shift is integral to the liberal mode of government and its form of economy, and not a departure from it. In its first formulation, liberal governance is pre-social. We have seen that pauperism is conceptually separated from considerations of poverty, and strategies of its management rest on the assumption that it is, in principle, capable of being institutionally isolated. The aim of the strategy of less-eligibility embodied in the use of the workhouse was to prevent the spread of pauperism, not only by containing it in an enclosed space but also by deterring applications for relief from the propertyless labourer. Such a strategy assumes labour to be a moralising force, and hence holds in esteem the virtues of the 'independent labourer', and addresses the propertyless as rational subjects of exchange.

In a later formulation, however, liberal governance needs to pose a social question. Here, pauperism inhabits the entire terrain of the labouring population. It is no longer simply a cause but a symbol in which is condensed all the symptoms of demoralisation. The conditions which produce pauperism, and coincident disease, crime, and political threat, are those under which wage-labourers must subsist. The liberal mode of government must not only remove the barriers to the constitution of a class of wage-labourers but also be able to expunge those modes and conditions of life of the poor which threaten the maintenance of the labouring population.

In this shift, labour has ceased to be an unambiguous element of the moralisation of the poor. The poor-law reforms assumed that erecting a barrier of less-eligibility would ensure that the demoralisation of the labouring population would cease. Public-health reform, on the other hand, charged that the new urban conditions of labour brought about the 'co-incidence of pestilence and moral disorder' (Chadwick 1965: 199). The *1842 Report* quoted the evidence of Alison who found that the manufacturing cities contained such a class, 'whose moral perceptions have been obliterated and they might be said to be characterised by a ferocious indocility which makes them prompt to wrongs and violences, destroys their social nature and transforms them into something little better than wild beasts' (1965: 199). 'Government through the economy', which sought to locate the poor as the motor-force of civilisation, is shown to bring about a multiplication of the demoralising conditions of poverty.

This liberal mode of government of poverty is undoubtedly conceived as a series of preventive measures, concerned with the fostering of a space of individual autonomy and with minimising state action. The quest for prevention, nevertheless, calls forth not only the quasi-private monitoring of the poor by philanthropy but, more importantly, the massive extension of those means of state administration which bear upon the lives of the poor. If this liberal mode of government is distinguished by its aim of incorporating self-responsibility and familial duty within the lives of the propertyless, it does so by multiplying the institutional and administrative networks which surround poverty. Liberal government does not simply withdraw from poor relief to give free reign to the natural laws of domestic and individual life, as Malthus and the propagandists of abolitionism had advocated it would, but specifies and promotes a specific, patriarchal conduct of life by a multiplicity of means. If the liberal mode of government presents itself as merely following the dictates of the natural laws of the economy, it does so to build the administrative structures which secure the vital conditions for the operation of this economy.

The liberal mode of government of the nineteenth century presented itself as a mere adjustment to the bioeconomic laws which governed humankind and to the ethical consequences which followed. In fact, however, this government embodied a distinctive project of social transformation. It goes without saying that this project was highly successful and has left its lasting legacy.

Conclusion

The event of pauperism, in which poverty was constituted at the end of the eighteenth century, can be understood as marking a fundamental transformation in modes of governance, and the emergence of a new, liberal style of administration which entailed a reworking of the older systems of police around conceptions of self- and familial responsibility. This transformation involves, at a minimum, the redefinition of the field of action of the state, which is at once a withdrawal of state responsibility for relief to specific categories of the propertyless, and a centralisation and bureaucratisation of the apparatus of the administration of relief. But it also bears upon much broader concerns involving the particular conduct of life of the propertyless population and the generalisation of wage-labour within the transformed framework of patriarchal relations. Let us conclude with questions on the consequences of the liberal *break*, first in relation to the accounts of the formation of capitalism of Marx and Weber, and, second, with respect to issues of rupture and continuity in the governance of poverty.

What follows are some all too brief remarks which are simply intended to suggest the broader implications of this study in relation to the classical theorists of capitalist transformation, Marx and Weber, whose work introduced this study and entered into consideration at several important junctures in the course of it. The part of Marx's account which is pertinent here is that concerning the expropriation of the rural population, the classic formulation of which is to be found in Part 8 of the first volume of *Capital* (1974, 1: 667–693; but see also Marx 1973: 459–514). The approach embodied there stands in contrast to earlier approaches Marx and Engels made to the problem of the historical genesis of the capitalist mode of production, such as that found in *The German Ideology* (1964: 64–77). Where he had earlier emphasised the role of mercantile activity, the growth of towns, and the expansion of world markets and trade, Marx now insists that the 'process which clears the way' for capitalism is none other than that which strips the labourer of the possession of the means of production: 'The secret of the primitive accumulation . . . is nothing else than the historical process of divorcing the producer from the means of production' (1974, 1: 688). Marx's version of this process constitutes an impressively marshalled historical interpretation of a process 'written in the annals of mankind in letters of blood and fire' followed by an equally forceful account of the 'bloody legislation against the expropriated' from Tudor times (686–693).

Nevertheless, this account only shows how there came to be a large propertyless and landless plebeian mass. There is no necessity for such a mass to become wage-labourers even given the existence of a class of owners of money and means of production. Marx's analysis of expropriation can only ever be a genealogy of the historical preconditions for the emergence of the class of wage-labourers which would be drawn into capitalist relations of production. Indeed Marx appears to realise this in the *Grundrisse* when he notes that it is a matter of 'historic record' that the propertyless tried a life of 'begging, vagabondage and robbery' before they tried wage-labour (1973: 507). They were, he argues, driven off this former 'road by gallows, stocks and whippings, onto the narrow path of the labour market', and successive governments were conditions of 'the historical dissolution process' of the old mode of production. Leaving aside the problem that the anti-vagrancy legislation Marx alludes to may well be intelligible as a shoring-up of feudal relations of servitude and a clamping down on the dispossessed peasantry (as both Anderson's study of absolutism (1974), and our own account of the nature and functions of police in the eighteenth century would imply), Marx does seem to underestimate the difficulties presented by other, non-repressive forms of governmental practice to the formation of the labour market. The question of how the propertyless are made to sell their labour-power *freely* is further glossed over when he argues that it can be answered by reference to capitalist production itself: 'The advance of capitalist production develops a working-class, which by education, training, habit, looks upon the conditions of that mode of production as self-evident laws of Nature' (Marx 1974, 1: 689). The present study would suggest that before this could occur the structure of the administration of the poor would first have to be subject to a liberal transformation in its governance. By seeking to tell that story, we have pursued just some of the means of the conversion of the propertyless into wage-labourers and, in this regard, have made a case-study in the formation of the working class. The proletariat was not a product of the process of expropriation so vividly described by Marx, although that process is a necessary precondition of its formation. Rather, it must now be said that the formation of a class which relies solely or largely on the sale of labour-power for its subsistence and reproduction was in large part due to a mode of government of poverty which instituted such conditions as would promote a form of life organised around the wage-labourer/breadwinner.

The participation in wage-labour is, however, only one aspect of the *conduct of life*, the *Lebensführung*, which is promoted by this liberal government of poverty. This theme brings us closer to those concerns of Max Weber which we have attempted to incorporate into this study.

It is well known that the relation between Protestantism and the capitalist spirit, which is posited in Weber's famous study (1985), is irreducible to a causal one. Moreover, it is also true that Weber situates the analysis of the Protestant ethic in a wide-ranging, complex, multi-factorial discussion of the necessary preconditions of capitalism, as, for example, in Part 4 of his *General Economic History* (1927: 275–369). However, what requires attention here is not the general historical interpretation Weber offers as his thesis but rather his insistence on the effects of changes in religious ethics which are manifested in a specific mode of life. The methodical and disciplined conduct of life which arises from the psychological consequences (Weber speaks (1985: 104), for instance, of 'inner loneliness') of this ascetic, rationalist ethic bears more than a passing resemblance to the form of life – with its virtues of moral restraint, thrift, economy, and hard work – which are promoted under the Malthusian ethic of self-responsibility. Does that mean that the genealogy of the governance of the poor is simply an adjunct to a more fundamental change in *values*? At times, indeed, Weber himself suggests that the changes to the Tudor poor law after the Civil War are an embodiment of a Puritan ethos (1927: 349).

To distinguish the implications of the present study from Weber's famous thesis, a number of immediate contrasts must be made. Where the efficacy of Calvinism over its adherents has to do with the *subjective* consequences engendered in them by the doctrine of predestination (Weber, 1985: 98–128), the liberal transformation of governance, at least in the first instance, sought to give effect to a self-responsible conduct of life by the deterrent institutional form of the workhouse. The ethic of patriarchal self-responsibility identified in the present study may have been preached from countless pulpits and embodied in many forms of consciousness, but its social implantation was, in its primary formula-tion, to be promoted by its inscription in the conditions placed upon poor relief by a system of central state superintendence.

A second contrast that must be made concerns the nature of the mercantilist work-police. Weber argues that, after the Civil War, the treatment of the poor was deeply affected by Puritan values (1927: 349–351). This is certainly not in doubt, particularly in light of the work of Christopher Hill (e.g. 1986: 247–273). Yet, Weber also seeks to claim that the Puritan-inspired poor law can be interpreted as the mechanism of the recruitment of the new capitalist labour-force (1927: 306–307).

This is at best doubtful. Weber fails to recognise the vastly different roles of the governance of the poor in the late seventeenth and eighteenth centuries, the period of forced labour schemes in the late eighteenth and early nineteenth centuries, when it acted to shore up the supply of agricultural labour, and after 1834. It is only in this latter period that the poor law can be said to secure the conditions of the capitalist labour market. Like Marx, Weber too easily reads earlier state administration and legislation through the *telos* of capitalism. Both prematurely identify the role of the state in legislation towards the idle and industrious Poor (in poor, labour, and vagrancy legislation) as functioning to promote capitalism. By contrast we have sought to contribute to a non-reductive and non-teleological analysis of what is indeed a highly complex genealogy of the governance of the Poor. At a minimum, the present study implies that eighteenth-century discourses and governmental practices concerning the Poor cannot be understood simply by reference to their functions in terms of capitalist social relations.

Moreover, it will be noted that this study has eschewed the use of the notion of 'traditionalism' as it appears in Weber's history (1985: 58–72). There are several problems with this notion, not the least of which is that it implies an opposition between a past, in which economic activities are ethically regulated under patriarchal relations, and a present of rational, demoralised, economic activity entered into by contract. Weber styles traditionalism as the 'exclusive reliance upon such trade and industry as have come down from the *fathers*' (1927: 355, emphasis added; cf Weber 1948: 296). He adds that, although master–slave relations could be 'subjected to immediate ethical regulation . . . the relations between the mortgage creditor and the property which was pledged for the debt, or between an endorser and bill of exchange, would at least be exceedingly difficult, if not impossible, to moralize' (357–358). On such a logic, the relation between the wage-labourer and the labour-contract would be similarly divested of moral concerns. The transition from traditional to modern economic relations would appear to be a break between a patriarchal, ethically regulated past and an individualist, ethically neutral present.

The present study has shown, on the contrary, that there are implicit moral characteristics of wage-labour, whether formulated in terms of the imperative to exchange in Smith, or as obedience to bioeconomic laws in classical political economy. Most important of these is the dual nature of the civil status of the wage-labourer as worker and head of household, the latter involving his patriarchal mastery in the private, domestic sphere. Rather than opposing a set of powerful religious ethics to the sanctity of patriarchal tradition, and assuming that religion formed 'a powerful, unconsciously refined organisation for the production of capitalistic individuals' (368), the present study has located the rise of a form of life, of the wage-labourer as patriarchal breadwinner, in the ethic of self-responsibility which came to be embodied in the transformation of an older system of police. If, as has been pointed out many times, trade unions would come to demand a living wage for the worker and *his* family, this would not so much be due to survival of traditional, patriarchal ethics, but a result of the moral efficacy of this liberal mode of governance of poverty.

This study has sought to underline how fundamental the liberal break was, and how the genealogy of what we would today call social policy must grasp its full significance. This should not be taken to imply that the liberal mode is entirely discontinuous with earlier systems of relief, provision, and administration of the poor. The liberal mode of government did not emerge fully formed *ex nihilo*. It evinced a rationality which was cobbled together from disparate elements, minor transitions, and local practices. Thus although Malthus' principle of population was capable of providing an articulate case for abolition of the old systems of relief, and marked a rupture with earlier conceptions of population, it is highly unlikely that its author took a conscious theoretical step away from his predecessors. The principle of population was a fundamental break, but one which appropriated and transformed, perhaps even deformed, earlier conceptions of the relations of population to subsistence. Similarly, the notion of the workhouse as a deterrent, the centrepiece of the new strategy of 1834, had already been tried in the early eighteenth-century turn towards repressive measures, and had achieved legislative form in the 1723 Act. The *1834 Report* itself based its remedies on the strategies already undertaken in various poor-law unions created under eighteenth-century legislation (Poynter 1969: 310–316).

Benthamism places in full relief the vexed question of the liberal mode's ability to appropriate, transform, and utilise discursive and governmental schemas founded on pre-liberal presuppositions. There are grounds for arguing a special contribution of Bentham's pauper management to the reformed poor-law administration of the 1830s, namely the conceptual distinction between indigence and poverty on which both rested, and the practical strategy for the maintenance of such a distinction by making the condition of the pauper *appear* less eligible than that of the 'independent labourer'. If the New Poor Law was not a transcription of Bentham's system of pauper management, it at least borrowed the latter's crucial conceptual delineation of the legitimate field of intervention and the means by which relief could be restricted to such a field. Moreover, there is the issue of the centralisation of relief administration. While many historians notice this to be a feature of both Bentham's pauper management and the post-1834 poor law, they do not ask of either the aim of this centralisation, on what principles central administration was to operate, or what was constituted as its administrable domain. Because the historians fail to address such questions, they fail to comprehend that both the New Poor Law and Bentham's plan constitute virtually identical targets of national administration based on the same principle which sought to achieve the same ends. Centralised, professional, bureaucratic state administration cannot be understood merely as an empty, universal form but must be placed in relation to the specific rationality it embodies, the strategies in which it is embedded, and the objectives it seeks. We must remain cautious about those definitions of 'modernity' which maintain a purely *formal* approach to the reform of institutions.

The liberal mode of government of poverty, and its form of economy, never finally broke with the methods and concerns of 'cameralist' police in the German case (Tribe 1984), and one senses something of this in England, even given its undeveloped pre-liberal conception of police. The New Poor Law provided the most radical attempt at severing all the hierocratic, paternalist, and police elements from the administration of poor relief in order to constitute or set free the individuality of the propertyless, male labourer as an answer to both the requirements of the economy and the demoralisation of the character of the poor. Its Benthamite less-eligibility solutions assumed an inherent capacity of the poor to consult their own self-interest and take up the more eligible condition of independent labourer. Yet there is a tension between merely semio-technical measures, which assume the problem of self-responsibility to be a question of overcoming artificial obstacles and replacing them with the appropriate signs to guide the choices of the poor, and more positive measures which seek to create interventions which actively shape the conditions under which choice is made. Indeed, John Stuart Mill, as early as 1838, was to reproach Bentham for ignoring 'self-education' which is more important than the regulation of 'outward actions' (1950: 70–71; cf Corrigan 1977: 12). The same point can be made of the *1834 Report*'s strategy of dispauperisation. The destiny of liberal governance would be to establish its own positive measures of moral, educational, and medical police. This can be detected as early as the political economists' demand for the 'intervention of the State as universal educator' (Halévy 1928: 490). It exists also, but in a more developed fashion, in Whig-liberalism's administrative vision in which the superintendence of relief and its potentially demoralising effects must be complemented with positive measures of the state in relation to the living and working conditions of the population.

A final point which cannot go unnoticed when discussing the issue of the illiberality of the liberal mode of government, and continuities with earlier systems of oeconomy and police, is that of patriarchy. One might be tempted to oppose the *status* of the poor within the patriarchalism of mercantilist police to a form of governance which seeks only to encourage them as juridical subjects of the wage-*contract*. By emphasising that the responsibilising of the poor was crucially about the construction of the 'independent labourer' as wage-labourer *and* male breadwinner, and wives and children as their dependants, this study has sought to stress that the liberal mode, no matter how ruptural in the history of police, was a break *within* patriarchy. Strategies of responsibilisation seek to promote certain patriarchal relations, regardless of their degree of appropriateness, in the conduct of life of the poor. To use Carole Pateman's language (1988), we might say that the paternal patriarchalism of the police of the Poor in the eighteenth century gave way to the obligations, and rights, of *fraternal* patriarchy with the emergence of a liberal mode of government. If one of the functions of the marriage-contract is to secure patriarchal property rights among the rich, for the propertyless poor it would henceforth be used to define the limits of state responsibility for relief and subsistence.

It is also necessary to return briefly to the issue of the *social*. If we are to understand the attack on pauperism and political economy as together forming the discovery of the natural science of society, as does Polanyi, then the state policy closely allied with it can be legitimately called *social* policy. It is necessary to resist such an inference for two reasons. First, the debate on pauperism should be understood as a 'surface of emergence' of the social, rather than being a social problem itself. The discussion of poverty which preceded and included the great watershed of the *1834 Poor Law Report*, and the forms of knowledge which figured in this discussion, cannot be regarded as the site of the formation of 'the social question', if that phrase implies an interrogation of the lives, habits, conditions, and circumstances of the labouring population as an effect of the organisation of society.[1] These discourses were, rather, a necessary preliminary to the emergence of a field of social governance. They sought to establish the institutional conditions for the formation and reproduction of that which was to be interrogated by the social question, a class of wage-labourers and their families. It is only then that 'the working class' was both formed as a clearly unified entity for state administration and political calculation, and also displaced earlier notions of 'the labouring Poor' or the 'labouring class*es*'. The social question, which would make problematic the urban and industrial conditions of the new class, can only be posed from a liberal perspective after the implementation of a regime of poor relief which constitutes wage-labour as a solution to the fiscal and moral crisis of pauperism.

Moreover, Polanyi's position misses the importance of the crucial distinction between *political* economy and *social* economy enunciated by those such as Buret. The social always implies some distance from, or dissonance within, political economy as a programme of government. The viewpoint of the social presupposes a breakdown of the claims of the economy to leave the governance of human affairs to the operation of bioeconomic laws. Polanyi's 'self-protection of society' pitted against the regime of a market economy is better understood as the capacity of the liberal mode of governance to shift from the implantation to the effective reproduction of the conditions of such an economy. Doubtless, the degree to which the economic sphere succeeds in subordinating the political order, and in erecting a realm of interests, is the degree to which a space is opened for a new field of knowledge and governance concerned with defining the state's content in relation to the private sphere. This is the space occupied by the social.

Liberal govern*mentality*, whether in regard to state or non-state measures, is overwhelmingly concerned with the establishment of those conditions – both negative and positive – which make the poor responsible for what later generations would term their 'standard of living'. It is around the tactics of responsibilisation that the liberal economy always contained within itself the possibility of interventions in favour of a specific form of life for the labouring population. All of this allows us to question accounts of philanthropic notions of 'self-help', 'self-restraint', etc., as so many instances of a 'bourgeois ideology' concerned simply with the establishment of forms of consciousness appropriate to capitalism. The ethos of self-help certainly concerns the withdrawal of the liberal state from definite obligations to certain social categories, but it is also about the autonomy and mobility of the worker/breadwinner outside the moral paternalism of earlier forms of police, and an implicit recognition of workers' patriarchal rights over their wives in a newly privatised domestic sphere. This pay-off for propertyless men may no doubt partially explain why such an ethos lends itself to alternative uses, such as in the advocacy of friendly societies or in working-class co-operative societies in the 1840s and after. The notion of self-responsibility is the key to the gaining/granting of civil individuality on the part of the male labouring poor. It also implies some definite limits to forms of governance which even Benthamite pauper management, for all its ambivalence to such limits, found it had to respect.

The liberal mode of government in the nineteenth century traced a double spiral. In the first turn the problem of pauperism leads to the production of the conditions of wage-labour. In the second, in factory legislation, in public-health, policing, and educational measures, the path of the first circle is retraced through the concern with the effective reproduction of the conditions of wage-labour through the crucial mediation of a familial structure organised around the male breadwinner.

In this second path, the question of morality and poverty could still be conceived in terms of ensuring the preference for labour over relief or, in the Malthusian sense, of the obedience of the poor to bioeconomic necessity. However, morality had also become, in the British and French social investigations of this time, a question of the comparison and evaluation of the habits, behaviours, and modes of existence of various sectors of the poor. It is at this point that the liberal mode of government would begin to address the specific content of the position of housewife and mother within the working-class family, an issue taken up in Donzelot's study (1979). It was at the same time that philanthropy would be reorganised as a 'sacrament of moralising intervention' (Procacci 1978: 68) which would convert the issue of relief into one of personal economic morality (Donzelot 1979: 55). Thus, one could cite examples from Chalmers' celebrated scheme in the Tron parish of Glasgow (Young and Ashton 1956: 70–71), to the work of the Charity Organisation Society among the casual poor of London in the 1870s (Stedman Jones 1984: 271–280). Each intervention, from the field of philanthrophy to the public-health measures, would be conceived as a moralising one, monitoring and attempting to transform the minute details of the domestic lives of the poor. If the first circle of liberal governance drew upon the workhouse to enforce wage-labour, and the older semio-technique of less-eligibility, its second turn would increasingly find the need for a network of measures which sought actively to encourage the ethic of personal responsibility and to target women as its agents. But we have only here begun to map the path of this second turn, which will no doubt form the basis of future studies on the formation of the concept of unemployment, the notion of the 'residuum', and a new ecological theory of urban degeneration, which emerge amidst the crises of the late nineteenth century (Stedman Jones 1984: 281–290).

The continuous thread is provided by prevention. Ultimately, the liberal government of morals would be concerned with the prevention of those modes of existence which elevate poverty to a 'social danger' (Chevalier 1973: 141–144). It was perhaps Buret who captured this final aspect of the problem of poverty most acutely. It was not poverty itself which was the object of his study but distress ('la misère'), which he defined as 'poverty felt morally' (142). The more the working class becomes aware of distress, he concluded, the less 'resigned' they become: 'The poor have already engendered their theoreticians, who maintain that political institutions are the cause of people's sufferings. Let governments beware!' (143). Let us hope, too, that such theoreticians are not lacking at the end of the twentieth century.

Notes

Introduction

1 The concept of the conditions of existence of capitalist social relations of production was developed in the context of the critique of the notion of social totality associated with certain developments in British Marxism in the 1970s (Cutler *et al* 1977, 1: 222–242). Such an approach is not so much a massive departure from Marx as a restatement of his own working methodology, particularly that of the historical sketch of economic relations and categories in the *Grundrisse* (1973: 459–514; also 1974, Part 8).

2 Recurrence is a concept which is derived from French traditions in the history of science, particularly from Georges Canguilhem. It is the phenomenon whereby history is rewritten in such a way as to make formalised scientific knowledge the *telos* of the multiplicity of prior modes of knowing and paths of investigation (Foucault 1972: 187–188; 1980a: 56).

3 Compare the following: 'The cause of the origin of a thing and its eventual utility, its actual employment and place in a system of purposes, lie worlds apart; whatever exists, having somehow come into being, is again and again reinterpreted to new ends, taken over, transformed and redirected by some power superior to it' (Nietzsche 1969: 77); 'When, then, the explanation of a social phenomemon is undertaken, we must seek separately the efficient cause which produces it and the function it fulfils' (Durkheim 1965: 95).

4 The term 'case-history' is central to Cousins' and Hussain's reading of Foucault's genealogical enterprise (1984: 3–4). A case-history is distinguished from conventional histories in that it is directed by questions of intelligibilty rather than exhaustiveness, and seeks progressively to understand particular dimensions of the past, which are always open to revision and extension, rather than a complete reconstruction.

5 Recent attempts to come to terms with Polanyi's legacy include that of Block and Somers (1984), which includes good material on his biography and on *The Great Transformation*, and a useful bibliography. There has appeared, importantly, a *Telos* special section on Polanyi

(1987) with items by Polanyi-Levitt and Mendell, Martinelli, Gislain, and Salsano, covering biography, concepts of economy, the state/market relation, and his anthropology.

6 The term 'the liberal mode of government' is employed extensively throughout Minson's recent study (1985). Despite differences in application, there are several overlapping themes: the use of the term government to imply both state and non-state forms of regulation, the accent on the constitution of a sphere of personal action, and the situation of the personal within particular legal and administrative co-ordinates. Moreover, I am indebted to Minson's discussion of the notion of police and his account of its transformation, as well as his introduction of issues concerning morality (see chapters three and six of the present study). See also Halévy (1928), on the antimonies of radicalism, and Rimlinger (1971) on the liberal break in policy. Walther's (1984) and Sherman's (1974) historical–theoretical critiques show why the notion of 'economic liberalism' needs displacing.

7 The term 'administrable domain' was coined by Robert Castel. A helpful account of its use is given in the review article of his *L'Ordre Psychiatrique* by Peter Miller (1980: 63–105). An administrable domain is formed when it is possible to delineate a specific historical complex of various practices – including theoretical discourse, more 'practical' knowledges, state and non-state interventions, and administrative techniques – which constitute a relatively coherent and distinct field, with definite objects of knowledge and targets of intervention, specific agents, modes of organisation, and aims. See Dean (1988, Introduction, Part 4).

8 For a re-reading of Weber's approach to issues of government and rationality in relation to Foucault's later lectures and fragments, see Gordon (1987). See also Hennis (1987).

1 The discourse of the poor

1 In discussing pre-liberal governance and discourses, the eighteenth-century convention of capitalising the term 'the Poor' and its sub-categories, such as 'the idle Poor', 'the industrious Poor', and so on, will be followed throughout this study. I have sought to remain consistent in this, which becomes difficult when discussing those passages or moments when such categories are undergoing decisive transformation. In those cases I have chosen to capitalise only when it is absolutely clear that the Discourse of the Poor is in operation. Thus, in chapter four, Townsend remains clearly within such a discourse, while Malthus does not. Where there is some ambiguity, as in the cases of the moral philosphers in chapter six and Adam Smith in chapter seven, I have used the lower case.

2 The knowledge of the population was of the utmost sensitivity in matters of the security and well-being of the nation. For example, census data was considered and treated as top secret in Austria and Sweden in the eighteenth century (Glass 1973: 13). William Wales expressed the fear

that a census in England would show a smaller population than its enemies believed and consequently encourage military adventures against it (Glass 1973: 17).

2 The problem of idleness

1 According to Thompson (1967: 80–81), the slow development of industrial capitalism in England served to foster a 'vigorous and licensed popular culture which the propagandists of discipline regarded with dismay'. It was this culture, he argues, which best offers an understanding of the severity of mercantilist doctrines. It is also worth noting that twentieth-century sociology has retained this critique of certain attitudes towards and practices of labour under the rubric of what Weber called 'traditionalism' (1985: 58–63).

2 Furniss (1957: 125–126) cites a host of opinions to this effect.

3 One well-known eighteenth-century text germane to the discussion of poor policy which has not been dealt with here is Bernard Mandeville's *The fable of the bees: or private vices, public benefits* of 1714. The text consists of a long allegorical poem, containing apparently paradoxical opinions, and an explanation of its lines and the sentiments they conveyed. A detailed examination of this text here would be simply repetitive of much of Landreth's (1975: 193–208) recent commentary. The main tenets of the text are those which are characteristic of the Discourse of the Poor. Landreth shows (1975: 198–202) that its position on both foreign trade and domestic matters of wages, the Poor, and population, was that of orthodox mercantilism. See also Dumont (1977) for a quite different analysis of Mandeville and 'economic ideology'.

3 The police of the poor

1 It is noteworthy that, when such reforms were tried at Ypres, near Bruges, the mendicant orders protested over the secular nature of their administration (Webb and Webb 1963a: 40–41). The local municipal authorities had the religious hierarchy on their side in the dispute (the bishop and even the papal legate). Upon the appeal of the orders, the Sorbonne pronounced favourably on the reforms.

2 The general argument that we need to look beyond religious ethics if we are to understand the treatment of the Poor does not mean that we should ignore the peculiarities of Puritanism in this matter which Hill (1986: 247–269) shows to have dissociated 'the Poor' from 'the people', and hence from inclusion in the political nation. Nor does our argument deny that the problem of idleness can be addressed from the perspective of religious ethics. George (1985: 286) shows that in the eighteenth century the chapel was a permanent fixture in most factory colonies and large employers such as Robert Peel favoured Methodist overlookers. For a critical review of conventional wisdom on the effects of the Puritan Revolution on poor relief, and an analysis of the London

Corporation of the Poor in 1649, see Pearl (1978).

3 In the following, I do not wish to enter into the debate over the 'Absolutist state' (Anderson 1974). However, Minson (1985: 102–108) locates police in terms of its conservative commitment to the 'absolutist condominium' and as an obstacle to the formation of the sovereign constitutional state. See also Strakosch (1967).

4 The quote is, significantly, contained in a letter from Scotland, where it states 'Police is still a great Office grown into *Desuetude*' (Radzinowicz 1956: 1). Smith and Blackstone are treated thoroughly in Radzinowicz (1956: 417–423), which must be the starting-point for research into 'that strange word "police"'. The vast literature on police has been more recently rediscovered by the pioneering work of Knemeyer (1980) and Pasquino (1978), although the earlier contributions to an understanding of the significance of the concept in the history of public health of 'medical police' by Rosen (1958, 1974), and, of course, the history of the 'Great Confinement' (Foucault 1965), warrant attention. The use of the term in historical research appears to be gaining ground. George (1985) uses the concept to construct an alternative to 'retrospective' accounts of textile history, while Hume (1981) employs it to explicate eighteenth-century conceptions of government. On the related issue of 'cameralism', see Tribe (1984).

5 This industrial police 'consisted of precise and highly detailed legal specifications which were designed to take into account a variety of contingencies, while its overall effect was to fix the statuses, rights and duties of the various categories of individuals according to their place in the great chain of being' (George 1985: 234). It enforced apprenticeship regulations and compulsory harvest-time agricultural services, and sought to erect barriers to labour migration and occupational changes (233–235). Industrial police, however, recognised the importance of regional differences, seasonal needs, local costs of necessities, and the various situations of chartered towns, trade guilds, mercantile companies, and so on. Again, the agents of this legislation were to be the justices of the peace.

6 The recognition that this is the case has a keen intellectual historian such as Hume (1981: 36) searching rather unconvincingly for the 'point of emancipation of political economy from police' in Smith or perhaps James Steuart. He is more convincing when he suggests that eighteenth-century 'political economy' can be understood 'as an amalgamation of oeconomy with some of those problems and categories of police which had been translated from a local to a national level'.

7 As in so many other aspects of the last two chapters, I am indebted to M.A. George's excellent M.Phil. thesis (1985: 250–251) for reminding me of aspects of Foucault's analysis pertinent here.

4 Population, subsistence, poverty

1 An informative account of the general context of the eighteenth-century population debate, and the respective contributions of, and links

between, Montesquieu, Wallace, and Hume, is provided by Glass (1973: 11–39). Glass' analysis shows *inter alia* the intimate connection between questions of population and the poor (12–21).

2 On how the dual identification of worker with wage-labourer and male breadwinner/head of household is characteristic of wages policy and census taking in liberal-capitalist societies, see Pateman (1988; 136–139). Malthus may be one of the earliest examples of what Diana Barker calls the 'dominant interpretation of Individualist philosophy in the nineteenth century' in which full legal citizenship is extended to all heads of households and in which individual obligation is carried out by them (1978: 256). On the masculinist 'social schizophrenia' by which the law, particularly in this crucial stage of English state formation, at once affirms and denies the position of women as autonomous individuals in the eyes of the law, see Corrigan and Sayer (1985: 131–134). On the contradictory effects of strategies to grant wives juridical equality with their husbands by legal reforms on the basis of market and contractual principles see Olsen (1983: 1530–1539). Malthus' ambiguities on the agency of moral restraint share such a schizophrenia but know none of the later contradictions! A similar sense of the way in which liberal political theory and the law both place women within and outside the fraternity of civil individuals or citizens pervades Pateman's major study (1988).

3 Pateman writes: 'Until late into the nineteenth century the legal and civil position of a wife resembled that of a slave. Under the common law doctrine of coverture, a wife, like a slave, was civilly dead. A slave had no independent legal existence apart from his master, and husband and wife became "one person", the person of the husband' (1988; 119). It is perfectly consistent of Malthus to draw the implication from this doctrine that a wife is entirely dependent on her husband for her subsistence.

4 I am indebted to Jeffrey Minson for raising this point. I would insist, however, that it is necessary to make plain that Malthus' remedy of moral restraint was conceived as a part of the 'natural' patriarchal prerogative, and not, as a recent study has claimed, as 'a part of what we would today term "responsible parenthood"' (Petersen 1979: 184). Huzel's article (1986: 138–145) contains enough evidence to convince us that not only Malthus but also government commissioners throughout the 1820s and 1830s held that it was indeed men who calculated the responsibilities of marriage.

5 The Malthusian effect

1 I cannot agree with the interpretation of pre-1834 relief as merely 'supplementary'. Wiliams argues (1981: 39) that given that just under one million received out-relief of just over three million pounds, the doles were too small to support an individual fully and must have been supplementary to other sources of income. He estimates that 'the weekly dole per pauper works out at just under one and a quarter (1.23)

shillings a week in an era when even an underpaid agricultural labourer could expect to earn the better part of ten shillings a week' (1981: 39). However, considering that able-bodied adults and children constituted 84 per cent of the total number of paupers, it is probable that a large proportion of these were able-bodied men and their dependants. If these families are taken as typically consisting of a man, a woman, and four children, as does Williams (1981: 42), then the average weekly dole figure would have to be multiplied by six to get some sense of its degree of contribution to the family budget. The result would mean relief was roughly three-quarters of the income of a lowly-paid labourer.

2 In contrast to the denial of relief to adult able-bodied males and those constructed as their dependants, the poor law after 1834 relieved large numbers of the aged and infirm, including those classed as insane, for the rest of the century. The adult 'non-able-bodied' accounted for over 40 per cent of all paupers for most of the second half of the century (Williams 1981: Table 4.23, 204–205). Pauperism declined throughout the nineteenth century from over 60 per 1,000 of total population in the 1840s to around 30 per thousand in the 1890s (Williams 1981: Graph 4. iv, 191). That the unemployed constituted only a negligible number of those relieved is indicated in the virtual absence of any correlation between fluctuations in unemployment rates and this gradual absolute decline in the number of paupers (Williams 1981: Graph 4. iv, 191).

6 From morality to economy?

1 Minson's definition is: 'Foundationalism . . . views ethical considerations as always grounding and therefore overriding other considerations. The ethical cannot be confined to one province of human and social life but rather subsumes all other provinces. This subsumption consists in always being entitled to subject economic, political, artistic, legal or any other apsects of a situation to its criteria of evaluation. Moral evaluation takes priority over other particularistic and consequently one-sided types of evaluation. These themselves lie under an injunction to attempt to take their cue from the ethic mode of evaluation which transcends them all. Evaluation takes the form of subjecting actions or states of affairs to the test of whether they conform to the first principles of that ethic' (1985: 149).

7 The moral economy of Adam Smith

1 See Meuret (1988) for an alternative reading of Smith within a quite different 'genealogy of political economy'. The present study agrees with Meuret that political economy 'would not so much express as institute' the economy: (227). It differs in the mechanism of that institution: in his case, by virtue of its better representation; in the present study, by the formation of a rationality which came to be embodied in various state-administrative practices.

8 The condition of poverty

1 The Adamite critique of the laws of settlement was repeated in this speech which upheld the familiar eighteenth-century line on population. This was the same speech which promised relief as 'a matter of right and an honour' for those with families (Poynter 1969: 58–59).

2 A more detailed discussion of these different conceptions of rent can be found in Dean (1988, Part Three).

9 Pauperism and the labour market

1 Digby: 'The Royal Commission on the Poor Laws of 1832–4, by focusing on the abuse of outdoor allowances to the able-bodied poor in the countryside, seemed to have provided remedies for the problems of rural poverty . . .' (1976: 149). Digby thus accepts that the definition of the problem of the 1834 Report was outdoor relief to all the able-bodied poor. Ashforth is more equivocal, giving two different definitions of the problem in the space of two sentences: 'The Royal Commission of 1832–4 directed attention towards the problem of the unemployed and underemployed adult able-bodied paupers. The 1834 Report assumed that . . . all able-bodied males could find employment in a free labour market' (1976: 129).

2 This notion of workhouse or indoor relief as 'less-eligible' is central to the official strategy of 1834. It is discussed at length in the following chapters.

3 Williams argues that Speenhamland is more a matter of 'methodological assumption than practical demonstration' (1981: 34) and Webb and Webb's characterisation of the pre-1834 poor law as flawed by the presupposition of a unitary meaning of relief practice. One cannot but agree with Williams' assertion that their account remains superior to recent poor-law historiography because it entails a willingness to pose questions of 'institutional configuration' which have since been effectively abandoned (e.g. Blaug 1963; Baugh 1975; Neuman 1972). Corrigan noted that 'the Poor Law operated to classify (i.e. mark) different poor people in different ways' (1977: 42). Such an insight pervades Williams' analysis in which specific phases of the poor law transform the ways in which paupers are differentiated as new strategies are adopted.

4 Williams considers and convincingly discounts three alternatives to such a conclusion: that relief took place indoors, that it was misrepresented under the sickness exception clauses, and that it was not returned at all (1981: 72–75).

5 This figure is arrived at from two sources. The number of 'ordinarily able-bodied' women without children receiving outdoor relief under sixty on a single day in 1906 was, according to the majority *Report* (1909: 66), approximately 2,700. The mean number of total paupers for any day of that year was, after Williams (1981: Table 4.5, 158–160), 892,000. Assuming that the total number of paupers was close to this

mean on the day cited in the *Report*, we arrive at the conclusion that the category in question comprised about one-third of 1 per cent of the pauper population.

6 Is Williams' account credible? Specialist reviews reciprocate the hostility his text evinces towards conventional historiography but offer no grounds for the rejection of Williams' position on the official strategy of 1834 or its effectiveness (e.g. Fraser 1982: 159–160). The specialists all find Williams' use of semiotics and his rejection of current historiographic methods perplexing and annoying. However, they are willing to concede the significance of his statistical analysis and tabulation and his conclusions. Brundage regards his analysis of the pre-1834 poor law as 'compelling' and the book overall as 'offbeat, quarrelsome and extremely important' (1982: 451–452). Harold Perkin is even more generous, calling the statistical tabulations 'a marvellous compendium of meticulously abstracted information which will change the whole interpretation of poor law history', and concluding that 'Saussure be praised that Dr Williams at least left us the statistics' (1982: 115–116).

10 Pauper-land

1 The debate over the relation of Bentham and Benthamism to the transformation of state administration in the 1830s, and in the nineteenth century more generally, has been hotly contested and multi-faceted. Starting with a sideline to the major debate first, there have been more than a few skirmishes on the relation between Bentham and the poor-law reform. Himmelfarb's (1970: 122n.) remarks that Bentham had not envisaged a central board administering relief such as was established under the 1834 Act has been described as 'wholly misleading' by Boralevi (1984: 103). Boralevi argues that the main issue was one of centralisation and cites the proposal for an Indigence Relief Ministry. Himmelfarb's reply to such arguments is contained in her later book (1984: 85–86). Her denial of the contribution of Bentham's thought to the reform of poor-law administration is symptomatic of a tendency within the much wider debate on the influence of Bentham and state transformation in Britain in the nineteenth century. The key to this debate is A.V. Dicey's classification of legislative phases (1914). One side (MacDonagh 1958; Roberts 1974) in the debate treated this account as a misguided orthodoxy. Their positions provoked considerable comment, most notably from Parris (1960), Hart (1965), and Hume (1967), who reasserted the Benthamite factor in the reform of state administration, but in ways which implied a considerable departure from the thesis attributed to Dicey. These arguments are treated at some length in Dean (1988, chapter eleven). An excellent summary of the divergent strands of the post-war debate(s) (1945–1976) on the revolution of government, including assessment of the roles of political economy, Benthamism, and the poor law, is provided by chapter one of Corrigan's thesis, in which he concludes that all these debates 'are

remarkable for their sustained sociological naivete' (1977: 58).
Sutherland's collection (1972) brings together some seminal pieces on
the wider question of the 'growth of government', including the article
by S.E. Finer on the transmission of Benthamite ideas which, together
with his book (1952), the views of John Stuart Mill (1950), and Elie
Halévy (1928), must form the basis for any assessment of the
significance of Bentham.

2 The passage comes from *Observations on the Nature, Extent and Effects
   of Pauperism, and the means of reducing it*, of 1826, by Thomas
   Walker, a stipendiary magistrate who was later consulted by the Poor
   Law Commission in 1833.

3 Whereas Foucault sought to analyse the Panopticon as an encapsulation
   of disciplinary mechanisms of power, the present concern is with the
   more modest project of understanding its place in Bentham's particular
   plans of 'pauper management'. In order to do this, however, certain
   aspects of Foucault's interpretation, dictated by the larger concern to
   characterise disciplinary power in terms of the process of
   'assujettissement' (1977a: 24–31, 217), must be put aside in the present
   context.

4 See the various articles from the reviews collected in *Population
   Problems in the Victorian Age* (1973).

11 The mechanisms of prevention

1 Despite the continuing interest of her article, there are problems with
   the distinction Procacci makes (1978: 60) between science and *savoir*,
   the latter mediating between the theoretical abstractions of science and
   practical issues. Her typology depends on the opposition between those
   discourses which form an object of knowledge by abstracting from an
   (extra-discursive) reality and those which place an object so derived in
   the relationships which are constitutive of such a reality. From the
   present perspective, this distinction is based on two spurious premises:
   first, that scientific discourse can be characterised by the epistemological
   project of forming a theoretical object in a process of abstraction from
   the real; and second, that other 'practical' discourses are able to take
   into account the 'concrete functioning' of the real in their calculations.
   For a fuller critique see Dean (1988, chapter 12).

2 The Academy of Moral Sciences organised a competition to answer the
   questions, 'What does distress consist in, by what signs is it observable
   in various countries, what are its causes?' (Chevalier 1973: 140, 460).
   Among the twenty-two essays submitted were Honore Fréiger's *Des
   classes dangereuses de la population dans les grandes villes*, and the
   winner of the highest award, Eugène Buret's study. Both were published
   in 1840.

Conclusion

1 In respect of Bentham, Corrigan's thesis maintains that he does have a conception of the 'social bond', and that his theory of government is based on an implicit sociology (1977: 15–16). I would suggest that this estimation does not apply to a system of pauper management employing semio-technical measures based on a theory of the rational individual. At best Bentham's problem is not of social reform but of the reform of the governmental conditions of individual choice. This would apply to all strategies of 'less-eligibility'.

Bibliography

Abrams, P. (1968) *The Origins of British Sociology 1834–1915*, Chicago:
University of Chicago Press.
—— (1980) 'History, sociology, historical sociology', *Past and Present* 87:
3–16.
—— (1982) *Historical Sociology*, Shepton Mallet: Open Books.
Anderson, P. (1974) *Lineages of the Absolutist State*, London: New Left Books.
Appleby, J.O. (1978) *Economic Thought and Ideology in Seventeenth-
Century England*, Princeton, N.J.: Princeton University Press.
Ashforth, D. (1976) 'The urban poor law', in D. Fraser (ed.) *The New
Poor Law in the Nineteenth Century*, London: Macmillan.
Bahmueller, C. (1981) *The National Charity Company: Jeremy Bentham's
Silent Revolution*, Berkeley: University of California Press.
Barker, D.L. (1978) 'Regulation of marriage', in G. Littlejohn, B. Smart,
J. Wakeford and N. Yuval-Davis (eds) *Power and the State*, London:
Croom Helm.
Baugh, D.A. (1975) 'The cost of poor relief in south-east England,
1790–1834', *Economic History Review* 28: 50–68.
Beales, H.L. (1946) *The Making of Social Policy*, Oxford: Oxford
University Press.
Bentham, J. (1843) *Works*, ed. J. Bowring, 11 vols, Edinburgh: William
Tait.
—— (1950) *The Theory of Legislation*, ed. C.K. Ogden, London: Routledge
and Kegan Paul.
Blackstone, Sir W. (1830) *Commentaries on the Laws of England*, 4, 17th
edn, ed. E. Christian, London: Dawsons of Pall Mall.
Blaug, M. (1963) 'The myth of the old poor law and the making of the
new', *Journal of Economic History* 23, 2: 151–184.
Block, F. and Somers, M.R. (1984) 'Beyond the economistic fallacy: the
holistic social science of Karl Polanyi', in T. Skocpol (ed.) *Vision and
Method in Historical Sociology*, Cambridge: Cambridge University
Press.
Bonar, J. (1885) *Malthus and his Work*, London: Macmillan.
Boralevi, L.C. (1984) *Bentham and the Oppressed*, Berlin: Walter de Gruyter.
Bowley, M. (1937) *Nassau Senior and Classical Economics*, London: Allen
and Unwin.

Bray, J.F. (1839) *Labour's Wrongs and Labour's Remedy*, Leeds: David Green.

Briggs, A. (1961) 'The welfare state in historical perspective', *Archives Européenes du Sociologie* 11: 221-258.

Bruce, M. (1968) *The Coming of the Welfare State*, 4th edn, London: B.T. Batsford.

Bruland, T. and Smith, K. (1981) 'Economic discourse and the capitalist order', *Economy and Society* 10, 4: 467-480.

Brundage, A. (1978) *The Making of the New Poor Law*, London: Hutchinson.

—— (1982) 'Review of *From Pauperism to Poverty*', *American History Review* 87, 2: 451-452.

Burke, E. (1826) *The Works of the Right Honourable Edmund Burke*, 16 vols, London: C. and V. Rivington.

Chadwick, E. (1837) *An Article on the Principles and Progress of the Poor Law Amendment Act*, reprinted from *Edinburgh Review*, London: C. Knight.

—— (1965) *Report on the Sanitary Conditions of the Labouring Population of Great Britain of 1842*, ed. M. Flinn, Edinburgh: Edinburgh University Press.

Chalmers, T. (1832) *On Political Economy, in Connexion with the Moral State and Moral Prospects of Society*, 1968 reprint, New York: A.M. Kelley.

—— (1912) *Problems of Poverty*, London: Nelson.

Checkland, S.G. and Checkland, E.O. (eds) (1974) *The Poor Law Report of 1834*, Harmondsworth: Penguin.

Chevalier, L. (1973) *Labouring Classes and Dangerous Classes in Paris in the First Half of the Nineteenth Century*, trans. F. Jellinek, New York: Howard Festig.

Child, Sir J. (1669) 'A New Discourse on Trade', 1968 reprint, in *Selected Works 1668-1697*, Farnborough: Gregg Press.

Coats, A.W. (1960) 'Economic thought and poor-law policy in the eighteenth century', *Economic History Review*, second series 13, 1: 39-51.

—— (1976) 'Relief of poverty, attitudes to labour, and economic change in England 1660-1782', *International Review of Social History* 21: 98-115.

Coleridge, S.T. (1972) *Collected Works*, ed. R.J. White, 16 vols, London: Routledge and Kegan Paul.

Colmer, J. (1959) *Coleridge: Critic of Society*, Oxford: Clarendon Press.

Colquhoun, P. (1805) *A Treatise on the Police of the Metropolis*, 6th edn, London. J. Mawman.

—— (1806) *A Treatise on Indigence*, London: J. Mawman.

—— (1814) *A Treatise on the Wealth, Power and Resources of the British Empire*, London: J. Mawman.

Corrigan, P. (1977) 'State formation and moral regulation in nineteenth-century Britain: sociological investigations', unpublished Ph.D. thesis, University of Durham.

Corrigan, P. and Corrigan, V. (1979) 'State formation and social policy until 1871', in N. Parry, M. Rustin, and C. Satyamurti (eds) *Social Work, Welfare and the State*, London: Edward Arnold.

Corrigan, P. and Sayer, D. (1985) *The Great Arch: English State Formation as Cultural Revolution*, Oxford: Basil Blackwell.

Cousins, M. and Hussain, A. (1984) *Michel Foucault*, London: Macmillan.

Cowherd, R.G. (1977) *Political Economists and the English Poor Laws: a Historical Study of the Influence of Classical Economics on Social Welfare Policy*, Athens: Ohio University Press.

Cunningham, W. (1912) *The Growth of English Industry and Commerce in Modern Times*, vol. 2: *The Mercantile System*, Cambridge: Cambridge University Press.

Cunningham Wood, J. (ed.) (1984) *Adam Smith: Critical Assessments*, 3 vols, London: Croom Helm.

Cutler, A., Hindess, B., Hirst, P.Q., and Hussain, A. (1977) *Marx's 'Capital' and Capitalism Today*, 1, London: Routledge and Kegan Paul.

D'avenant, C. (1771) *The Political and Commercial Works of that Celebrated Writer Charles D'avenant, L.L.D.*, 5 vols, 1967 reprint, Farnborough: Gregg.

Davies, D. (1795) *The Case of the Labourers in Husbandry Stated and Considered*, London.

de Tocqueville, A. (1986) 'On pauperism; memoire sur le pauperisme', *International Review of Community Development* 16 (56): 27–40.

Dean, M. (1986) 'Foucault's obsession with Western Modernity', *Thesis Eleven* 14: 44–61.

—— (1988) 'The constitution of poverty: a case-history in the genealogy of liberal government', unpublished Ph.D. thesis, University of New South Wales.

Dean, M. and Bolton, G. (1980) 'The administration of poverty and the development of nursing in nineteenth-century England', in C. Davies (ed.) *Rewriting Nursing History*, London: Croom Helm.

Defoe, D. (1704) *Giving Alms No charity and Employing the Poor a Grievance to the Nation*, 1970 reprint, New York: Johnson Reprint Corp.

Dicey, A.V. (1914) *Lectures on the Relation between Law and Public Opinion in England during the Nineteenth Century*, 2nd edn, London: Macmillan.

Digby, A. (1976) 'The rural poor law', in D. Fraser (ed.) *The New Poor Law in the Nineteenth Century*, London: Macmillan.

Donzelot, J. (1979) *The Policing of Families*, trans. R. Hurley, New York: Pantheon Books.

Dumont, L. (1977) *From Mandeville to Marx*, Chicago: University of Chicago Press.

Durkheim, E. (1965) *The Rules of the Sociological Method*, trans. S.A. Aolovay and J.H. Mueller, Chicago: University of Chicago Press.

Eden, Sir. F.M. (1797) *The State of the Poor: or a History of the Labouring Classes in England, from the Conquest to the Present Time*, 3 vols, London: J. Davis.

—— (1928) *The State of the Poor: a History of the Labouring Classes in England*, abridged and ed. A.G.L. Rogers, London: Routledge.

Engels, F. (1973) *The Condition of the Working Class in England*, Moscow: Progress Publishers.

Evans, R. (1982) *The Fabrication of Virtue: English Prison Architecture*, Cambridge: Cambridge University Press.

Finer, S.E. (1952) *The Life and Times of Sir Edwin Chadwick*, London: Methuen.

—— (1972) 'The transmission of Benthamite ideas 1820-50', in G. Sutherland (ed.) *Studies in the Growth of Nineteenth-century Government*, London: Routledge and Kegan Paul.

Flew, A. (1970) 'Introduction', in T.R. Malthus *An Essay on the Principle of Population*, Harmondsworth: Penguin.

Flinn, M.W. (1965) 'Introduction', in E. Chadwick *Report on the Sanitary Conditions of the Labouring Population of Great Britain of 1842*, Edinburgh: Edinburgh University Press.

Foucault, M. (1965) *Madness and Civilisation: a History of Insanity in the Age of Reason*, trans. R. Howard, London: Tavistock.

—— (1970) *The Order of Things: an Archaeology of the Human Sciences*, trans. A.M. Sheridan, London: Tavistock.

—— (1972) *The Archaeology of Knowledge*, trans. A.M. Sheridan Smith, London: Tavistock.

—— (1973) *The Birth of the Clinic*, trans. A.M. Sheridan, London: Tavistock.

—— (1977a) *Discipline and Punish: the Birth of the Prison*, trans. A. Sheridan, London: Allen Lane.

—— (1977b) 'Nietzsche, genealogy, history', in *Language, Counter-memory, Practice*, ed. D.B. Bouchard, Oxford: Basil Blackwell.

—— (1979a) 'Governmentality', *I and C* 6: 5-21.

—— (1979b) *The History of Sexuality*, vol. 1: *An Introduction*, trans. R. Hurley, London: Allen Lane.

—— (1980a) 'Georges Canguilhem, philosopher of error', *I and C* 7: 51-62.

—— (1980b) *Power/Knowledge: Selected Interviews and Other Writings 1972-1977*, ed. C. Gordon, Brighton: Harvester Press.

—— (1981) 'Questions of method', *I and C* 8: 3-14.

—— (1982) 'Afterword: the subject and power', in H. Dreyfus and P. Rabinow *Michel Foucault: beyond Structuralism and Hermeneutics*, Brighton: Harvester, 208-226.

Fraser, D. (1982) 'Review of *From Pauperism to Poverty*', *History* 67, 219: 159-160.

Furniss, E.S. (1957) *The Position of the Laborer in a System of Nationalism: a Study in the Labor Theories of the Late English Mercantilists*, New York: Kelley and Millman.

Gaskell, P. (1833) *The Manufacturing Population of England, its Moral, Social and Physical Conditions*, London: Baldwin and Cradock.

Gee, J.M.A. (1984) 'Adam Smith's social welfare function', in J. Cunningham Wood (ed.) *Adam Smith: Critical Assessments*, London: Croom Helm.

George, M.A. (1985) 'The concept of industrial revolution: textile history and the "histories" of discipline', unpublished M.Phil. thesis, Griffith University.

Gilbert, G. (1980) 'Economic growth and the poor in Malthus' Essay on Population', *History of Political Economy* 12, 1: 83–96.

Gislain, J-J. (1987) 'On the relation of state and market', *Telos* 73: 147–152.

Glass, D.V. (1953) 'Malthus and the limitation of population growth', in D.V. Glass (ed.) *Introduction to Malthus*, New York: John Wiley and Sons.

—— (1973) *Numbering the People: the Eighteenth-century Population Controversy and the Development of Census and Vital Statistics in Britain*, Farnborough: D.C. Heath.

Godwin, W. (1971) *An Enquiry Concerning Political Justice*, ed. K. Coddell Carter, Oxford: Clarendon Press.

Gordon, C. (1987) 'The soul of the citizen: Max Weber and Michel Foucault on rationality and government', in S. Whimster and S. Lash (eds) *Max Weber, Rationality and Modernity*, London: Allen and Unwin.

Grampp, W.D. (1974a) 'Classical economics and its moral critics', *History of Political Economy* 5, 2: 359–374.

—— (1974b) 'Malthus and his contemporaries', *History of Political Economy* 6, 3: 278–304.

Hale, Sir M. (1683) *A Discourse Touching Provision for the Poor*, London: William Shrowsbery.

Halévy, E. (1928) *The Growth of Philosophic Radicalism*, trans. M. Morris, London: Faber.

—— (1956) *Thomas Hodgskin*, trans. A.J. Taylor, London: Benn.

—— (1961) *England In 1815: A History of the English People in the Nineteenth Century*, 1, London: Ernest Benn.

Hammond, J.L. and Hammond, B. (1913) *The Village Labourer 1760–1830*, London: Longmans, Green & Co.

—— (1978) *The Village Labourer*, London: Longman.

Hart, J. (1965) 'Nineteenth-century social reform: a Tory interpretation of history', *Past and Present* 31: 39–61.

Harvey-Phillips, M.B. (1984) 'Malthus' theodicy: the intellectual background of his contribution to political economy', *History of Political Economy* 16, 4: 591–608.

Hennis, W. (1983) 'Max Weber's "central question" ', *Economy and Society* 12, 2: 135–180.

—— (1987) 'Personality and life orders: Max Weber's theme', in S. Whimster and S. Lash (eds) *Max Weber, Rationality and Modernity*, London: Allen and Unwin.

Henriques, U. (1979) *Before the Welfare State: Social Administration in Early Industrial Britain*, London: Longman.

Hill, C. (1964) *Society and Puritanism in Pre-revolutionary England*, London: Panther.

—— (1969) *Reformation to Industrial Revolution*, The Pelican Economic History of Britain vol. 2: 1530–1780, Harmondsworth: Penguin.

—— (1978) 'Sex, marriage and the family in England', *Economic History Review* 31: 450–463.

—— (1986) 'The poor and the people', in *The Collected Essays of*

Christopher Hill, vol. 3: *People and Ideas in 17th Century England*, Brighton: Harvester Press.

Himmelfarb, G. (1970) 'Bentham's Utopia: the National Charity Company', *Journal of British Studies* 10: 80–125.

—— (1984) *The Idea of Poverty: England in the Early Industrial Age*, New York: Alfred A. Knopf.

Hirschman, A.O. (1977) *The Passions and the Interests: Political Arguments for Capitalism before its Triumph*, Princeton: Princeton University Press.

Hodgskin, T. (1825) *Labour Defended against the Claims of Capital*, 1963 reprint, New York: A.M. Kelley.

—— (1827) *Popular Political Economy*, London: Chas. Tait.

—— (1832) *The Natural and Artificial Right of Property Contrasted*, London: B. Steil.

Hume, D. (1882) 'Of the populousness of ancient nations', in *Philosophical works*, 3, ed. T.H. Green and T.H. Grose, 1964 reprint. Germany: Scientia Verlag Aalen.

Hume, L.J. (1967) 'Jeremy Bentham and the nineteenth-century revolution in government', *The Historical Journal* 10, 4: 361–367.

—— (1981) *Bentham and Bureaucracy*, Cambridge: Cambridge University Press.

Huzel, J.P. (1986) 'Malthus, the poor law, and population in early nineteenth-century England', in J. Cunningham Wood (ed.) *Thomas Robert Malthus: Critical Assessments*, 4, London: Croom Helm.

Ingram, R. (1808) *Disquisitions of Population etc.*, London: J. Hatchard.

James, P. (1979) *Population Malthus: His Life and Times*, London: Routledge and Kegan Paul.

Jarrold, T. (1806) *Dissertations on Man: Philosophical, Physiological and Political*, London.

Kay, J.P. (1832) *The Moral and Physical Condition of the Working Classes Employed in the Cotton Manufacture in Manchester*, London: James Ridgway.

Knemeyer, F-L. (1980) 'Polizei', *Economy and Society* 9, 2: 172–196.

Landreth, H. (1980) 'The economic thought of Bernard Mandeville', *History of Political Economy* 7, 2: 193–208.

LeMahieu, D.L. (1979) 'Malthus and the theology of scarcity', *Journal of the History of Ideas* 40: 467–474.

Leslie, J. (1807) *A Summons of Awakening or the Evil Tendency and Danger of Speculative Philosophy etc*, Harwick: Robert Armstrong.

MacDonagh, O. (1958) 'The nineteenth-century revolution in government: a reappraisal', *The Historical Journal* 1, 1: 52–67.

MacFarlane, A. (1986) *Marriage and Love in England: Modes of Reproduction, 1300–1840*, Oxford: Basil Blackwell.

Malcomson, R.W. (1973) *Popular Recreations in English Society, 1700–1850*, Cambridge: Cambridge University Press.

Malthus, T.R. (1798) *An Essay on the Principle of Population as it Affects the Future Improvement of Society*, London: Johnson.

—— (1803) *An Essay on the Principle of Population, or a View of its Past and Present Effects on Human Happiness*, 2nd edn, 2 vols, London: J. Johnson.

—— (1826) *An Essay on the Principle of Population or a View of its Past and Present Effects on Human Happiness*, 6th edn, 2 vols, London: John Murray.

—— (1872) *An Essay on the Principle of Population etc.*, 7th edn, London: Reeves and Turner.

Mandeville, B. (1924) *The Fable of the Bees; or, Private Vices, Public Benefits*, Oxford: Clarendon Press.

Mannheim, K. (1936) *Ideology and Utopia: an Introduction to the Sociology of Knowledge*, London: Routledge and Kegan Paul.

Mantoux, P. (1961) *The Industrial Revolution in the Eighteenth Century: an Outline of the Beginnings of the Modern Factory System in England*, trans. M. Vernon, London: Jonathan Cape.

Marshall, T.H. (1972) 'Value problems of welfare capitalism', *Journal of Social Policy* 1, 1: 15–32.

—— (1983) 'Citizenship and social class', in D. Held, J. Anderson, B. Gieben, S. Hall, L. Harris, P. Lewis, N. Parker, and B. Tierok (eds) *States and Societies*, Oxford: Martin Robertson.

Martinelli, A. (1987) 'The economy as institutional process', *Telos* 73: 131–146.

Marx, K. (1973) *Grundrisse: Foundations of the Critique of Political Economy*, trans. M. Nicolaus, London: Penguin.

—— (1974) *Capital: a Critical Analysis of Capitalist Production*, 1, trans. S. Moore and E. Aveling, Moscow: Progress Publishers.

Marx, K. and Engels, F. (1964) *The German Ideology*, trans. S. Ryazanskaya, Moscow: Progress Publishers.

Meuret, D. (1981/2) 'Political economy and the legitimation of the state', *I & C* 9: 29–38.

—— (1988) 'A political genealogy of political economy', *Economy and Society* 17, 2: 225–250.

Mill, J. (1978) 'An essay on government', in J. Lively and J. Rees (eds) *Utilitarian Logic and Politics*, Oxford: Clarendon.

Mill, J.S. (1950) 'Bentham', in F.R. Leavis (ed.) *Mill on Bentham and Coleridge*, London: Chatto and Windus.

Miller, P. (1980) 'The territory of the psychiatrist: review of Robert Castel's "L'Ordre Psychiatrique" ', *I & C* 7: 63–105.

Minson, J. (1980) 'Strategies for socialists? Foucault's conception of power', *Economy and Society* 9, 1: 1–43.

—— (1985) *Genealogies of Morals: Nietzsche, Foucault, Donzelot and the Eccentricity of Ethics*, London: Macmillan.

Montagu, A. (1971) Foreword to J. Townsend *A Dissertation on the Poor Laws by a Well-wisher of Mankind*, Berkeley: University of California Press.

Neuman, M. (1972) 'Speenhamland in Berkshire', in E.W. Martin (ed.) *Comparative Development in Social Welfare*, London: Allen and Unwin.

Nietzsche, F. (1969) *On the Genealogy of Morals*, trans. W. Kaufmann and R.J. Holingdale, New York: Random House.

North, R. (1753) *A Discourse of the Poor*, London: M. Cooper.

Olsen, F.E. (1983) 'The family and the market: a study of ideology and legal reform', *Harvard Law Review* 96, 7: 1497–1578.

Otter, W. (1836) 'Memoir', in T.R. Malthus *Principles of Political Economy*, 2nd edn, London: William Pickering.

Owen, D. (1964) *English Philanthropy 1660–1960*, Cambridge, Mass: Harvard University Press.

Owen, R. (1818) *A New View of Society*, London: Longman, Hurst, Rees and Orme.

Oxley, G. (1974) *Poor Relief in England and Wales, 1601–1834*, London: D. and C. Newton Abbot.

Paley, W. (1794) *The Principles of Moral and Political Philosophy*, 1, 10th edn, London: R. Fauldner.

Parris, H. (1960) 'The nineteenth-century revolution in government: a reappraisal reappraised', *The Historical Journal* 3, 1: 17–36.

Pasquino, P. (1978) 'Theatricum politicum: the genealogy of capital–police and the state of prosperity', *Ideology and Consciousness* 4: 41–54.

Pateman, C. (1988) *The Sexual Contract*, Oxford: Polity Press.

Pearl, V. (1978) 'Puritans and poor relief: the London workhouse, 1649–1660', in D. Pennington and K. Thomas (eds) *Puritans and Revolutionaries: Essays in Seventeenth-century History Presented to Christopher Hill*, Oxford: Clarendon Press.

Pelling, M. (1978) *Cholera, Fever and English medicine 1825–1865*, Oxford: Oxford University Press.

Perkin, H. (1969) *The Origins of Modern English Society, 1780–1880*, London: Routledge and Kegan Paul.

—— (1982) 'Review of *From Pauperism to Poverty*', *Economic History Review* 35, 1: 115–116.

Petersen, W. (1979) *Malthus*, Cambridge, Mass: Harvard University Press.

Petty, Sir W. (1963) *The Economic Writings of Sir William Petty*, 1, ed. C.H. Hill, New York: A.M. Kelley.

Place, F. (1821) *Illustrations and Proofs of the Principle of Population*, London: Longman, Hurst, Rees, Orme and Brown.

Polanyi, K. (1957) *The Great Transformation*, Boston: Beacon Press.

Polanyi-Levitt, K. and Mendell, M. (1987) 'Karl Polanyi: a biographical sketch', *Telos* 73: 121–131.

Population Problems in the Victorian Age, vol. 1: *Theory* (1973), Farnborough: Gregg International.

Poverty in the Victorian Age: Debates on the Issue from Nineteenth-century Critical Journals (1973), 4 vols, intro. by A.W. Coats, Farnborough: Gregg International.

Poynter, J.R. (1969) *Society and Pauperism: English Ideas on Poor Relief 1795–1834*, London: Routledge and Kegan Paul.

Procacci, G. (1978) 'Social economy and the government of poverty', *Ideology and Consciousness* 4: 55–72.

Pullen, J.M. (1981) 'Malthus' theological ideas and their influence on his principle of population', *History of Political Economy* 13, 1: 39–54.

Radzinowicz, L. (1956) *A History of English Criminal Law and its*

Administration from 1750, vol. 3: *The Reform of the Police*, London: Stevens & Sons.

Report of the Royal Commission on the Poor Laws and the Relief of Distress (1909), 1, London: HMSO.

Ricardo, D. (1951) *The Works and Correspondence of David Ricardo*, 10 vols, ed. P. Sraffa with M. Dobb, Cambridge: Cambridge University Press.

Rimlinger, G.V. (1971) *Welfare Policy and Industrialisation in Europe, America and Russia*, New York: J. Wiley and Sons.

—— (1984) 'Smith and the merits of the poor', in J. Cunningham Wood (ed.) *Adam Smith: Critical Assessments*, 1, London: Croom Helm.

Roberts, D. (1960) *Victorian Origins of the British Welfare State*, New Haven: Yale University Press.

—— (1974) 'Jeremy Bentham and the Victorian administrative state', in B. Parekh (ed.) *Jeremy Bentham: Ten Critical Essays*, London: Frank Cass.

Rose, M.E. (1976) 'Settlement, removal and the New Poor Law', in D. Fraser (ed.) *The New Poor Law in the Nineteenth Century*, London: Macmillan.

Rosen, G. (1958) *A History of Public Health*, New York: M.D. Publications.

—— (1974) *From Medical Police to Social Medicine: Essays on the History of Health Care*, New York: Science History Publications.

Salsano, A. (1987) 'Polanyi, Braudel, and the king of Dahomey', *Telos* 73: 153–166.

Say, J-B. (1880) *A Treatise on Political Economy or the Production, Distribution and Consumption of Wealth*, trans. C.R. Prinsep, Philadelphia: Claxton, Rimsen and Haffelfinger.

Schumpeter, J.A. (1954) *History of Economic Analysis*, New York: Oxford University Press.

Senior, N.W. (1829) *Two Lectures on Population Delivered before the University of Oxford in Easter Term 1828*, London: Saunders and Otley.

—— (1938) *An Outline of the Science of Political Economy*, 7th edn, London: Allen and Unwin.

Sherman, D. (1974) 'The meaning of economic liberalism in mid-nineteenth-century France', *History of Political Economy* 6, 2: 171–199.

Skinner, A.S. and Wilson, T. (eds) (1975) *Essays on Adam Smith*, Oxford: Clarendon Press.

Smith, A. (1853) *The Theory of Moral Sentiments*, London: Bohn.

—— (1889) *An Inquiry into the Nature and Causes of the Wealth of Nations*, ed. J.R. McCulloch, Edinburgh: Adam and Charles Black.

—— (1956) *Lectures on Justice, Police, Revenue and Arms*, ed. E. Cannan, New York: Kelley & Millan. Reprint of 1896 edn.

—— (1976) *An Inquiry into the Nature and Causes of the Wealth of Nations*, 2 vols, ed. R.H. Campbell and A.S. Skinner, London: Oxford University Press.

Smith, K. (1951) *The Malthusian Controversy*, London: Routledge and Kegan Paul.

Spengler, J.J. (1973) 'Introduction', in *Population Problems in the*

Victorian Age, vol. 1: *Theory*, Farnborough: Gregg International.

Stedman Jones, G. (1984) *Outcast London: A Study in the Relationship between Classes in Victorian Society*, 2nd edn, Harmondsworth: Penguin.

Steuart, Sir J. (1966) *An Inquiry into the Principles of Political Oeconomy*, 2 vols, ed. A.S. Skinner, Edinburgh: Oliver & Boyd.

Stewart, D. (1966) *A Biographical Memoir of Adam Smith*, New York: A.M. Kelley.

Strakosch, H.E. (1967) *State Absolutism and the Rule of Law*, Sydney: University of Sydney Press.

Sumner, J.B. (1816) *A Treatise on the Records of Creation and on the Moral Attributes of the Creator*, 2 vols, London.

Sutherland, G. (ed.) (1972) *Studies in the Growth of Nineteenth-century Government*, London: Routledge and Kegan Paul.

Tawney, R.H. (1938) *Religion and the Rise of Capitalism*, Harmondsworth: Penguin.

Thomas, K. (1958) 'The double standard', *Journal of the History of Ideas* 20: 195–216.

Thompson, E.P. (1967) 'Time, work-discipline and industrial capitalism', *Past and Present*, 38: 56–97.

—— (1968) *The Making of the English Working Class*, Harmondsworth: Penguin.

—— (1971) 'The moral economy of the English crowd in the eighteenth century', *Past and Present* 50: 76–136.

—— (1974) 'Patrician society, plebeian culture', *Journal of Social History* 7, 4: 382–405.

—— (1978) *The Poverty of Theory*, London: Merlin.

Thompson, W. (1824) *An Inquiry into the Principles of the Distribution of Wealth Most Conducive to Human Happiness*, London: Longman, Hurst, Rees, Orme, Brown and Green.

Townsend, J. (1971) *A Dissertation on the Poor Laws by a Well-wisher of Mankind*, Berkeley: University of California Press.

Townsend, P. (ed.) (1970) *The Concept of Poverty*, London: Heinemann Educational.

Tribe, K. (1978) *Land, Labour and Economic Discourse*, London: Routledge and Kegan Paul.

—— (1981) *Genealogies of Capitalism*, London: Macmillan.

—— (1984) 'Cameralism and the science of government', *Journal of Modern History* 52, 2: 263–284.

Wallace, R. (1761) *A Dissertation of the Numbers of Mankind*, 1969 reprint, New York: Kelley.

Walther, R. (1984) 'Economic liberalism', *Economy and Society* 13, 2: 178–207.

Webb, S. and Webb, B. (1963a) *English Poor Law History, Part One: the Old Poor Law*, Hamden: Archon Books.

—— (1963b) *English Poor Law History, Part Two: the Last Hundred Years*, 1, Hamden: Archon Books.

Weber, M. (1927) *General Economic History*, trans. F.A. Knight, London: Allen and Unwin.

—— (1948) *From Max Weber: Essays in Sociology*, trans. and ed. H.H. Gerth and C. Wright Mills, London: Routledge and Kegan Paul.

—— (1985) *The Protestant Ethic and the Spirit of Capitalism*, trans. T. Parsons, London: Unwin.

Williams, K. (1981) *From Pauperism to Poverty*, London: Routledge and Kegan Paul.

Williams, R. (1976) *Keywords*, Glasgow: Fontana.

Wilson, T. and Skinner, A.S. (1976) *The Market and the State: Essays in Honour of Adam Smith*, Oxford: Clarendon Press.

Winch, D. (1987) *Malthus*, Oxford: Oxford University Press.

Young, A. (1768) *A Six Weeks Tour through the Southern Counties*, London: Nicoll.

—— (1771) *A Six Months Tour through the North of England*, 4 vols. 2nd edn, London: W. Strahan.

Young, A.F. and Ashton, E.T. (1956) *British Social Work in the Nineteenth Century*, London: Routledge and Kegan Paul.

Zeigler, P. (1970) *The Black Death*, London: Collins.

Name index

Subject index